CAD for Interiors Beyond the Basics

▶ JOSEPH A. FIORELLO, JR., ASSOCIATE, IIDA

AUTODESK AUTHORIZED AUTHOR

CAD for Interiors Beyond the Basics

WILEY

John Wiley & Sons, Inc.

Library of Congress Cataloging-in-Publication Data

Fiorello, Joseph A., 1963–
  CAD for interiors: beyond the basics / by Joseph A. Fiorello, Jr.
    p. cm.
  Sequel to: CAD for interiors : basics.
  ISBN 978-0-470-43885-5 (pbk. : alk. paper)
  1. Interior decoration—Computer-aided design. 2. Space (Architecture)—Computer-aided design. 3. AutoCAD. I. Title.
  NK2114.F57 2010
  747.0285'536—dc22
                                        2009037619

Printed in the United States of America

10 9 8 7 6 5 4 3 2 1

Contents

Preface

CAD for Interiors: Beyond the Basics was developed as a follow-up to CAD for Interiors: Basics. After successfully using CAD for Interiors: Basics as the required text for beginning AutoCAD courses, I clearly realized that an additional AutoCAD instruction book would help fine-tune one's AutoCAD skillsets for advanced AutoCAD courses.

CAD for Interiors: Beyond the Basics not only introduces end users to some advanced AutoCAD commands and functions, it also exposes them to the 2D Drafting and Annotation Workspace and the 3D Modeling Workspace. Understanding both of these workspaces is key to understanding CAD for Interiors because some functions can be accessed only by utilizing them.

Remaining consistent with CAD for Interiors: Basics, the style of instruction in this book is the same. The advanced instruction is presented with easy-to-follow, step-by-step instructions accompanied by the visual outcome of the commands performed. To reinforce the learning process, this book also comes with a companion DVD containing command/function explanations, chapter reviews, practice exercises, etc.

My hope is that the information presented will allow you to become a credible, productive member of the interior design profession.

Acknowledgments

I developed this book after teaching several beginning and advanced AutoCAD courses at colleges in and around the metropolitan Boston area. It became clear to me that in order to successfully master the software, my students needed to be exposed to the most up-to-date methods for interacting with AutoCAD. This book was designed to fine-tune their experience and expose them to all that AutoCAD offers, so they can become credible, productive members of the industry.

I would like to thank all of my students and fellow instructors for the opportunities they have afforded me. Not only have these experiences and relationships challenged me, they have also enriched the student experience. The accolades and success stories are truly rewarding.

Also greatly appreciated are the support and enthusiasm of Paul Drougas, Acquisitions Editor for John Wiley & Sons, Inc. Paul offered me this wonderful opportunity and has remained a true gentleman.

Finally, I'd like to thank my wife, Maureen, and my children, Joe and Alexa, for their support and understanding throughout the process of writing this book.

Introduction

Technology is constantly moving faster than the speed of light; AutoCAD is no exception. A new release of AutoCAD becomes available every year. Usually, these releases offer additional tools to help end users become more efficient in their drawing habits, thereby becoming more productive. However, the past few releases of AutoCAD have been major revamps to the software, including the 2D Drafting and Annotation Workspace, the 3D Modeling Workspace, and a totally new model space interface.

To remain competitive, users need to constantly utilize or at least be exposed to the newest features of the software. To make it easier for you to use, this advanced book uses the same style of instruction as *CAD for Interiors: Basics*. The advanced instruction is presented with easy-to-follow, step-by-step instructions accompanied by the visual outcome of the commands performed. To reinforce the learning process, this book also comes with a companion DVD. The following is a summary of each chapter:

Chapter 1: Introducing the AutoCAD 2D Interface This chapter introduces the user to the 2D Drafting and Annotation Workspace for AutoCAD releases 2008, 2009, and 2010. The software model space interface for each release is briefly discussed in order to explain how to interact with the software release the student is currently using.

Chapter 2: Advanced Drawing and Modifying Commands This chapter offers step-by-step instructions of some useful and advanced drawing/modifying commands. Although the instructions use AutoCAD release 2010 with the accompanying screen shots, students using AutoCAD release 2008 or 2009 should easily be able to interact.

Chapter 3: Advanced Annotation Tools This chapter explains how to use the 2D Drafting and Annotation Workspace and covers advancements made to annotating a drawing.

Chapter 4: Introducing Isometric Drawing This chapter reviews the method of utilizing AutoCAD to prepare simple isometric drawings.

Chapter 5: Introducing AutoCAD 3D Drawing This chapter reviews the 3D Modeling Workspace and introduces the student to drawing simple 3D solids and surfaces, as well as the basic solid/surface editing commands.

Chapter 6: The Commercial Office Space This chapter provides information about the Commercial Office Space project that will be used as an example to prepare millwork details for balance of the book.

Chapter 7: Starting the Millwork Detail Drawings This chapter provides step-by-step instructions to create the millwork details for the following items for the commercial office space:

- The Wood Base detail for the conference room and the reception areas
- The wood shelves and matching wall-support standards for the library

Chapter 8: Continuing the Millwork Detail Drawings This chapter provides step-by-step instructions to create the millwork details for the cabinet/bookshelf in the conference room.

Chapter 9: Progressing the Millwork Detail Drawings This chapter provides step-by-step instructions to create the millwork details for the reception desk.

Chapter 10: Completing the Millwork Detail Drawings This chapter provides step-by-step instructions to create the millwork details for the two-person workstation.

CAD for Interiors Beyond the Basics

CHAPTER 1

Introducing the AutoCAD 2D Interface

AFTER COMPLETING THIS CHAPTER, YOU WILL UNDERSTAND:

▶ The 2D interface of AutoCAD 2008, 2009, and 2010

▶ The differences between the AutoCAD Workspaces for 2D drawing

▶ Some of the pertinent new features of each release

When this book was written, AutoCAD 2010 was the current AutoCAD release. Because significant changes were made to the AutoCAD 2008 and 2009 interface, understanding those changes is prudent. AutoCAD usually releases a new version of AutoCAD every year. With each new release, toolbars, commands, and the user interface are enhanced. Sometimes these changes are significant. Because these new features can help you streamline the drawing process and increase productivity, you should explore them and become familiar with them. Typically, a New Features Workshop prompt will launch the first time AutoCAD is opened, allowing you the option to review the new features or wait until later. (See Figure 1.1.) These new features can also be accessed via the AutoCAD Help menu at any time.

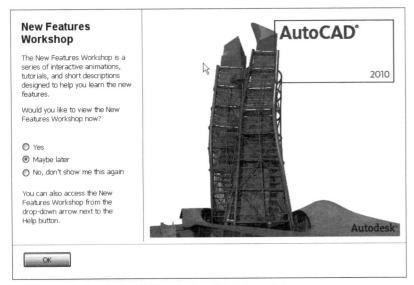

▶ **FIGURE 1.1:** The AutoCAD 2010 New Features Workshop window

If you have been using an earlier release of AutoCAD, chances are that you have been interacting with the software via the AutoCAD Classic Workspace and are familiar with it. Although this workspace is still available, the significant new features for each new release are accessed via the 2D Drafting and Annotation Workspace. While all of the commands can still be accessed using either the command line or the pulldown menus via the AutoCAD Classic Workspace, it is prudent to become familiar with the 2D Drafting and Annotation Workspace for 2D drawing. You can toggle your display between these workspaces. (See Figures 1.2 through 1.4.)

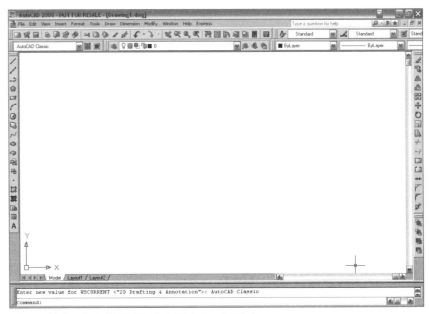

▶ **FIGURE 1.2:** AutoCAD 2008: The AutoCAD Classic Workspace

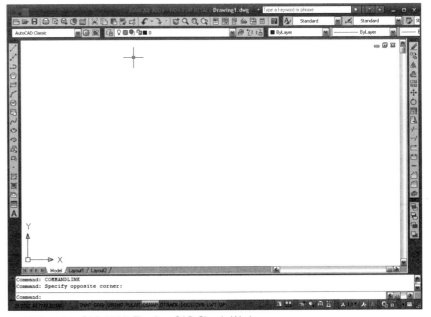

▶ **FIGURE 1.3:** AutoCAD 2009: The AutoCAD Classic Workspace

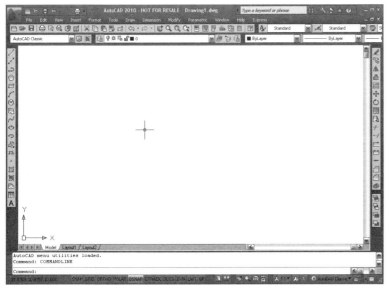

▶**FIGURE 1.4:** AutoCAD 2010: The AutoCAD Classic Workspace

If you are proficient with a recent AutoCAD release, you should have little difficulty getting up to speed. This chapter will provide an overview of some of the newest 2D drawing features of AutoCAD for releases 2008, 2009, and 2010. Refer to the particular AutoCAD release you wish to learn. For the most part, the instructions assume that you are familiar with AutoCAD. All of the instructions utilize the 2D Drafting and Annotation Workspace. Although this chapter reviews releases 2008 and 2009, later chapters will focus on AutoCAD 2010 and its features.

AutoCAD 2008

Major 2D drawing capabilities were added to the release of AutoCAD 2008—*annotative documentation,* in particular. This new feature allows you to add notes, tags, symbols, dimensions, etc. at the appropriate size for the scale of your drawing. Annotative documentation takes the guesswork out of the equation and ensures global standardization based on the scale of the drawing.

To begin, start by launching AutoCAD 2008 either via the icon on your desktop or using the Start menu. The 2D Drafting and Annotation Workspace might load when your version of AutoCAD 2008 is launched. If it does not load, do the following:

1. Position the cursor over the Workspaces Toolbar menu located at the top-left of the model space interface and click on it with the left mouse button. (See Figure 1.5.)

▶**FIGURE 1.5:** AutoCAD 2008: Launching the 2D Drafting and Annotation Workspace

This action will launch a menu of workspaces from which to choose.

2. Position the cursor over the 2D Drafting and Annotation Workspace option and click on it with the left mouse button.

This action will launch the 2D Drafting and Annotation Workspace (Figures 1.6 and 1.7). Some of its significant new 2D drawing features are listed here:

- The Information Center
- The Dashboard
- The addition of Annotation Scaling and Visibility to the Status toolbar
- The Clean Screen icon
- The Maximize/Minimize Viewport icon in layout space

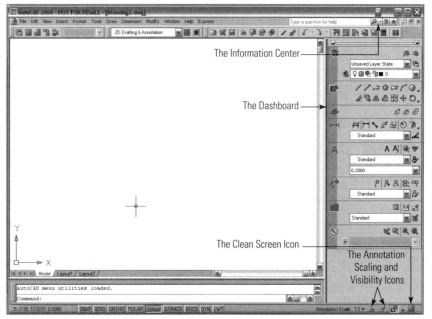

▶**FIGURE 1.6:** AutoCAD 2008: The 2D Drafting and Annotation Workspace's significant features in model space

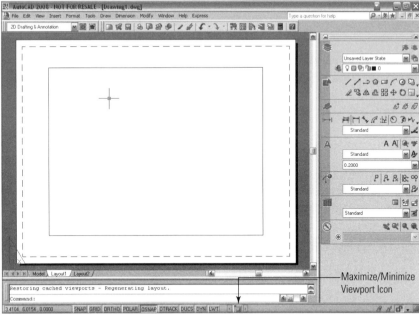

▶ **FIGURE 1.7:** AutoCAD 2008: The 2D Drafting and Annotation Workspace's significant features in layout space

The Information Center

The Information Center not only allows an additional way to access the Help menu, it also allows you to save past Help menu searches to a Favorites folder, and it allows you to exchange information about your product with Autodesk. (See Figures 1.8 through 1.10.)

▶ **FIGURE 1.8:** AutoCAD 2008: The Information Center window and icon

 ▶ **FIGURE 1.9:** AutoCAD 2008: The Communications Center icon

 ▶ **FIGURE 1.10:** AutoCAD 2008: The Favorites icon

The Dashboard

This interface improvement is quite significant because it neatly organizes all of the major commands and toolbars within a docked Dashboard (Figure 1.11) for easy access. The organization strongly reinforces a "point and click" mentality for performing many AutoCAD functions. The Dashboard includes the following toolbars:

- The Layers toolbar
- The 2D Draw toolbar
- The Annotation Scaling toolbar (new)
- The Dimensions toolbar
- The Text toolbar
- The Multileaders toolbar
- The Tables toolbar
- The 2D Navigate toolbar

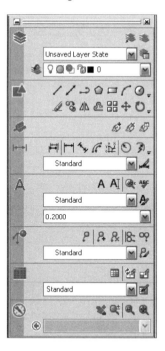

▶ **FIGURE 1.11:** AutoCAD 2008: The Dashboard

The Layers Toolbar

This toolbar still allows access to the Layer Properties Manager, as well as various other layer functions available to you, such as the function to isolate a layer or to set a layer current. (See Figure 1.12.)

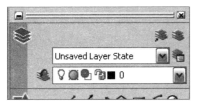

▶ **FIGURE 1.12:** AutoCAD 2008: The Dashboard's Layer toolbar

As an added feature, the Layers toolbar allows layers to be faded within model space and active viewports within layout tabs. To access this option, do the following:

1. Position the cursor over the Layers icon and click on it with the left mouse button to expand the toolbar (Figure 1.13).

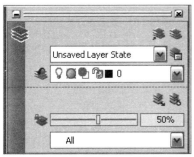

▶ **FIGURE 1.13:** AutoCAD 2008: The Dashboard's Layer toolbar (expanded)

Reducing the visual complexity in a drawing is referred to as *fading layers*. This technique can be useful when you need to keep specific layers active in a drawing in order to add information that may be contingent on the placement of items already drawn. For example, you might want to fade the Furniture layer of a drawing in order to add electrical or lighting information, because the placement of the furniture might need to be visible in order to line up electrical outlets or center lighting fixtures, etc.

A layer must be locked before it can be faded. This action will automatically fade any layer in the drawing that is currently locked. When the layers appear in their faded state, the visible geometry can utilize osnaps. Additionally, the fade can be adjusted and toggled between On and Off by clicking the AutoCAD Lock icon.

The 2D Draw Toolbar

The 2D Draw toolbar (Figure 1.14) allows access to all of the 2D drawing and modifying icons via the Dashboard. The top row consists of all of the drawing icons, and the bottom row consists of all of the modifying icons.

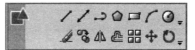

▶ **FIGURE 1.14:** AutoCAD 2008: The Dashboard's 2D Draw toolbar

To access additional drawing icons, do the following:

1. In the 2D Draw toolbar, position the cursor over the pulldown arrow at the end of the top row of icons and click it with the left mouse button.

This action will launch a flyout menu (Figure 1.15) showing the additional drawing icons.

▶ **FIGURE 1.15:** AutoCAD 2008: The Dashboard's 2D Draw toolbar and the Additional Drawing Icons flyout menu

Additional modifying icons can be accessed similarly. (See Figure 1.16.)

▶ **FIGURE 1.16:** AutoCAD 2008: The Dashboard's 2D Draw toolbar and the Additional Modifying Icons flyout menu

The Annotation Scaling Toolbar

Annotations are any items (such as symbols, text, and dimensions) added to a drawing. Scaling these objects has become significantly easier with the Annotation Scaling toolbar (Figures 1.17 and 1.18).

▶ **FIGURE 1.17:** AutoCAD 2008: The Dashboard's Annotation Scaling toolbar

▶ **FIGURE 1.18:** AutoCAD 2008: The Dashboard's Annotation Scaling icon

Now whenever any annotation is added to model space, it can be added with an annotative property. This property will automatically define the appropriate size of an object, text, or dimension style based on the chosen scale of your drawing in a Layout tab. Additional scales can be defined or deleted, and based on the scale of a given viewport, they will display appropriately. Prior to inserting any annotative object into the drawing, make sure to check the Annotation Visibility controls. These icons are located on the Status toolbar at the bottom-right of the AutoCAD interface. In order for the annotative objects to be visible when inserted into the drawing, these settings need to be turned On. To verify that they are, do the following:

1. Refer to the lower-right of the Status toolbar to visually verify that the Annotation Visibility icon is On. (See Figure 1.19.)

This is easy to determine. If the Sun icon appears, then Annotation Visibility is On. This designation will show annotative objects for all scales.

▶ **FIGURE 1.19:** AutoCAD 2008: The Annotation Visibility icons

If the Sun icon is shaded, the annotative objects will appear for the current scale only. If the icon is shaded, do the following:

1. Position the cursor over the Annotation Visibility icon and click on it with the left mouse button.

Also, verify that the Annotation icon located directly adjacent to the Annotation Visibility icon is also set to the On position. When this icon is set to the On position, it will appear with a yellow lightning bolt and AutoCAD will automatically add scales to annotative objects when the annotation scale changes. If this setting is not set accordingly, follow the previous step.

Symbols can be accessed using the Annotation Scaling toolbar. To access the tool palettes of the available symbols (Figure 1.20), do the following:

1. Position the cursor over the Annotation Scaling icon in the Annotation Scaling toolbar on the Dashboard, and click on it with the left mouse button.

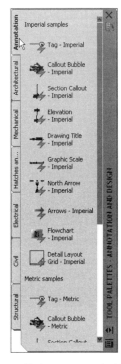

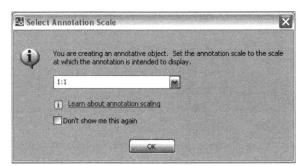

▶**FIGURE 1.20:** AutoCAD 2008: The
Annotation Scaling tool palettes

To insert a symbol into a drawing, do the following:

2. Position the cursor over the desired symbol in the Annotation tab on the tool
   palette and click on it with the left mouse button.

This action will launch the Select Annotation Scale window (Figure 1.21). It will
automatically default to a scale of 1:1.

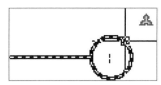

▶**FIGURE 1.21:** AutoCAD 2008: The Select Annotation Scale window

To change the annotation scale to ¼″ = 1′-0″ of that symbol, do the following:

3. Position the cursor over the pulldown arrow of the Annotation Scale control,
   scroll through the menu, select ¼″ = 1′-0″, and click on it with the left mouse
   button. Click the OK button with the left mouse button, and select an insertion
   point in the drawing by clicking it with the left mouse button.

This action will insert the symbol within model space at the correct size for a
drawing, which will ultimately be plotted at a scale of ¼″ = 1′-0″ and end the command. (See Figure 1.22.)

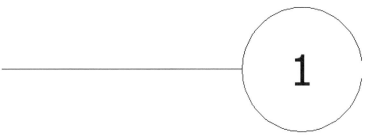

▶**FIGURE 1.22:** AutoCAD 2008: An annotation tag inserted in the drawing

An Annotative icon (Figure 1.23) will appear when the cursor is positioned over
an object that has annotative properties.

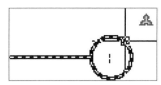

▶**FIGURE 1.23:** AutoCAD 2008: Annotative icon

The Annotation Scale of the drawing will be updated to ¼″ = 1′-0″. Refer to the
Status toolbar in the lower-right corner of the model space interface (Figure 1.24).

▶**FIGURE 1.24:** AutoCAD 2008: Annotation
Scale in the Status toolbar

Additional scales can also be added to annotative objects from the Annotation
Scaling toolbar (Figure 1.25).

► **FIGURE 1.25:** AutoCAD 2008:
The Add/Delete Scales icon

The Dimensions Toolbar

The Dimensions toolbar (Figure 1.26) still allows you to add all of the various dimensions to a drawing, as well as some new enhancements such as adding a jog to a linear dimension and breaking an extension line when it intersects with existing geometry. Additionally, dimensions can be added to a drawing as annotative objects.

► **FIGURE 1.26:** AutoCAD 2008: The Dimensions toolbar

The Text Toolbar

The Text toolbar (Figure 1.27) allows you to add multiline and single text to a drawing, as well as new text styles. An additional enhancement is the Spell Check option. Additionally, text can be added to a drawing as annotative objects.

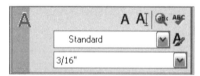

► **FIGURE 1.27:** AutoCAD 2008: The Text toolbar

The Multileaders Toolbar

The Multileaders toolbar (Figure 1.28) allows you to add a multileader style, as well as arrange and align leaders in the drawing.

► **FIGURE 1.28:** AutoCAD 2008: The Multileaders toolbar

The Tables Toolbar

The Tables toolbar (Figure 1.29) still allows you to add tables to your drawing, as well as other enhancements to create better quality tables with the addition of options such as borders and margins.

► **FIGURE 1.29:** AutoCAD 2008: The Tables toolbar

The 2D Navigate Toolbar

The 2D Navigate toolbar (Figure 1.30) still allows you to zoom into and pan across your drawing in real time.

► **FIGURE 1.30:** AutoCAD 2008: The 2D Navigate toolbar

Clean Screen

As you may have noticed, the drawing display area in the 2D Drafting and Annotation Workspace is somewhat limited because of the addition of the Dashboard. There are two options to remedy this. The first option is to simply modify the size of the Dashboard by stretching its limits, or you can use the Clean Screen icon. The Clean Screen icon (Figure 1.31) is significantly easier to use, and it allows you to toggle back and forth. The Clean Screen function basically hides all of the toolbars within the display, allowing the drawing space to take over the complete display (Figure 1.32).

► **FIGURE 1.31:** AutoCAD 2008:
The Clean Screen icon

To start the Clean Screen function, do the following:

1. Position the cursor over the Clean Screen icon in the bottom-right corner of the display, and click on it with the left mouse button.

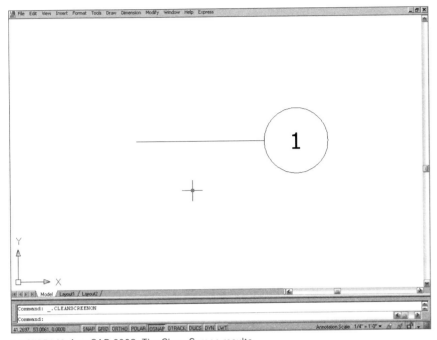

▶ **FIGURE 1.32:** AutoCAD 2008: The Clean Screen results

To disengage the Clean Screen function, do the following:

2. Position the cursor over the Clean Screen icon in the bottom-right corner of the display, and click on it with the left mouse button.

This action will return the display to the 2D Drafting and Annotation Workspace.

Maximize/Minimize Viewport

The Maximize/Minimize icon (Figures 1.33 and 1.34) is a significant enhancement to the Layout tab. This icon easily allows you to select/activate a viewport within any Layout tab.

▶ **FIGURE 1.33:** AutoCAD 2008: The Maximize Viewport icon

▶ **FIGURE 1.34:** AutoCAD 2008: The Minimize Viewport icon

To practice using this tool, make sure that your display is set to a Layout tab and do the following:

1. Position the cursor over the Maximize Viewport icon, and click on it with the left mouse button.

This action will maximize the viewport of the current Layout tab (Figure 1.35). It will appear as a red, dashed border. To deselect the viewport, do the following:

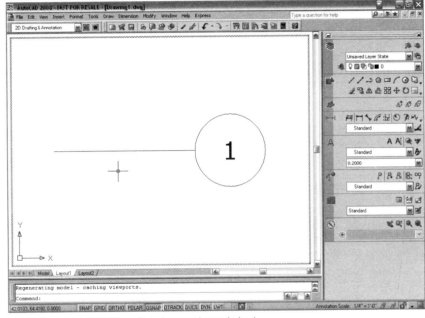

▶ **FIGURE 1.35:** AutoCAD 2008: The viewport is maximized.

2. Position the cursor over the Minimize Viewport icon, and click on it with the left mouse button.

This action will return the display to the Layout tab and deactivate the viewport.

AutoCAD 2009

The first thing you will notice is that the AutoCAD 2009 user interface has changed dramatically. Interacting with AutoCAD is much the same as interacting with the new Microsoft Office 2007 interface. The Dashboard has been replaced with a Ribbon that neatly organizes all of the commands you will use. The goal is to visually present the tools in a concise manner, thereby increasing the end user's productivity.

To begin, start by launching AutoCAD 2009 either via the icon on your desktop or via the Start menu. The 2D Drafting and Annotation Workspace may load when your version of AutoCAD 2009 is launched. If it does not load, do the following:

1. Position the cursor over the pulldown menu of the Workspaces toolbar located at the upper-left of the model space interface, or access the Workspace Switching icon (Figure 1.36 and Figure 1.37) in the lower-right of the model space interface on the Status toolbar. Click it with the left mouse button.

▶ **FIGURE 1.36:** AutoCAD 2009: Launching the 2D Drafting and Annotation Workspace

▶ **FIGURE 1.37:** AutoCAD 2009: The Workspace Switching icon

This action will launch a menu of workspaces from which to choose.

2. Position the cursor over the 2D Drafting and Annotation Workspace option, and click on it with the left mouse button.

This action will launch the 2D Drafting and Annotation Workspace. Some of the significant new 2D drawing features (Figure 1.38) are listed here:

- The Menu browser
- The Ribbon
- The Standard Annotation toolbar
- Improvements made to the Status toolbar
- Improved tooltips

The Menu Browser

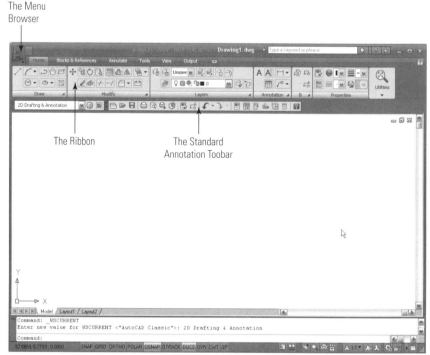

▶ **FIGURE 1.38:** AutoCAD 2009: The 2D Drafting and Annotation Workspace's significant features in model space

The Menu Browser

The Menu browser neatly organizes the dropdown menus that formerly appeared at the top of the model space interface within the AutoCAD Classic Workspace. Its icon (Figure 1.39) is located at the top-left of the model space interface.

▶ **FIGURE 1.39:** AutoCAD 2009: The Menu Browser icon

To access the Menu browser, do the following:

1. Position the cursor over the Menu Browser icon located at the top-left of the model space interface, and click on it with the left mouse button.

This action will open the Menu browser and allow access to commands in a way similar to that of the dropdown menus of the AutoCAD Classic Workspace. To interact with AutoCAD via the Menu browser (Figure 1.40), simply do the following:

2. Hover the cursor over the category to access, position the cursor over the command to launch, and click on it with the left mouse button.

▶ **FIGURE 1.40:** AutoCAD 2009: The Menu browser (expanded)

The Ribbon

Keeping in step with the new Microsoft Office 2007 interface, the new Ribbon replaces the Dashboard panel. Now all of the commands can be accessed using the Ribbon tabs located at the top of the user interface. (See Figure 1.41.)

▶ **FIGURE 1.41:** AutoCAD 2009: The Ribbon's Home tab

When the 2D Drafting and Annotation Workspace launches, the Home tab is the active tab on the Ribbon. This tab houses all of the basic commands used to draw and modify objects, annotate objects (add text and dimensions), and access layer controls. A new feature has been added to AutoCAD 2009 that allows the user to pin an action or a toolbar. This feature works in a fashion similar to the flyout menus you may be used to using. The major difference is that it allows the user to actually pin the expanded toolbar. To pin a toolbar on the Home tab, do the following:

1. Hover the cursor over the Modify toolbar on the Home tab of the Ribbon (Figure 1.42), and click on the pulldown arrow in the lower-right corner with the left mouse button.

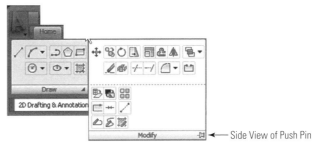

◄— Side View of Push Pin

▶ **FIGURE 1.42:** AutoCAD 2009: The Modify toolbar (prior to pin)

This action will launch the additional icons located on the Modify toolbar. The Push Pin icon is located in the lower-right corner of the toolbar. In order to pin this toolbar, simply do the following:

2. Hover the cursor over the side-view Push Pin icon, and click on it with the left mouse button to pin the toolbar in place. (See Figure 1.43.)

◄— Top View of Push Pin

▶ **FIGURE 1.43:** AutoCAD 2009: The Modify toolbar (pinned in place)

The pin will change to a top view. To return the toolbar to the previous position on the Ribbon, do the following:

3. Hover the cursor over the top-view Push Pin icon, and click on it with the left mouse button to return the toolbar to the Ribbon.

The Ribbon contains other categories of toolbars, which are described in the following text.

The Blocks and References Tab

The Blocks and References tab (Figure 1.44) houses the toolbars to create and edit blocks and block attributes, as well as attaching images and external references to the AutoCAD file.

▶ **FIGURE 1.44:** AutoCAD 2009: The Ribbon's Blocks and References tab

The Annotate Tab

The Annotate tab (Figure 1.45) houses the toolbars to dimension and add text to the file, as well as the toolbars, to create tables and multileaders and add or adjust annotation scales.

▶ **FIGURE 1.45:** AutoCAD 2009: The Ribbon's Annotate tab

The Tools Tab

The Tools tab (Figure 1.46) houses the toolbars to customize, query, and audit the drawing file.

▶ **FIGURE 1.46:** AutoCAD 2009: The Ribbon's Tools tab

The View Tab

The View tab (Figure 1.47) houses the toolbars to change the Universal Coordinate System (UCS) designation of the drawing file, as well as the toolbar to create and modify viewports.

▶ **FIGURE 1.47:** AutoCAD 2009: The Ribbon's View tab

The Output Tab

The Output tab (Figure 1.48) houses the toolbars to plot/publish and transmit the drawing file.

▶ **FIGURE 1.48:** AutoCAD 2009: The Ribbon's Output tab

The Standard Annotation Toolbar

The Standard Annotation Toolbar (docked directly below the Ribbon) houses the frequently used commands such as New, Save, Open, Undo/Redo. This toolbar (Figure 1.49) offers quick access to these commands.

▶ **FIGURE 1.49:** AutoCAD 2009: The Standard Annotation toolbar

The Status Toolbar

The Status Toolbar (located at the bottom of the model space interface) has been updated significantly. This toolbar (Figure 1.50) houses all of the icons from the former releases of AutoCAD, and new icons have been added to it. It is now possible to access 2D navigation tools to pan and zoom, control the annotation visibility of items in the drawing file, and access layout space as well. Object snaps are still located on the Status toolbar. You can now choose to display them as icons (Figure 1.51).

▶ **FIGURE 1.50**: AutoCAD 2009: The Status toolbar

To change the object snap's radio buttons to icons, do the following:

1. Hover the cursor over any of the object snaps, and click the radio button with the right mouse button.

   This action will launch a tooltip window.

2. Hover the cursor over the Use Icons option, and click on it with the left mouse button to change the appearance of the object snaps to icons.

▶ **FIGURE 1.51**: AutoCAD 2009: On the Status toolbar, object snaps are displayed as icons.

Improved Tooltips

AutoCAD's tooltips have also been dramatically improved. With a focus on productivity, the improved tooltips provide an easy way to learn more about a particular icon without having to access the Help menu. As in the past, when you hover the cursor over a particular icon, a small tooltip window will appear with the name of that icon. Now, when you hover the cursor over any icon, a small tooltip window appears with the name of the icon and a brief explanation. The longer the cursor hovers over the icon, the more additional information appears. (See Figures 1.52 and 1.53.)

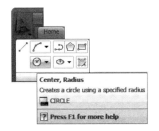

▶ **FIGURE 1.52**: AutoCAD 2009: The tooltip window

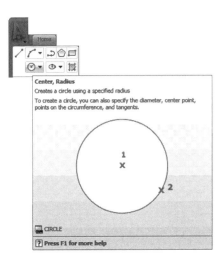

▶ **FIGURE 1.53**: AutoCAD 2009: The tooltip window (expanded)

AutoCAD 2010

AutoCAD 2008 and 2009 set a fast pace with improvements to the 2D AutoCAD; AutoCAD 2010 takes the AutoCAD 2009 interface a bit further. Because the new Microsoft Office 2007–style interface has been retained, you will notice a significantly expanded Ribbon. Some tools and commands have been improved and are easily accessed to reinforce end user productivity. One such improvement is *dynamic blocks*: it is now possible to edit a block in place without creating a whole new block to accommodate a different size or shape of a given component in that block. Another significant improvement is that PDF files can now be used as underlays in an AutoCAD drawing. In addition, the Menu browser and Application menu have been completely remodeled.

This portion of the chapter will offer a significantly abbreviated introduction because the balance of the book will cover the advanced improvements in AutoCAD 2010.

To begin, start by launching AutoCAD 2010 either via the icon on your desktop or via the Start menu. The 2D Drafting and Annotation Workspace may load when your version of AutoCAD 2010 is launched. If it does not load, do the following:

1. Position the cursor over the pulldown menu of the Workspace Switching icon in the lower-right of the model space interface on the Status toolbar (Figure 1.54). Click it with the left mouse button.

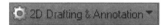

►FIGURE 1.54: AutoCAD 2010:
The Workspace Switching icon

This action will launch a menu of workspaces from which to choose.

2. Position the cursor over the 2D Drafting and Annotation Workspace option, and click on it with the left mouse button.

This action will launch the 2D Drafting and Annotation Workspace (Figure 1.55). Some of the significant new 2D drawing features are listed here:

- The Menu browser (completely remodeled)
- The Application menu (completely remodeled)
- The Quick Access toolbar
- An improved Help menu
- The Ribbon (completely expanded)

The Menu   The Quick
Browser   Access Toolbar

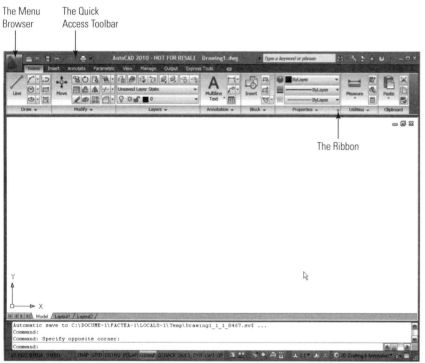

The Ribbon

►FIGURE 1.55: AutoCAD 2010: The 2D Drafting and Annotation Workspace's significant features in model space

The Menu Browser

The Menu browser has been completely remodeled. This new browser basically houses all of the commands that were formerly found on the File pulldown menu. In addition, the Application menu for the corresponding command prompts has also been remodeled. The Menu Browser icon (Figure 1.56) is located at the top of the model space interface within the AutoCAD Classic Workspace. This icon is located at the top-left corner of the model space interface.

►FIGURE 1.56: AutoCAD 2010:
The Menu Browser icon

To access the Menu browser, do the following:

1. Position the cursor over the Menu Browser icon located at the top-left of the model space interface, and click on it with the left mouse button.

This action will open the Menu browser (Figure 1.57), allowing access to commands in a way similar to that of the dropdown menus in the AutoCAD Classic Workspace. To interact with AutoCAD using the Menu browser, simply do the following:

2. Hover the cursor over the category to access, position the cursor over the command to launch, and click on it with the left mouse button.

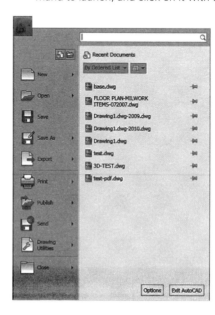

►FIGURE 1.57: AutoCAD 2010:
The Menu browser (expanded)

The Application Menu

The Application Menu browser (Figure 1.58) has been completely remodeled too. Now, when the Menu browser is accessed, the Application Menu browser launches with larger icons and an explanation of the function.

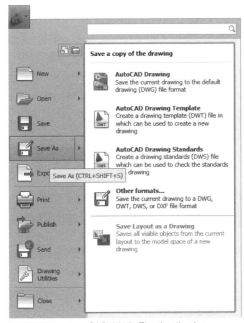

▶ **FIGURE 1.58:** AutoCAD 2010: The Application Menu browser (expanded)

To access the Application Menu browser once the Menu browser has been expanded, do the following:

1. Position the cursor over the Save As category located on the Menu browser, and click on it with the left mouse button.

This action will launch an expanded view of the Save As function. To interact with AutoCAD via this menu, simply do the following:

2. Position the cursor over the AutoCAD Drawing option, and then click on it with the left mouse button. (See Figure 1.59.)

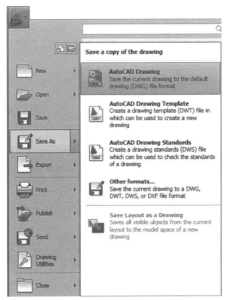

▶ **FIGURE 1.59:** AutoCAD 2010: Saving a drawing file as an AutoCAD drawing

This action will allow the drawing to be saved as an AutoCAD drawing. Simply follow the typical steps to save the file.

The Quick Access Toolbar

The Quick Access toolbar (docked to the right of the Menu Browser icon) houses the frequently used commands such as New, Save, Open, and Undo/Redo. This toolbar offers quick access to these commands. (See Figures 1.60 and 1.61.)

▶ **FIGURE 1.60:** AutoCAD 2010: The Quick Access toolbar

▶ **FIGURE 1.61:** AutoCAD 2010:
The Quick Access toolbar
(expanded)

Help Menu Improvement

You can still access information about AutoCAD commands and tools either using the Information Center located at the top-right of the model space interface or by pressing the F1 key on the keyboard. Although these methods are useful, you have to access the Contents, Index, or Search tabs in the Help menu. Sometimes these search options list an unrelated item or you need to scroll through many items to find the information you need. However, you don't have to go to so much trouble anymore. Now you can find information about a particular icon with minimal effort.

For example, to find additional information about the Line icon, do the following:

1. Hover the cursor over the Line icon and press the F1 key on the keyboard.

This action will launch the section of the Help menu that refers to information about the Line icon. (See Figure 1.63.)

Not only can basic commands be accessed via this toolbar, but it is totally customizable. The basic commands (which are listed) can be removed from the toolbar and additional commands/icons can be added. To customize this toolbar, do the following:

1. Hover the cursor over the pulldown arrow tab located on the right side of the Quick Access toolbar, and click on it with the left mouse button.

This action will launch the Customize Quick Access Toolbar tooltip window. Note that all of the icons that appear on the toolbar have a check mark to the right of the name of the command in this tooltip window. In order to remove an icon from the toolbar, do the following:

2. Hover the cursor over the command option for Plot, and click on it with the left mouse button.

This action will remove the Plot icon from the Quick Access toolbar and allow you to customize the toolbar with an additional icon if you like (Figure 1.62).

▶ **FIGURE 1.62:** AutoCAD 2010: The Quick Access toolbar (without the Plot icon)

To return the Plot icon to the Quick Access toolbar, do the following:

3. Hover the cursor over the pulldown arrow tab located on the right side of the Quick Access toolbar, and click on it with the left mouse button. Then, hover the cursor over the command option for Plot, and click on it with the left mouse button.

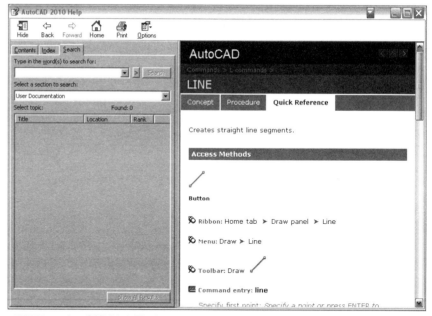

▶ **FIGURE 1.63:** AutoCAD 2010: The improved Help Menu window

The Ribbon (Expanded)

Keeping in step with the new Microsoft Office 2007–style interface, the new Ribbon replaces the Dashboard panel. Now all of the commands can be accessed via the Ribbon tabs located at the top of the user interface. (See Figure 1.64.)

▶ **FIGURE 1.64:** AutoCAD 2010: The Ribbon's Home tab

When the 2D Drafting and Annotation Workspace launches, the Home tab is the active tab on the Ribbon. This tab houses all of the basic commands used to draw and modify objects, as well as annotate objects (add text and dimensions to objects) and layer controls. A measuring toolbar is also added to this tab.

The Insert Tab

The Insert tab (Figure 1.65) houses the toolbars used to create and edit blocks and block attributes, as well as attach images and external references to an AutoCAD file.

▶ **FIGURE 1.65:** AutoCAD 2010: The Ribbon's Insert tab

The Annotate Tab

The Annotate tab (Figure 1.66) houses the toolbars used to dimension and add text to the file, as well as the toolbars to create tables and multileaders and to add/adjust annotation scales.

▶ **FIGURE 1.66:** AutoCAD 2010: The Ribbon's Annotate tab

The Parametric Tab

The Parametric tab (Figure 1.67) houses the toolbars used to draw with geometric and dimensional constraints. Basically, this toolbar allows you to draw 2D geometry with a restriction on particular elements or associations of a given object based on the relationship of a given angle, dimension, or size and distance of an object, etc. This ability is useful in the manufacturing field.

▶ **FIGURE 1.67:** AutoCAD 2010: The Ribbon's Parametric tab

The View Tab

The View tab (Figure 1.68) houses the toolbars used to change the UCS designation of the drawing file, the toolbar to create and modify viewports, and the toolbar to control the Status toolbar.

▶ **FIGURE 1.68:** AutoCAD 2010: The Ribbon's View tab

The Manage Tab

The Manage tab (Figure 1.69) houses the toolbars used to customize AutoCAD.

▶ **FIGURE 1.69:** AutoCAD 2010: The Ribbon's Output tab

The Output Tab

The Output tab (Figure 1.70) houses the toolbars used to plot/publish and transmit a drawing file.

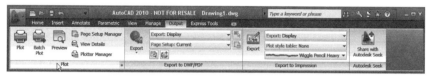

▶**FIGURE 1.70:** AutoCAD 2010: The Ribbon's Output tab

The Express Tools Tab

The Express Tools tab (Figure 1.71) houses toolbars with additional options that let you perform expanded commands such as placing text on an arc or enclosing it in a circle.

▶**FIGURE 1.71:** AutoCAD 2010: The Ribbon's Express Tools tab

CHAPTER 2

Advanced Drawing and Modifying Commands

AFTER COMPLETING THIS CHAPTER, YOU WILL UNDERSTAND:

▶ How to use the expanded Ribbon

▶ How to pin and unpin toolbars

▶ How to use advanced drawing techniques

▶ How to modify commands and tools

As discussed in Chapter 1, the AutoCAD 2010 interface resembles the Microsoft Office 2007 interface. A significant improvement to AutoCAD 2009 is the expansion of the Ribbon. More tools have been added to make it even easier to draw and increase productivity. To get the most out of AutoCAD 2010, it is prudent to work within the 2D Drafting and Annotation Workspace. This workspace houses the expanded Ribbon.

This chapter will introduce you to some of the advanced drawing/modifying commands and tools for 2D drawing. To keep the introduction brief, not every command, icon, and toolbar will be explained. Hopefully, after completing this chapter, you will explore other commands that were not reviewed. Other commands will be explained in the appropriate chapters.

To begin this introduction, launch AutoCAD 2010 using the icon on your desktop or via the Start menu. (See Figure 2.1.)

▶ **FIGURE 2.1:** AutoCAD 2010: The Desktop Shortcut icon

The 2D Drafting and Annotation Workspace may load when your version of Auto-CAD 2010 is launched. If it does not load, do the following:

1. Access the Workspace Switching icon in the lower-right of the model space interface at the Status toolbar, and click on the 2D Drafting and Annotation Workspace.

2. Access the Application menu via the Menu browser located in the upper-right corner of the model space interface, click the Drawing Utilities folder, and click Units. (See Figure 2.2.)

3. Set the drawing units to Architectural.

4. In the Status toolbar, set the Ortho and Osnap functions to On.

5. Set the Ribbon to Home. (See Figure 2.3.)

You are now ready to begin. Typically, the AutoCAD drawing file should be saved prior to working on it. However, because this chapter is meant to be interactive, there's no need to save the file.

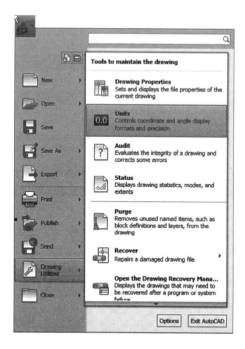

▶ **FIGURE 2.2:** Use the Application menu to set the drawing units.

▶ **FIGURE 2.3:** The Ribbon's Home tab

The Draw Toolbar

So that you can easily access some of the expanded icons available on the Ribbon, you can *pin* some of the toolbars. This feature, which was added to the AutoCAD 2009 release, is similar to the flyout menus you have probably used. The major difference is that you can actually pin the expanded toolbar. To pin the Draw toolbar on the Home tab, do the following:

1. Hover the cursor over the Draw toolbar on the Home tab of the Ribbon, and click on the pulldown arrow in the lower-right corner with the left mouse button.

This action will launch the additional icons located on the Draw toolbar. The Push Pin icon is located in the lower-right corner of the toolbar. In order to pin this toolbar, simply do the following:

2. Hover the cursor over the side-view icon of the pin, and click on it with the left mouse button to pin the toolbar in place. (See Figure 2.4.)

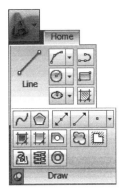

▶ FIGURE 2.4: The Draw toolbar (pinned in place)

The Center Ellipse Command

The Ellipse tool can be used to draw 2D and 3D ellipses. To create a 2"-wide by 4"-high vertical ellipse using the Center Ellipse icon, do the following:

1. Click the Center Ellipse icon (Figure 2.5) with the left mouse button.

▶ FIGURE 2.5: The Center Ellipse icon

The following prompt appears on the command line:
```
Command: _ellipse
Specify axis endpoint of ellipse or [Arc/Center]: _c
Specify center of ellipse:
```

2. Left-click the center point of the ellipse anywhere in model space.

The following prompt appears on the command line:
```
Specify endpoint of axis:
```

3. Make sure the Ortho function is On, position the cursor in the west direction, type **1**, and right-click.

The following prompt appears on the command line:
```
Specify distance to other axis or [Rotation]:
```

4. Position the cursor in the north direction, type **2**, and press the Enter key.

This action will end the command and create a 2" × 4" ellipse. If you are unable to see the ellipse within the model space display, you may be zoomed in too close. To view the ellipse on your display, do the following:

1. Type **Z** and press the Enter key, and then type **E** and press the Enter key.

This action will zoom the ellipse to fit within your model space display. (See Figure 2.6.)

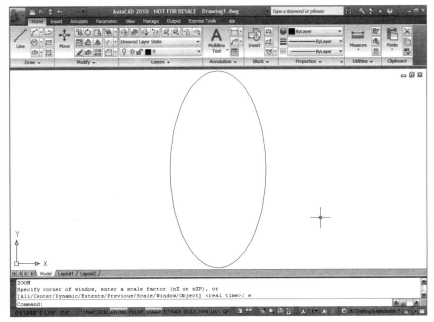

▶ FIGURE 2.6: The completed ellipse

The Spline Command

The Spline tool creates a polyline with smooth curved surfaces.

1. Click the Spline icon with the left mouse button (Figure 2.7).

▶ FIGURE 2.7: The Spline icon

The following prompt appears on the command line:
```
Command: _spline
Specify first point or [Object]:
```

2. Left-click the start point of the spline anywhere in model space.

The following prompt appears on the command line:
```
Specify next point:
```

3. Ensure the Ortho function is On, position the cursor in the east direction, type **1**, and right-click.

The following prompt appears on the command line:
```
Specify next point or [Close/Fit tolerance] <start tangent>:
```

4. Position the cursor in the north direction, type **2**, and press the Enter key.

5. To end the command, press the Enter key.

The following prompt appears on the command line:
```
Specify start tangent:
```

6. Press the Enter key.

The following prompt appears on the command line:
```
Specify end tangent:
```

7. Press the Enter key to end the command. (See Figure 2.8.)

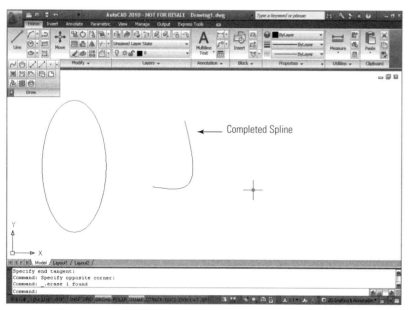

Completed Spline

▶ **FIGURE 2.8:** The completed spline

The Revision Cloud Command

The Revision Cloud tool creates a cloud-like polyline around changes made to construction documents once they have already been issued. The arc length of the revision cloud can be controlled based on the graphic presentation desired. The maximum arc length is 4′. To create a revision cloud with a maximum arc length of 1″, do the following:

1. Click the Revision Cloud icon (Figure 2.9) with the left mouse button.

▶ **FIGURE 2.9:** The Revision Cloud icon

The following prompt appears on the command line:
```
Command: _revcloud
Minimum arc length: 4' Maximum arc length: 4' Style: Normal
Specify start point or[Arc length/Object/Style] <object>:
```

2. Type **A** and press the Enter key to assign a new arc length.

The following prompt appears on the command line:
```
Specify minimum length of arc <4'>:
```

3. Type **1** and press the Enter key.

The following prompt appears on the command line:
```
Specify maximum length of arc <4'>:
```

4. Type **1** and press the Enter key.

The following prompt appears on the command line:
```
Specify start point or[Arc length/Object/Style] <object>:
```

5. Click the starting point of the revision cloud.

The following prompt appears on the command line:
```
Guide crosshairs along cloud path…
```

6. Move the cursor in a clockwise motion to continue the revision cloud.

To close the revision cloud, do the following:

7. Position the cursor over the start point of the revision cloud.

The following prompt appears on the command line:
```
Revision cloud finished.
```

These steps will create a completed revision cloud (Figure 2.10).

THE DRAW TOOLBAR 23

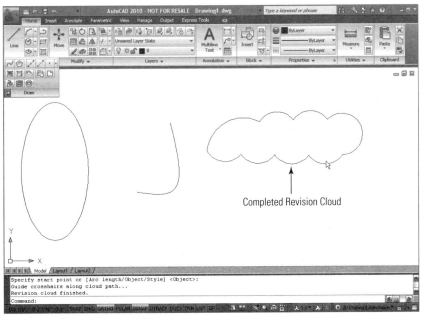

►**FIGURE 2.10**: The completed revision cloud

The Donut Command

The Donut tool allows you to either draw a filled (solid-hatch) ring or circle. To draw a 2″ diameter ring with a 1″ diameter circle, do the following:

1. Click the Donut icon (Figure 2.11) with the left mouse button.

►**FIGURE 2.11**: The Donut icon

The following prompt appears on the command line:
```
Command: DONUT
Specify inside diameter of donut <0'-0">:
```

2. Type **1** and press the Enter key to assign the inside diameter.

The following prompt appears on the command line:
```
Specify outside diameter of donut <0'-0">:
```

3. Type **2** and press the Enter key.

The following prompt appears on the command line:
```
Specify center of donut of <exit>:
```

4. Left-click a point within the model space display and press the Enter key. This action will create a filled, 2″ diameter donut ring with a 1″ diameter.

To create a solid filled circle, simply specify an inside diameter of zero for the donut. (See Figure 2.12.)

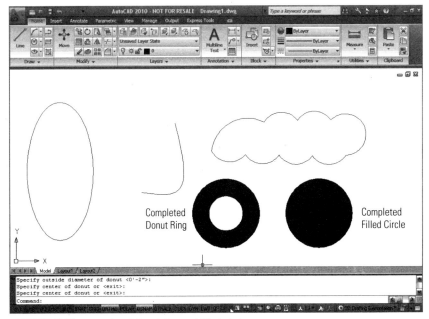

►**FIGURE 2.12**: The completed donut ring and filled circle

The Divide Command

The Divide tool allows you to assign evenly spaced divisions to an object. To divide a line segment into three evenly spaced divisions, do the following:

1. Ensure the Ortho function is On, and draw a horizontal line of any length.

2. Click the Divide icon (Figure 2.13) with the left mouse button. This icon appears as a flyout under the Multiple Points icon.

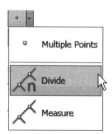

► **FIGURE 2.13:** The Divide icon

The following prompt appears on the command line:
```
Command: _divide
Select object to divide:
```

3. Position the cursor over the previously drawn horizontal line and click on it with the left mouse button.

The following prompt appears on the command line:
```
Enter the number of segments or [Block]:
```

4. Type **3** and press the Enter key.

This action will end the command and assign Node points to the line segment at three equal intervals. To prove this, do the following:

1. Check the osnap settings in your drawing, and make sure the Node setting is checked and the Ortho function is On.

2. Start the Line command, hover the cursor over the implied end of the first division segment until the Node osnap is highlighted, and draw a vertical line from that point. (See Figure 2.14.)

► **FIGURE 2.14:** The Node point is positioned at the first division.

3. Start the Line command, hover the cursor over the implied end of the second division segment until the Node osnap is highlighted, and draw a vertical line from that point. (See Figures 2.15 and 2.16.)

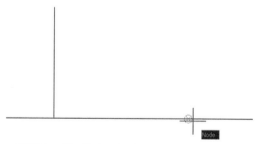

► **FIGURE 2.15:** The Node point is positioned at the second division.

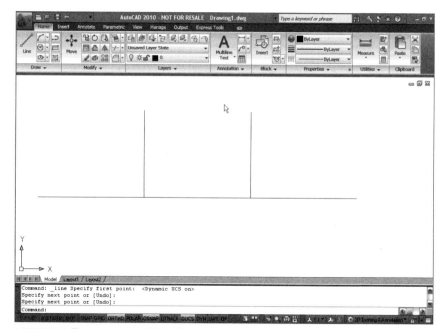

► **FIGURE 2.16:** The completed, divided line segment

The Modify Toolbar

In order to review some of the expanded icons available on the Modify toolbar, do the following:

1. Hover the cursor over the Modify toolbar on the Home tab of the Ribbon and click on the pulldown arrow in the lower-right corner with the left mouse button.

This action will launch the additional icons located on the Draw toolbar. In order to pin this toolbar, simply do the following:

2. Hover the cursor over the side-view Push Pin icon and click on it with the left mouse button to pin the toolbar in place. (See Figure 2.17.)

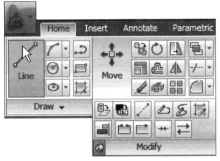

►**FIGURE 2.17:** The Modify toolbar (pinned in place)

The Scale Command

The Scale tool allows you to change the size of selected geometry while keeping all of the components proportionate. To demonstrate the Scale command, do the following:

1. Create a 2″ × 2″ square using the Rectangle command.

2. Click the Scale icon (Figure 2.18) with the left mouse button.

 ►**FIGURE 2.18:** The Scale icon

The following prompt appears on the command line:
Command: _scale
Select objects:

3 Click the previously drawn square.

The following prompt appears on the command line:
Specify base point:

4. Press the Enter key.

The following prompt appears on the command line:
Select objects: 1 found
Select objects:

5. Ensure the Osnap function is On, and click the bottom-left endpoint of the rectangle.

The following prompt appears on the command line:
Specify scale factor or [Copy/Reference] <0'-1">:

6. Make sure the Osnap function is On, and click the bottom-left endpoint of the square.

The following prompt appears on the command line:
Specify scale factor or [Copy/Reference] <0'-1">:

This action will allow you to scale the rectangle to any random size (either larger or smaller) by simply moving your cursor.

7. To scale the square to a 3″ × 3″ square, type **1.5** and press the Enter key.

This action will scale the rectangle to one and half times its original size (3″ × 3″) and end the command (Figure 2.19).

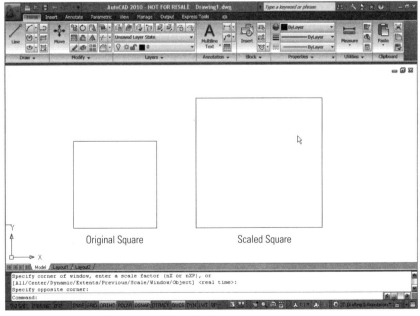

Original Square   Scaled Square

►**FIGURE 2.19:** The original square and the scaled square

The Fillet Command

The Fillet tool allows you to add a curved radius at the intersection of two line segments. Using the previously scaled 3″ × 3″ square, do the following:

1. Click the Fillet icon (Figure 2.20) with the left mouse button.

▶ **FIGURE 2.20**: The Fillet icon

The following prompt appears on the command line:
Command: _fillet
Current settings: Mode = Trim, Radius 0'-0"
Select first object or [Undo/Polyline/Radius/Trim/Multiple]:

Because the current radius is set to 0′-0″, a new radius must be set. Keep in mind that a radius must not exceed the distance of the line segment.

2. Type **R** and press the Enter key.

The following prompt appears on the command line:
Specify fillet radius: <0'-0">

To fillet the upper-left corner of the rectangle with a radius of ¾″, do the following:

3. Type **¾″** and press the Enter key.

The following prompt appears on the command line:
Select first object or [Undo/Polyline/Radius/Trim/Multiple]:

4. Left-click the top horizontal line of the square closest to the upper-left corner.

The following prompt appears on the command line:
Select second object or shift-select to apply corner:

5. Left-click the left vertical line of the square closest to the upper-left corner.

This action will add a curved radius of ¾″ to the upper-left side of the square and end the command (Figure 2.21).

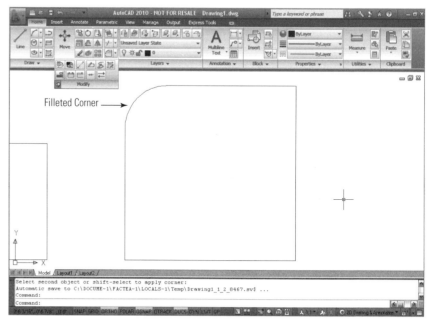

Filleted Corner

▶ **FIGURE 2.21**: A square with the upper-left corner filleted

The Chamfer Command

The Chamfer tool allows you to add beveled edge at the intersection of two line segments. Using the previously scaled 3″ × 3″ square, do the following:

1. Click the Chamfer icon (Figure 2.22) with the left mouse button.

▶ **FIGURE 2.22**: The Chamfer icon

The Chamfer icon is located on the flyout menu with the Fillet icon on the Modify toolbar.

The following prompt appears on the command line:
Command: _chamfer
(Trim mode) Current chamfer Dist1= 0'-0", Dist2 = 0'-0"
Select first line or [Undo/Polyline/Distance/Angle/Trim/mEthod/Multiple]:

Because the current distances are set to 0′-0″, a distance for each direction must be set. Again, keep in mind that the distance must not exceed the distance of the line segment.

2. Type **D** and press the Enter key.

   The following prompt appears on the command line:
   `Specify first chamfer distance: <0'-0">`

   To chamfer the lower-right corner of the square with a distance of ¾", do the following:

3. Type ¾" and press the Enter key.

   The following prompt appears on the command line:
   `Specify second chamfer distance <0'-0 ¾">`

4. Type ¾" and press the Enter key.

   The following prompt appears on the command line:
   `Select first line or [Undo/Polyline/Distance/Angle/Trim/mEthod/Multiple]:`

5. Left-click the bottom horizontal line of the square closest to the lower-right corner.

   The following prompt appears on the command line:
   `Select second object or shift-select to apply corner:`

6. Left-click the right vertical line of the square closest to the lower-right corner.

   This action will add a beveled edge of ¾" to the lower-right side of the square and end the command (Figure 2.23).

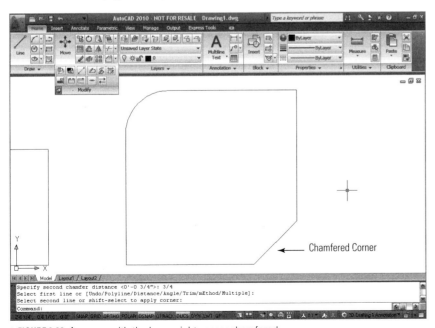

▶**FIGURE 2.23:** A square with the lower-right corner chamfered

The Edit Polyline Command

The Edit Polyline tool allows you to edit a previously drawn polyline. Many options are available to edit a polyline, such as the width or the linetype, etc. To change the width of the previously modified 3" × 3" square, do the following:

1. Click the Polyline Edit icon (Figure 2.24) with the left mouse button.

   ▶**FIGURE 2.24:** The Edit Polyline icon

   The following prompt appears on the command line:
   `Command: _pedit Select polyline or[Multiple]:`

2. Click the previously modified square.

   The following prompt appears on the command line:
   `Enter an option [Open/Join/Width/Edit vertex/Fit/Spline/Decurve/Ltype gen/Reverse/Undo]:`

   To change the width of the polyline, do the following:

3. Type **W** and press the Enter key.

   The following prompt appears on the command line:
   `Specify second chamfer distance <0'-0 ¾">`

4. Type ¾" and press the Enter key.

   The following prompt appears on the command line:
   `Specify new width for all segments:`

5. Type ¼" and press the Enter key.

   The following prompt appears on the command line:
   `Enter an option [Open/Join/Width/Edit vertex/Fit/Spline/Decurve/Ltype gen/Reverse/Undo]:`

6. Press the Enter key.

   This action will change the width of the modified square to a thickness of ¼" (Figure 2.25).

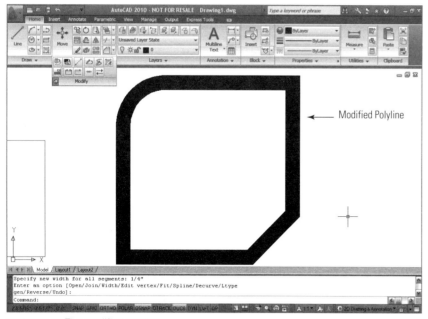

▶ **FIGURE 2.25:** The modified polyline

The Lengthen Command

The Lengthen tool allows you to lengthen a line segment by a given amount. This tool also allows you to either trim or extend geometry. To lengthen a line segment, do the following:

1. Make sure the Ortho function is On, and draw a 2″ horizontal line.

2. Click the Lengthen icon (Figure 2.26) with the left mouse button.

▶ **FIGURE 2.26:** The Lengthen icon

The following prompt appears on the command line:
```
Command: _lengthen
Select an object or[Delta/Percent/Total/Dynamic]:
```

3. Left-click the previously drawn line segment.

The following prompt appears on the command line:
```
Current length: 0'-2"
Select an object or[Delta/Percent/Total/Dynamic]:
```

To lengthen the line segment an additional inch, do the following:

4. Type **DE** and press the Enter key.

The following prompt appears on the command line:
```
Enter delta length or [Angle]: <0'-0">:
```

5. Type **1″** and press the Enter key.

The following prompt appears on the command line:
```
Select an object to change or [Undo]:
```

6. Click the 2″ horizontal line segment.

The following prompt appears on the command line:
```
Select an object to change or [Undo]:
```

7. Press the Enter key.

This action will lengthen the line segment to 3″ and end the command.

The Break Command

The Break tool allows you to *break* a selected piece of geometry at a given point. To break the previously lengthened line segment, do the following:

1. Make sure the Osnap function is On.

2. Click the Break icon (Figure 2.27) with the left mouse button.

▶ **FIGURE 2.27:** The Break icon

The following prompt appears on the command line:
```
Command: _break Select object:
```

3. Left-click the previously lengthened 3″ line segment.

The following prompt appears on the command line:
```
Specify second break point or[First point]:
```

To break the line segment at the midpoint, do the following:

4. Type **F** and press the Enter key.

The following prompt appears on the command line:
```
Specify first break point:
```

5. Left-click the midpoint of the line segment.

The following prompt appears on the command line:
```
Specify second break point:
```

6. Left-click the midpoint of the line segment.

This action will break the line segment into two separate line segments at the midpoint of the original line segment. To prove this point, select both line segments to expose the grips. (See Figure 2.28.)

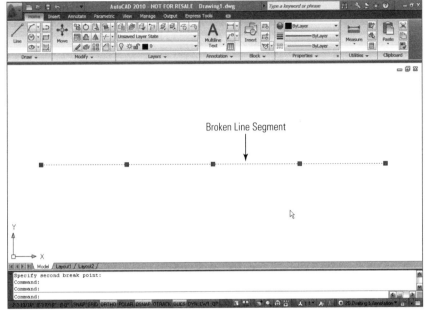

▶ **FIGURE 2.28:** The broken line segment

The Join Command

The Join tool allows you to join selected pieces of geometry on the same plane and convert them to a single segment. To join the previously broken line segments, do the following:

1. Ensure the Ortho function is On and move the previously broken line segments slightly away from each other.

2. Click the Join icon (Figure 2.29) with the left mouse button.

▶ **FIGURE 2.29:** The Join icon

The following prompt appears on the command line:
Command: _join Select source object:

3. Left-click one of the line segments.

The following prompt appears on the command line:
Select lines to join to source:

4. Left-click the other the line segment.

The following prompt appears on the command line:
Select lines to join to source:

5. Press the Enter key.

This action will join the two previously broken line segments and make them a single piece of geometry. To prove this point, simply click the joined line segment.

The Align Command

The Align tool allows you to align objects with other points on objects. To align the previously chamfered edge of the square with the previously joined line segment, do the following:

1. Make sure the Osnap function is On.

2. Click the Align icon (Figure 2.30) with the left mouse button.

▶ **FIGURE 2.30:** The Align icon

The following prompt appears on the command line:
Command: _align
Select objecst:

3. Left-click the chamfered edge of the square and press the Enter key.

The following prompt appears on the command line:
Specify first source object:

4. Left-click the chamfered edge endpoint of the bottom horizontal line of the square.

The following prompt appears on the command line:
Specify first destination point:

5. Left-click the left endpoint of the horizontal line.

The following prompt appears on the command line:
Specify second source point:

6. Left-click the chamfered edge endpoint of the bottom vertical line of the square.

The following prompt appears on the command line:
Specify first destination point:

7. Left-click the right endpoint of the horizontal line.

The following prompt appears on the command line:
Specify third source point or <continue>:

8. Press the Enter key.

The following prompt appears on the command line:
Scale objects based on alignment points? [Yes/No] <N>:

9. Press the Enter key again.

This action will align the lower-right chamfered edge of the square with the horizontal line and end the command. (See Figures 2.31 and 2.32.)

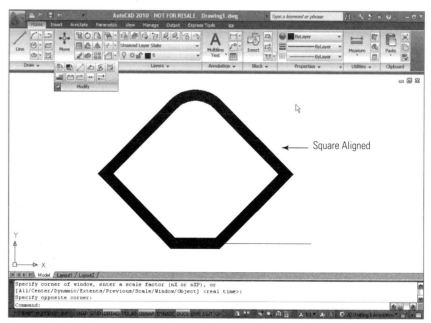

▶ **FIGURE 2.32:** The chamfered edge of the square aligned with horizontal line

The Utilities Toolbar

A useful icon on the Utilities toolbar (Figure 2.33) is the Distance icon.

▶ **FIGURE 2.33:** The Utilities toolbar

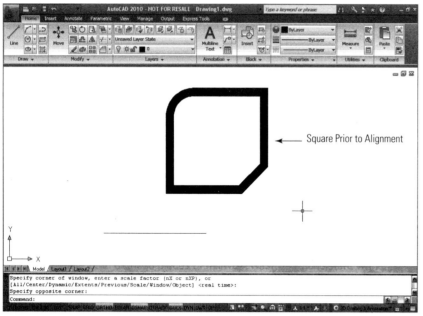

▶ **FIGURE 2.31:** The square prior to alignment with horizontal line

The Distance Command

The Distance tool allows you to measure the length between two points. To measure the distance between two endpoints of a line segment, do the following:

1. Make sure the Ortho function is On, and draw a line segment at any random length.

2. Click the Distance icon (Figure 2.34) with the left mouse button.

▶ **FIGURE 2.34:** The Distance icon

> *The following prompt appears on the command line:*
> Command: _MEASUREGEOM
> Enter an option [Distance/Radius/Angle/Area/Volume] <Distance>:
> _distance:
> Specify first point:

3. Left-click one of the endpoints of the previously drawn line.

> *The following prompt appears on the command line:*
> Specify second point or [Multiple points]:

4. Left-click the opposite endpoint of the previously drawn line.

This action will launch the dimension of the line segment and also list the information in the command line (Figure 2.35).

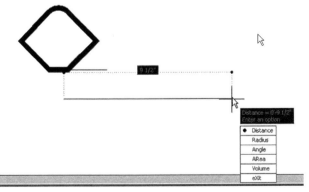

▶ **FIGURE 2.35:** The Distance command is executed

The Ribbon View Tab

The View tab (Figure 2.36) houses several useful tools that will help drawing with AutoCAD easier. Some of these tools include navigating the 2D model space, changing views when drawing isometric objects, and an additional way to control the Status toolbar.

▶ **FIGURE 2.36:** The Ribbon's View tab

The Palettes Toolbar

▶ **FIGURE 2.37:** The Palettes toolbar

The Tool Palettes Command

The Tool Palettes tool houses multiple tags and other annotative items for use when labeling floor plans and elevations. To insert a tag, do the following:

1. Click the Tool Palettes icon (Figure 2.38) with the left mouse button.

▶ **FIGURE 2.38:** The Tool Palettes icon

> *The following prompt appears on the command line:*
> Command: _toolpalettes

The Tool Palettes – All Palettes window will also launch (Figure 2.39).

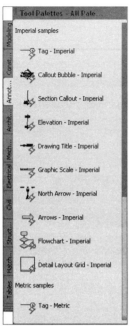

▶**FIGURE 2.39:** The Tool Palettes –
All Palettes window

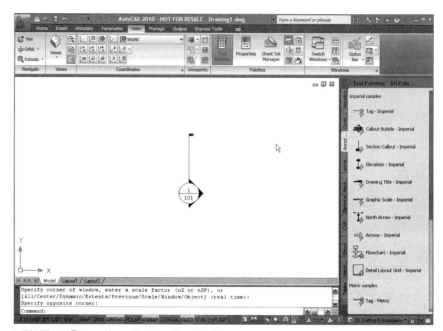

▶**FIGURE 2.40:** The section callout tag (inserted)

To insert a section callout tag, do the following:

2. Left-click the Annotation Tab on the left side of the Tool Palettes window.

   The following prompt appears on the command line:
   ```
   Duplicate definition of block Section Callout - Imperial ignored
   Specify insertion point or [Basepoint/Scale/X/Y/Z/Rotate]:
   ```

3. Position the cursor anywhere within the model space display and left click.

This action will place the tag in the drawing and end the command. To close the Tool Palettes – All Palettes window, simply click the X in the upper-right corner of the window. (See Figure 2.40.)

The Command Line Command

The Command Line tool can be very useful if additional space is required within the model space.

This tool allows you to temporarily suppress the command line from view. To accomplish this, do the following:

1. Click the Command Line icon (Figure 2.41) with the left mouse button.

▶**FIGURE 2.41:** The Command Line icon

A Command Line – Close Window dialog box will launch. To suppress the command line, do the following:

2. Click the Yes button with the left mouse button.

Conversely, to relaunch the command line, simply click the Command Line icon. (See Figures 2.42 and 2.43.)

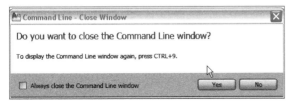

▶ **FIGURE 2.42:** The Command Line – Close Window dialog box

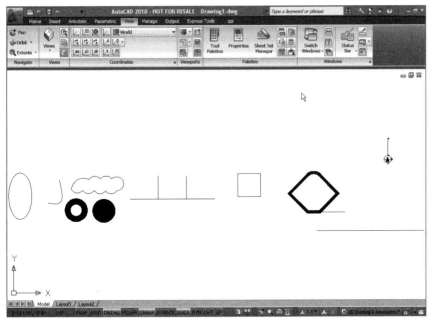

▶ **FIGURE 2.43:** The command line (suppressed)

The Ribbon's Express Tools Tab

The Ribbon's Express Tools tab (Figure 2.44) houses commands that you may use to add items to your drawing such as text aligned on an arc or explode attributes to blocks, etc.

▶ **FIGURE 2.44:** The Ribbon's Express Tools tab

The Draw Toolbar

▶ **FIGURE 2.45:** The Draw toolbar

The Break-Line Symbol Command

The Break-Line Symbol tool is used to graphically represent either a break in the item that is being drawn or to signify that the item continues on, but it is not important to show the entire length of the object. The break-line symbol is housed on the Ribbon within the Express Tools tab. To draw this symbol, do the following:

1. Make sure the Ortho and the Osnap functions are On, draw a vertical line segment at any random length, and then offset that line by 6″.

2. Click the Break-Line Symbol icon (Figure 2.46) with the left mouse button.

▶ **FIGURE 2.46:** The Break-Line Symbol icon

The following prompt appears on the command line:
```
Command: breakline
Block= BRKLINE.DWG, Size=0", Extension=0"
Specify first point for breakline or [Block/Size/Extension]:
```

The size of the area that will be graphically pleasing will vary, depending on the item that the break-line will cover. For our purpose, because the lines are spaced only 6″ apart, the size of the break should be 1″. To assign the size of the break, do the following:

3. Type **S** and press the Enter key.

The following prompt appears on the command line:
```
Breakline symbol size <0'-0">:
```

4. Type **1″** and press the Enter key.

The following prompt appears on the command line:
```
Specify first point for breakline or [Block/Size/Extension]:
```

To set the extension beyond the limit of the item, do the following:

5. Type **E** and press the Enter key.

The following prompt appears on the command line:
```
Breakline extension distance <0'-0">:
```

6. Type **3⁄16″** and press the Enter key.

The following prompt appears on the command line:
```
Specify first point for breakline or [Block/Size/Extension]:
```

7. Left-click the bottom endpoint of the left vertical line.

The following prompt appears on the command line:
```
Specify second point for breakline :
```

8. Left-click the top endpoint of the right vertical line.

The following prompt appears on the command line:
```
Specify location for break symbol <Midpoint>:
```

9. Press the Enter key.

These steps will place the Break symbol on a diagonal angle between the two lines and end the command. (See Figure 2.47.)

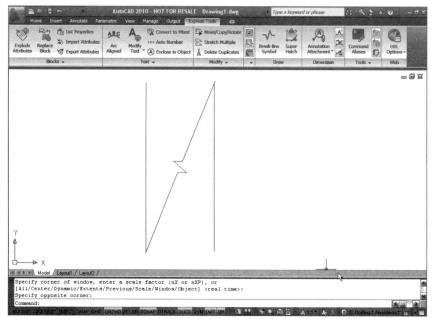

▶ **FIGURE 2.47:** The Break-Line symbol (completed)

CHAPTER 3

Advanced Annotation Tools

AFTER COMPLETING THIS CHAPTER, YOU WILL BE ABLE TO:

- ▶ Understand drawing annotations
- ▶ Create an annotative text style
- ▶ Create an annotative dimension style
- ▶ Create an annotative multileader style
- ▶ Understand annotation scaling
- ▶ Use the Annotate tab on the Ribbon

Annotations are notes, objects, tags, symbols, etc. used to add information to a drawing. When adding these items to a drawing, you should understand how to use them. Using them correctly is critical to help explain your design; therefore, it is important for them to be the appropriate size, based on the scale of the drawing, in order to be legible.

AutoCAD now supports annotative objects. *Annotative objects* are predefined items that can be controlled and changed based on any given scale within your drawing. No longer is it necessary, for example, to determine the plot scale factor for a given scale in order to determine the correct size of the text or dimensions in your drawing. AutoCAD does all of the work for you by simply identifying the text or dimension style as annotative. It is also possible to insert and control tags and symbols into your drawing.

This chapter will be devoted to explaining annotative objects and how to create and control them. To begin, do the following:

1. Launch AutoCAD 2010 either via the icon on your desktop or via the Start menu.

2. Make the 2D Drafting and Annotation Workspace current.

3. Update the Drawing Units for your drawing to Architectural.

You are now ready to begin. Typically, the AutoCAD drawing file should be saved prior to working on it. However, because this chapter is meant to be interactive, there's no need to save the file.

Creating an Annotative Text Style

In this section, you will create an annotative text style for the drawing. Keep in mind that this text style, as well as any other annotative styles, will have the ability to scale appropriately for any given scale within your drawing. This control is housed within the Home tab on the Annotation toolbar. In order to create an annotative text style, do the following:

1. Set the Ribbon to the Home tab, and pin the Annotation toolbar (Figure 3.1).

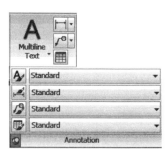

▶ **FIGURE 3.1:** The Annotation toolbar (pinned)

2. Position the cursor over the Text Style icon and click on it with the left mouse button.

   This action will launch a Text Style window (Figure 3.2).

3. Position the cursor over the Annotative option in the Styles category located at the upper-left of the Text Style window and click on it with the left mouse button.

   This action will update the Size category by placing a green check mark in the Annotative field.

4. Position the cursor over the pulldown arrow of the Font Name field in the Font category with the left mouse button, scroll through the available fonts, and select the City Blueprint font by clicking on it with the left mouse button.

5. Position the cursor over the Set Current button at the top of the window and click on it with the left mouse button. Then, position the cursor over the Close button at the bottom of the window and click on it with the left mouse button.

   These steps will ensure that any text added to the drawing will have annotative qualities.

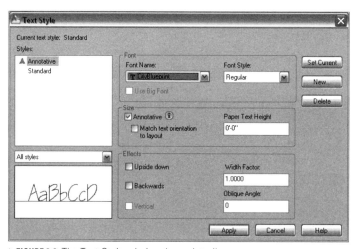

▶ **FIGURE 3.2:** The Text Style window (completed)

Creating an Annotative Dimension Style

In this section, you will create an annotative dimension style for the drawing. This dimension style will reference the annotative text style already made. This control is also housed within the Home tab on the Annotation toolbar. In order to create an annotative dimension style, do the following:

1. Position the cursor over the Dimension Style icon and click on it with the left mouse button.

   This action will launch a Dimension Style Manager window.

2. Position the cursor over the Annotative option in the Styles category located in the upper-left of the Dimension Style Manager window (Figure 3.3) and click on it with the left mouse button.

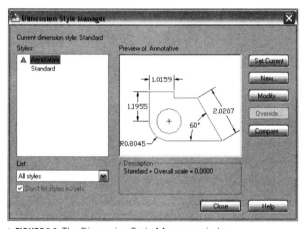

▶ **FIGURE 3.3:** The Dimension Style Manager window

3. Position the cursor over the Modify button on the right side of the Dimension Style Manager window and click on it with the left mouse button.

   This action will launch a Modify Dimension Style: Annotative window. This window has a series of tabs at the top. To continue, do the following:

4. Position the cursor over the Lines tab and click on it with the left mouse button.

In order for the dimensions in a drawing to be legible, the extension lines of the dimension string must appear lighter than the other components of the dimension. To do this:

5. Position the cursor over the pulldown arrow in the Color field of the Extension Lines category located in the lower-left corner, and click on it. Select Gray Color 8 by clicking on it. Then, in the same category, position the cursor over the pulldown arrow of the Lineweight field and select the 0.13mm option by clicking on it with the left mouse button. (See Figure 3.4.)

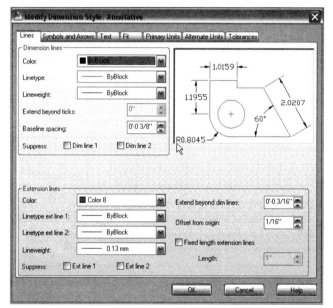

▶ **FIGURE 3.4:** The Lines tab in the Modify Dimension Style: Annotative window (completed)

6. Position the cursor over the Symbols and Arrows tab at the top of the window and click on it with the left mouse button. Position the cursor over the pulldown arrow of the first field in the Arrowheads category and select the Architectural Tick option with the left mouse button, then position the cursor in the Arrow Size window and change it to ⅟₁₆″. (See Figure 3.5.)

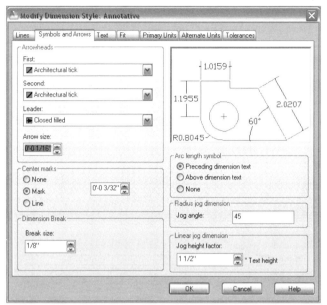

▶ **FIGURE 3.5:** The Symbols and Arrows tab in the Modify Dimension Style: Annotative window (completed)

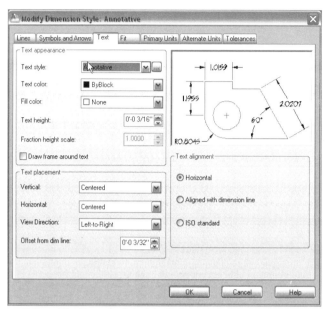

▶ **FIGURE 3.6:** The Text tab of the Modify Dimension Style: Annotative window (completed)

7. Position the cursor over the Text tab at the top of the window and click on it with the left mouse button. In the Text Appearance field, position the cursor over the pulldown arrow of the Text Style field and click on it with the left mouse button. Position the cursor over the Annotative option and click on it with the left mouse button. (See Figure 3.6.)

8. Position the cursor over the Primary Units tab at the top of the window and click on it with the left mouse button. Position the cursor over the pulldown arrow of the Units Format field in the Linear Dimensions category and click on it with the left mouse button. Select the Architectural Units option with the left mouse button. (See Figure 3.7.)

9. Click the OK button with the left mouse button, hover over the Set Current button and click on it with the left mouse button, and then click the Close button with the left mouse button.

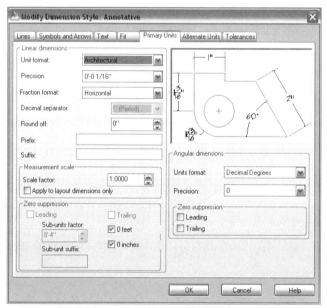

▶ **FIGURE 3.7:** The Primary Units tab of the Modify Dimension Style: Annotative window (completed)

Creating an Annotative Multileader Style

In this section, you will create an annotative multileader style for the drawing. This multileader style will also reference the annotative text style already made. This control is housed within the Home tab on the Annotation toolbar. In order to create an annotative multileader style, do the following:

1. Position the cursor over the Multileader Style icon and click on it with the left mouse button.

   This action will launch a Multileader Style Manager window.

2. Position the cursor over the Annotative option in the Styles category located in the upper-left of the Multileader Style Manager window (Figure 3.8) and click on it with the left mouse button.

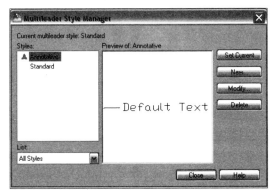

▶ FIGURE 3.8: The Multileader Style Manager window

3. Click the Modify button on the right side of the Multileader Style Manager window and click on it with the left mouse button.

   This action will launch a Modify Multileader Style: Annotative window. This window also has a series of tabs at the top. To continue, do the following:

4. Position the cursor over the Leader Format tab (Figure 3.9) and click on it with the left mouse button.

   To set the appropriate size of the arrowhead for the multileader, do the following:

5. Position the cursor over the (down) pulldown arrow in the Size field of the Arrowhead category and select ¹⁄₁₆" by clicking on it twice with the left mouse button.

6. Position the cursor over the Content tab (Figure 3.10) and click on it with the left mouse button. Position the cursor over the pulldown arrow of the Text Style field in the Text Options category and select the Annotative Text Style option by clicking on it with the left mouse button.

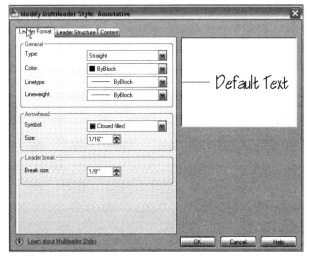

▶ FIGURE 3.9: The Leader Format tab of the Modify Multileader Style: Annotative window (completed)

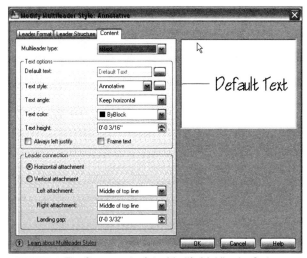

▶ FIGURE 3.10: The Content tab of the Modify Multileader Style: Annotative window (completed)

7. Click the OK button with the left mouse button, hover over the Set Current button and click on it with the left mouse button and then click the Close button with the left mouse button.

The Annotation Scaling Toolbar

Now that you have created several annotative styles, using them in your drawing is quite easy. Scaling these objects has become significantly easier with the Annotation Scaling tools, which are located on the Status toolbar at the bottom-right of the model space interface. (See Figure 3.11.)

►**FIGURE 3.11:** The Annotation Scaling icons

Prior to inserting any annotative object into your drawing, you will need to verify the Annotation Scaling controls. Keep in mind that additional scales can be defined or deleted, as well. You can also suppress the visibility of certain scales within your drawing. To set the Annotation Scaling controls for ¼″ = 1′-0″ scale, do the following:

1. Position the cursor over the Annotation Scale pulldown arrow located in the lower-right of the Status toolbar and click it with the left mouse button. (See Figure 3.12.)

This action will launch a tooltip window with all of the scales available to set within the drawing.

2. Scroll through the menu and select ¼″ = 1′-0″ and click on it with the left mouse button.

This action will update the annotation scale of the drawing file to ¼″ = 1′-0″.

►**FIGURE 3.12:** The Annotation Scale control (¼″ = 1′-0″)

Next, so that the annotative objects are displayed at their appropriate size, verify that the Annotation Visibility controls are On. The icons are located on the Status toolbar adjacent to the Annotation Scale Control icon at the bottom-right of the Auto-CAD interface. To check this, do the following:

3. Check the Annotation Visibility icon (Figure 3.13) to determine its status. The status is easy to determine. If it appears as the Sun icon, then it is On. This designation will show annotative objects for all scales.

►**FIGURE 3.13:** The Annotation Visibility icons

If the icon appears and the Sun icon is shaded, this designation will show annotative objects for the current scale only. If the icon is shaded, do the following:

4. Position the cursor over the Annotation Visibility icon and click on it with the left mouse button.

Also, verify that the Annotation icon located directly adjacent to the Annotation Visibility icon is set to the On position. When this icon is set to the On position, it will appear with a yellow lightning bolt and AutoCAD will automatically add scales to annotative objects when the annotation scale changes. If this setting is not set accordingly, click on the Annotations icon.

An Annotative icon will appear when the cursor is positioned over an object that has annotative properties.

The Annotate Tab

Annotations such as text, dimensions, and multileaders can easily be added to a drawing via the Home tab on the Ribbon. However, to access additional Annotation icons, it is prudent to use the Annotate tab on the Ribbon (Figure 3.14).

►**FIGURE 3.14:** The Ribbon's Annotate tab

To see how inserted annotations will appear in your drawing, do the following:

1. Set the Ribbon to the Annotate tab.
2. Draw a 10′ × 10′ square with the lower-left corner at 0,0.
3. Refer to the Text toolbar.

The Text Toolbar

The Text toolbar (Figure 3.15) allows you to add multiline and single-line text to a drawing, as well as apply new text styles. Notice that the current text style is set to the annotative text style that was previously created. An additional enhancement is the Spell Check option.

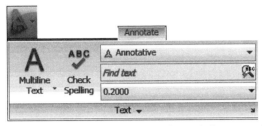

▶ **FIGURE 3.15:** The Text toolbar on the Ribbon's Annotate tab

Annotative Multiline Text

Inserting annotative multiline text into a drawing is no different than entering standard text (Figure 3.16). To enter annotative multiline text, do the following:

1. Click the Multiline Text icon on the Text toolbar.
2. Create a multiline of text to the right of the 10′ × 10′ square.

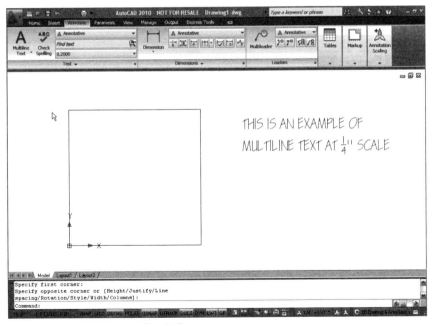

▶ **FIGURE 3.16:** Multiline text at ¼″ = 1′-0″

The Leaders Toolbar

Inserting an annotative multileader into a drawing is quite simple. To enter an annotative multileader, do the following:

1. Click the Multileader icon on the Leaders toolbar (Figure 3.17).
2. Create a leader at the bottom-right of the 10′ × 10′ square. (See Figure 3.18.)

▶ **FIGURE 3.17:** The Leaders toolbar on the Ribbon's Annotate tab

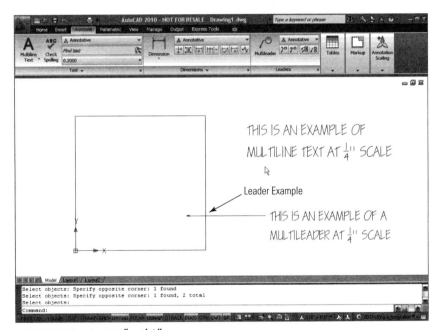

▶ **FIGURE 3.18:** Leader at ¼″ = 1′-0″

The Dimensions Toolbar

The Dimensions toolbar (Figure 3.19) allows you to add additional types of dimensions to your drawing. You can still access the most commonly used dimension types such as linear, continue, angled, etc. Plus, you can access the new dimension type icons that have been added. To demonstrate some of the new dimension types, do the following:

1. Create a horizontal linear dimension at the top of the square.

2. Create a vertical linear dimension at the right side of the square. (See Figure 3.20.)

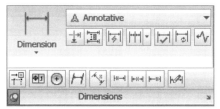

▶ **FIGURE 3.19:** The Dimensions toolbar (pinned) on the Ribbon's Annotate tab

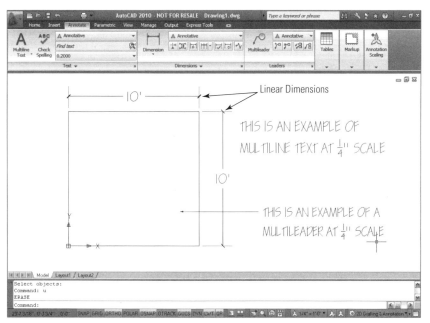

▶ **FIGURE 3.20:** Horizontal and vertical linear dimensions of the square

The Break Dimension Command

Graphic quality is paramount. Annotations that are added to the drawing should help clearly explain the design intent, not hamper it. The Break Dimension tool can be used to break a dimension string so that it does not interfere with other leaders or

notes. To add a dimension break to the vertical linear dimension previously drawn, do the following:

1. Click the Dimension Break icon (Figure 3.21) with the left mouse button.

▶ **FIGURE 3.21:** The Break Dimension icon

The following prompt appears on the command line:
```
Command: _DIMBREAK
Select dimension to add/remove break or [Multiple:]
```

2. Left-click the vertical linear dimension.

The following prompt appears on the command line:
```
Select object to break dimension or [Auto/Manual/Remove] <Auto>:
```

3. Position the cursor over the leader previously drawn and click on it with the left mouse button.

The following prompt appears on the command line:
```
Select object to break dimension:
```

4. Press the Enter key to end the command.

This action will break the dimension string where the leader intersects it, allowing the annotations to be read clearly. (See Figure 3.22.)

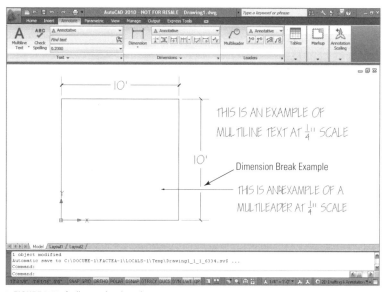

▶ **FIGURE 3.22:** A dimension break

The Oblique Dimension Command

The Oblique Dimension tool allows you to add an oblique angle to the extension lines of the dimension string. This can be useful if limited space is available to add a dimension in an area. *Oblique dimensions* are used to modify an existing dimension. To modify an existing dimension, do the following:

1. Click the Oblique Dimension icon (Figure 3.23) with the left mouse button.

 ▶**FIGURE 3.23**: The Oblique Dimension icon

> ### The following prompt appears on the command line:
> ```
> Command: _dimedit
> Enter type of dimension editing [Home/New/Rotate/Oblique] <Home>: _o
> Select objects:
> ```

2. Left-click the horizontal linear dimension and press the Enter key.

> ### The following prompt appears on the command line:
> ```
> Enter obliquing angle [press ENTER for none]:
> ```

3. Type **45** and press the Enter key.

This action will end the command and modify the existing horizontal dimension with 45-degree angled extension lines. (See Figure 3.24.)

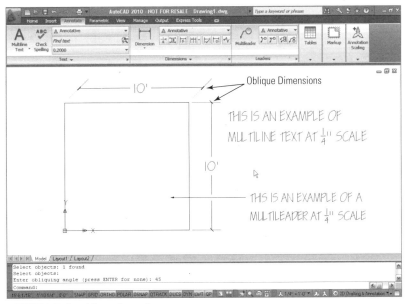

▶**FIGURE 3.24**: An oblique dimension

The Text Angle Dimension Command

The Text Angle Dimension tool allows you to add an oblique angle to the text of the dimension string. Again, this is useful if limited space is available to add a dimension in an area. *Text angle dimensions* are used to modify an existing dimension. To modify an existing dimension, do the following:

1. Click the Text Angle Dimension icon (Figure 3.25) with the left mouse button.

 ▶**FIGURE 3.25**: The Text Angle Dimension icon

> ### The following prompt appears on the command line:
> ```
> Command: _dimtedit
> Select dimension:
> ```

2. Left-click the vertical linear dimension and press the Enter key.

> ### The following prompt appears on the command line:
> ```
> Specify new location for dimension text or [Left/Right/Center/Home/
> Angle]: _a
> Specify angle for dimension text:
> ```

3. Type **45** and press the Enter key.

This action will end the command and modify the existing vertical dimension with text at a 45-degree angle. (See Figure 3.26.)

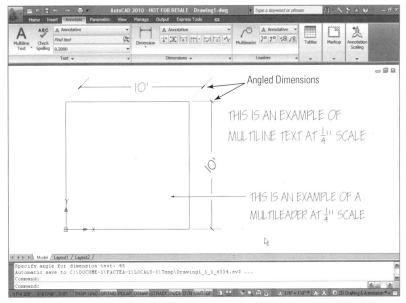

▶**FIGURE 3.26**: A text angle dimension

The Annotative Symbol

You should always try to use annotative styles in your drawings. Doing so will make it significantly easier to modify a drawing to a different scale if necessary. To identify annotative objects in your drawing, do the following:

1. Hover the cursor over the object in question.

   If the object is annotative, the annotative symbol will identify it as annotative. (See Figures 3.27 and 3.28.)

 ▶**FIGURE 3.27:** An Annotative symbol

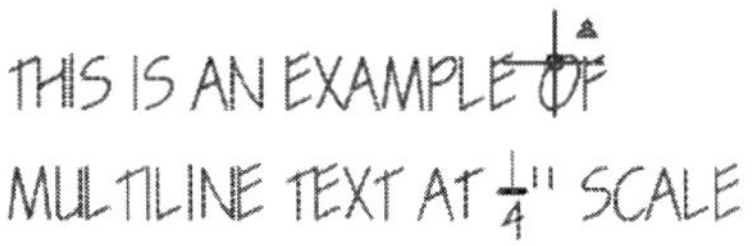

THIS IS AN EXAMPLE OF
MULTILINE TEXT AT $\frac{1}{4}$" SCALE

▶**FIGURE 3.28:** The Annotative symbol in use

Adding Scale to Annotative Objects

In closing, let's demonstrate the ease in which you can add an additional scale to your drawing. Do the following:

1. Access the Annotation Scale control on the Status toolbar.

2. Select ½" = 1'-0". This action will change the annotation scale of the drawing file to ½" = 1'-0". (See Figure 3.29.)

   Notice how all of the annotative objects changed when the scale was changed. To verify that the annotative objects in your drawing are associated with more than one annotation scale, do the following:

1. Hover the cursor over any annotative object.

   This action will launch two annotative symbols, indicating that the annotative object is associated with more than one annotation scale. (See Figure 3.30.)

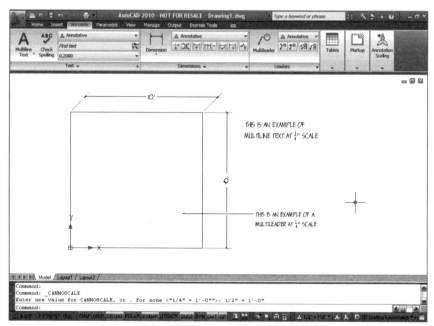

▶**FIGURE 3.29:** The Annotation Scale control (updated to ½" = 1'-0")

▶**FIGURE 3.30:** Multiple annotative symbols

CHAPTER 4

Introducing Isometric Drawing

AFTER COMPLETING THIS CHAPTER, YOU WILL BE ABLE TO:

- ▶ Understand isometric drawings
- ▶ Understand the isoplane polar coordinates
- ▶ Understand the isoplane polar faces of objects
- ▶ Apply isometric settings to a drawing
- ▶ Understand the behavior of the X- and Y-axes
- ▶ Draw simple isometric shapes
- ▶ Draw an isometric circle

There are several types of axonometric drawings. The most common is isometric. Objects drawn in isometric view are placed on a 30-degree angle.

Although isometric drawings are used to show objects in three dimensions, do not mistake an isometric drawing for a 3D drawing. Unlike 3D objects, objects drawn in isometric view are flat and have no volume; 3D objects have volume. Isometric drawings are usually drawn within the AutoCAD Classic Workspace or the 2D Drafting and Annotation Workspace.

As previously mentioned, isometric drawings are placed on a 30-degree angle to show the three-dimensional aspects of an object. The three isometric axes are 30 degrees left, 30 degrees right, and vertical (Figure 4.1).

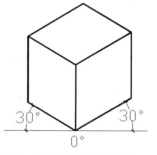

THREE ISOMETRIC AXES

▶ **FIGURE 4.1:** The isometric axes

When drawing an isometric object, you need to understand the isoplane polar coordinates and isoplane views/faces of an object (Figures 4.2 and 4.3).

ISOPLANE POLAR COORDINATES

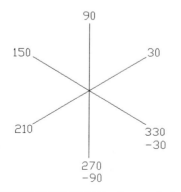

▶ **FIGURE 4.2:** The isoplane polar coordinates

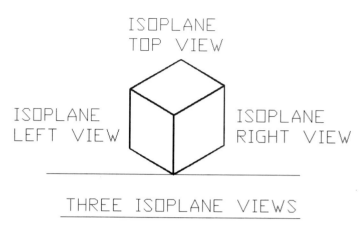

THREE ISOPLANE VIEWS

▶ **FIGURE 4.3:** The isoplane views

Isometric drawing is quite easy once you decide to draw an object by changing isoplane faces/views or by entering polar coordinates. Both procedures will be explained. This chapter will be devoted to explaining the isoplane axes, faces, and polar coordinates used to draw isometric objects. In order to draw isometric objects, you need to understand how the X- and Y-axes behave.

To begin, do the following:

1. Launch AutoCAD 2010 either via the icon on your desktop or via the Start menu.

2. Make the 2D Drafting and Annotation Workspace current.

3. Update the Drawing Units for your drawing to Architectural.

4. Set the Ribbon to the Home tab.

You are now ready to begin. Typically, the AutoCAD drawing file should be saved prior to working on it. However, because this chapter is meant to be interactive, there's no need to save the file.

Applying Isometric Settings

To begin drawing an isometric object, it is prudent to apply an isometric setting to your drawing. By applying this setting, you will be able to toggle through the three isoplane faces/views of an object and draw specific shapes in isometric view. To apply this isometric setting, refer to the Snap button on the Status toolbar and do the following:

1. Position the cursor over the Snap button and right-click. Then hover the cursor over Settings in the tooltip window and left-click.

This action will launch the Drafting Settings window (Figure 4.4).

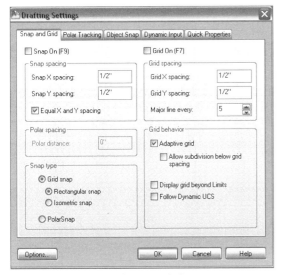

▶ **FIGURE 4.4:** The Drafting Settings window

To apply the isometric setting to the drawing, refer to the Snap and Grid tab and then do the following:

2. Refer to the Snap Type category in the lower-left corner of the window, left-click the Isometric Snap field, and then left-click the OK button.

This action will change the appearance of the cursor/crosshairs in the drawing (Figure 4.5).

▶ **FIGURE 4.5:** The Isometric crosshairs (top plane view)

By applying the Isometric Snap setting to your drawing, the view of your drawing changes to the Isoplane Top - View. You can use this view when you enter isometric polar coordinates or draw the top or bottom face of an object. (See Figure 4.6.)

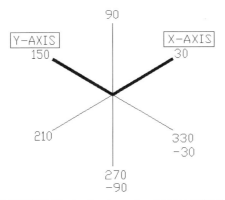

▶ **FIGURE 4.6:** The top isoplane view, polar coordinates, and X- and Y-axes

Notice that the X- and Y-axes have also changed in this view. When the Ortho function is On, the X-axis moves along the 30-to-210–degrees axis, and the Y-axis moves along the 150-to-330–degrees axis.

Changing the Isoplane View

Changing the isoplane view is easy. To change the isoplane view (Figure 4.7 through Figure 4.10), do the following:

1. Press the F5 key on the keyboard.

   The following prompt appears on the command line:
   Command: <Isoplane Right>

▶ **FIGURE 4.7:** The Isometric crosshairs (right plane view)

This action places the view of your drawing to the Isoplane Right–View. You can use this view when you are drawing the right face of an object.

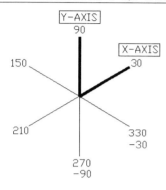

► **FIGURE 4.8:** The right isoplane view, polar coordinates, and the X- and Y-axes

Notice that the X- and Y-axes changed in this view also. When the Ortho function is On, the X-axis moves along the 30-to-210–degrees axis, and the Y-axis moves along the 90-to-270–degrees axis.

Pressing the F5 key allows you to toggle through the three isometric plane views. To change the isoplane view again, do the following:

1. Press the F5 key.

   The following prompt appears on the command line:
   Command: <Isoplane Leftt>

► **FIGURE 4.9:** The Isometric crosshairs (left plane view)

This action places the view of your drawing to the Isoplane Left - View. You can use this view when you are drawing the left face of an object.

Notice that the X- and Y-axes have changed in this view also. When the Ortho function is On, the X-axis moves along the 150-to-330–degrees axis, and the Y-axis moves along the 90-to-270–degrees axis.

Set the isoplane view back to the Isoplane Top - View.

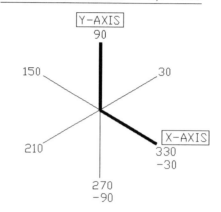

► **FIGURE 4.10:** The left isoplane view, polar coordinates, and the X- and Y-axes

Drawing an Isometric Object with Polar Coordinates

Now that you understand isoplane views and polar coordinates, you can draw a simple isometric object. There are two methods for drawing isometric objects with AutoCAD. One way is to draw an isometric object by entering the polar coordinates; the other way is by toggling through the isoplane views. For this exercise, you will begin drawing a simple isometric object by entering polar coordinates. When polar coordinates are used to draw an isometric shape, the drawing view should be set to the Isoplane Top–View. The other isoplane views can be ignored.

The isometric object you will draw consists of two interlocked rectangles that are 2' deep × 3'. One rectangle is 6" high and the other is 1' high. (See Figures 4.11 through 4.15.)

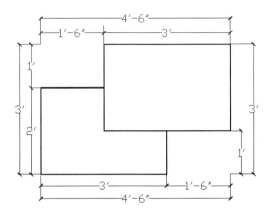

INTERLOCKED RECTANGLES – PLAN VIEW

▶ **FIGURE 4.11:** Interlocked rectangles (plan view)

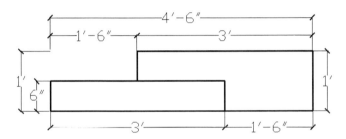

INTERLOCKED RECTANGLES – FRONT VIEW

▶ **FIGURE 4.12:** Interlocked rectangles (front view)

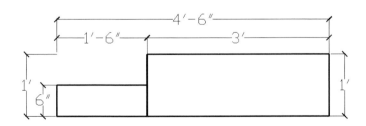

INTERLOCKED RECTANGLES – REAR VIEW

▶ **FIGURE 4.13:** Interlocked rectangles (rear view)

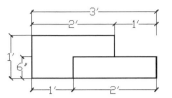

INTERLOCKED RECTANGLES – LEFT SIDE VIEW

▶ **FIGURE 4.14:** Interlocked rectangles (left side view)

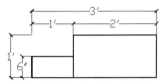

INTERLOCKED RECTANGLES – RIGHT SIDE VIEW

▶ **FIGURE 4.15:** Interlocked rectangles (right side view)

To begin drawing, do the following:

1. Verify that the Isometric Snap is set.
2. Turn on the Ortho and Osnap function.
3. Verify that the current view is set to Isoplane Top.

Begin drawing the bottom view of the object from the lower-left hand corner.

1. Start a line at the coordinates 0,0 and press the Enter key.
2. Continue the line segment by typing **@36<30**, and then press the Enter key.
3. Type **@12<150** and press the Enter key.
4. Type **@18<30** and press the Enter key.
5. Type **@24<150** and press the Enter key.
6. Type **@36<210** and press the Enter key.
7. Type **@12<330** and press the Enter key.
8. Type **@18<210** and press the Enter key. To end the command, type **C** and press the Enter key.

This action will complete the bottom portion of the object and end the command. (See Figure 4.16.)

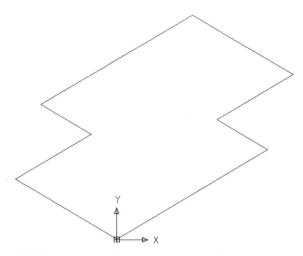

▶ **FIGURE 4.16:** Interlocked rectangles in progress (bottom view)

When you first start drawing an isometric object, depending on the complexity of the shape, it helps to draw all of the lines of the shape so that they are shown as a wire model form, even though all of the lines won't show up due to the angle. From this point on, we will draw only the lines that will actually appear. Having said that, there may be an instance or two when a line will need to be drawn and later erased or trimmed. To continue, refer to the rectangle on the left side. This rectangle is 6″ high on three sides.

9. Start a line at the coordinates 0,0 and press the Enter key.

10. Continue the line segment by typing **@6<90**, and then press the Enter key twice.

11. Copy that line from the lower endpoint (0,0) to the other two intersections of the lower rectangle and end the command.

12. Start a line at the coordinates 0,6 and press the Enter key.

13. Continue the line segment by typing **@36<30** and then press the Enter key twice.

14. Start a line at the coordinates 0,6 and press the Enter key.

15. Continue the line segment by typing **@24<150** and then press the Enter key.

16. Continue the line segment by typing **@18<30** and then press the Enter key twice.

Next, refer to the rectangle on the right side. This rectangle is 1′ high on three sides. To continue, do the following:

17. Start a line at the intersection of the corner directly opposite of the coordinates 0,0 and press the Enter key.

18. Continue the line segment by typing **@12<90**, and then press the Enter key twice.

19. Copy that line from the lower endpoint to the other two intersections of the higher rectangle and end the command.

20. Start a line at the top endpoint of the line at the intersection of the corner directly opposite the coordinates 0,0 and press the Enter key.

21. Continue the line segment by typing **@36<210**, and then press the Enter key.

22. Type **@12<330**, and then press the Enter key.

23. Continue the line segment by positioning the cursor directly over the endpoint of the line below and left-click.

If you have drawn everything correctly so far, this point should be the edge of the higher rectangle that is closest to you.

24. Continue the line segment by typing **@12<330**, and then press the Enter key.

25. Type **@18<30**, and then press the Enter key twice. (See Figure 4.17.)

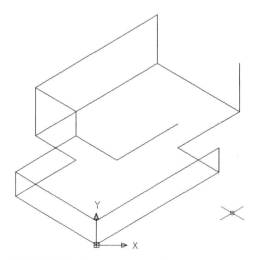

▶ **FIGURE 4.17:** Interlocked rectangles in progress (top view)

To draw the other side of the higher rectangle, do the following:

26. Start a line at the top endpoint of the line at the intersection of the corner directly opposite the coordinates 0,0 and press the Enter key.

27. Continue the line segment by typing **@24<330**, and then press the Enter key.

28. Continue the line segment by positioning the cursor directly over the endpoint of the line below and left-click.

29. Continue the line segment by typing **@12<330**, and then press the Enter key twice.

To finish drawing the top rectangle, do the following:

30. Start a line at the intersection of the corner of the higher rectangle closest to you and press the Enter key.

31. Continue the line segment by typing **@6<90**, and then press the Enter key.

32. Type **@12<150**, and then press the Enter key twice.

33. Start a line at the top endpoint at the intersection of the corner of the higher rectangle closest to you and press the Enter key.

34. Continue the line segment by typing **@18<30**, and then press the Enter key twice.

This completes the isometric object. Now that you have drawn and understand how to construct the shape you just made, you can erase and trim any extraneous lines. (See Figure 4.18.)

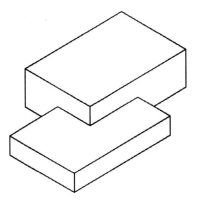

INTERLOCKED RECTANGLES - ISOMETRIC VIEW

▶**FIGURE 4.18:** Interlocked rectangles (completed)

Drawing an Isometric Object Using Isoplane Views

Isometric objects can also be drawn using isoplane views. According to some users, this is the preferred method for drawing an isometric object.

The isometric object you will draw is a stepped rectangle with a hole in the cavity of the upper step. The overall dimensions of this object are 1' wide × 1'-6" long × 1'-6" high. Each step is 6" high × 6" deep. The upper step has a 4"-diameter circle within the cavity. (See Figures 4.19 through 4.21.)

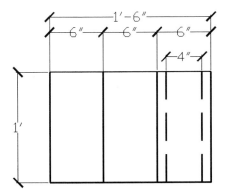

STEPPED RECTANGLE - PLAN VIEW

▶**FIGURE 4.19:** The stepped rectangle (plan view)

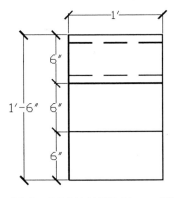

STEPPED RECTANGLE - FRONT VIEW

▶**FIGURE 4.20:** The stepped rectangle (front view)

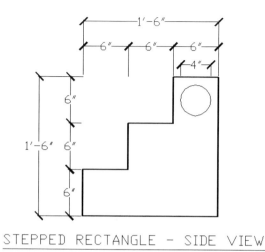

STEPPED RECTANGLE - SIDE VIEW

▶ **FIGURE 4.21:** The stepped rectangle (side view)

To begin drawing, do the following:

1. Verify that the Isometric Snap is set.

2. Turn on the Ortho and Osnap function.

3. Verify that the current view is set to Isoplane – Right.

You will begin drawing from the lower-right corner of the object and draw the right face (Figure 4.22).

1. Start a line at the coordinates 0,0 and press the Enter key.

2. Continue the line segment by moving the cursor in the north direction, and then type **6** and left-click.

3. Move the cursor in the east direction and type **6**, and then press the Enter key.

4. Move the cursor in the north direction and type **6**, and then press the Enter key.

5. Move the cursor in the east direction and type **6**, and then press the Enter key.

6. Move the cursor in the north direction and type **6**, and then press the Enter key.

7. Move the cursor in the east direction and type **6**, and then press the Enter key.

8. Move the cursor in the south direction and type **18**, and then press the Enter key.

To complete the side face, do the following:

9. Type **C** and then press the Enter key.

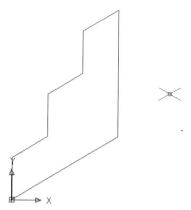

▶ **FIGURE 4.22:** The stepped rectangle in progress (right face)

Now to draw the front edge of each step (Figure 4.23), do the following:

10. Press the F5 key to set the current view to Isoplane–Left.

11. Start a line at the coordinates 0,0 and press the Enter key.

12. Continue the line segment by moving the cursor in the west direction, and then type **12** and left-click.

13. Move the cursor in the north direction and type **6**, and then press the Enter key.

14. Move the cursor in the east direction and type **12**. Press the Enter key twice.

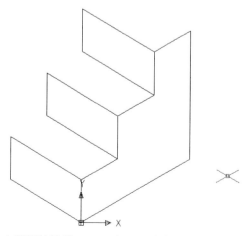

▶ **FIGURE 4.23:** The stepped rectangle in progress (left face)

This action will draw the bottom front face of the left side of the object. To complete the other front faces of the steps, do the following:

15. Copy the three lines that were previously drawn to form the left front face of the lower step. Select 0,0 as the base point and copy the lines to the intersections of the steps drawn on the right front face and end the command.

16. Start a line from the rear endpoint of the highest step and move the cursor in the west direction. Type **12** and press the Enter key twice.

To connect the lines on the opposite side of each step, do the following:

17. Press the F5 key to set the current view to Isoplane–Top.

18. Draw a line from the endpoint to the opposite endpoint of each step.

To draw the 4"-diameter circle at the top step, you will need a guideline. To select this guideline, do the following:

19. Copy the top-vertical right-hand line of the top step, and select the base point as the top endpoint of that line. Paste it to the midpoint of the top step on the right face. (See Figure 4.24.)

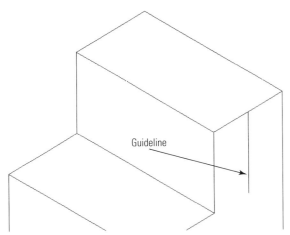

▶ FIGURE 4.24: Stepped rectangle with guideline for circle

Drawing an Isometric Circle

In order to draw a circle on an isometric object, you will actually need to use the Ellipse tool. The correct term for an isometric circle is *isocircle*. The correct ellipse icon to select is the Ellipse Axis, End icon (Figure 4.25). In order for this ellipse to be an option to choose, your Isometric Snap must be enabled.

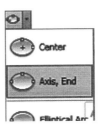

▶ FIGURE 4.25: The Ellipse Axis, End icon

The Ellipse Axis, End icon is located on the Ribbon's Home tab on the Draw toolbar. To place the 4"-diameter isocircle in the cavity of the top step, make sure that the current view is set to Isoplane–Right and do the following:

1. Click the Ellipse Axis, End icon with the left mouse button.

   The following prompt appears on the command line:
   Command: _ellipse
   Specify axis endpoint of ellipse or [Arc/Center/Isocircle]:

2. Type **I** and press the Enter key.

   The following prompt appears on the command line:
   Specify center of isocircle:

3. Position the cursor over the midpoint of the guideline at the top step and left-click.

   The following prompt appears on the command line:
   Specify radius of isocircle or [Diameter]:

4. Type **d** and press the Enter key.

   The following prompt appears on the command line:
   Specify diameter of isocircle

5. Type **4** from the keyboard and press the Enter key.

This action will place the isocircle at the midpoint of the guideline at the top step and end the command. (See Figure 4.26.)

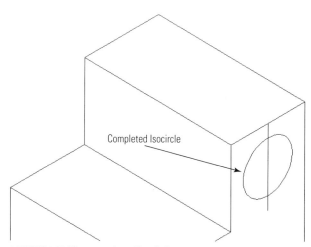

▶ **FIGURE 4.26:** The completed isocircle

To complete the stepped rectangle isometric drawing with the dashed lines, verify that the dashed linetype is loaded to your drawing and that the current view is set to Isoplane – Left.

6. Draw a line from the upper-right quadrant of the isocircle to the line on the opposite side of the top step, and press the Enter key twice. (See Figure 4.27.)

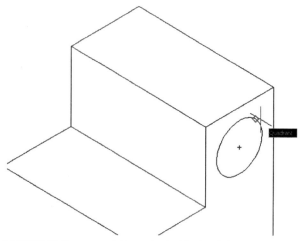

▶ **FIGURE 4.27:** The upper-right quadrant of the isocircle

Repeat step 6 for the lower-left quadrant of the isocircle and update the lines to a dashed linetype. (See Figure 4.28.)

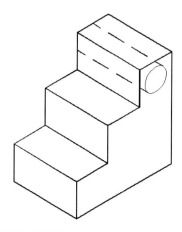

STEPPED RECTANGLE – ISOMETRIC VIEW

▶ **FIGURE 4.28:** The stepped rectangle (completed)

CHAPTER 5

Introducing AutoCAD 3D Drawing

AFTER COMPLETING THIS CHAPTER, YOU WILL:

▶ Understand the AutoCAD 2010 3D interface

▶ Be able to apply settings to the 3D Modeling Workspace

▶ Be able to apply additional tiled viewports to the 3D Modeling Workspace

▶ Understand the pertinent 3D Drawing/Modifying toolbars on the Ribbon

▶ Be able to navigate within the 3D Modeling Workspace

▶ Be able to draw basic primitive objects

▶ Be able to edit basic primitive objects

Drawing a 3D object is relatively simple. Until now you have been drawing within the 2D Drafting and Annotation Workspace, which utilized the X- and Y-axes. The 3D Modeling Workspace utilizes the X-, Y-, and Z-axes. The Z-axis is used to represent the vertical height of the 3D objects. The key to drawing in three dimensions is to have some sort of strategy. A good strategy is to break down the object you want to model into a simple shape or a combination of shapes. AutoCAD 3D provides a number of simple premade shapes from which to choose. These shapes are referred to as *solids*. Solid modeling allows you to create 3D objects that are easy to use and modify.

New to AutoCAD 2010 is free-form 3D design. This improvement allows you to design virtually anything in 3D quite simply. Free-form 3D design is referred to as *mesh modeling*. This type of 3D modeling allows you to create solids with complex elements and control the smoothness of the shapes and surface plane.

3D modeling also allows you to do the following:

- View an object from any station point
- Create 2D objects and sections from the 3D model
- Add lighting and shade settings
- Create an animation file of the 3D object

Adding rendered qualities to 3D objects is an advanced skill that will not be covered in this chapter. This chapter will be devoted to reviewing the 3D Modeling Workspace, navigating the interface, drawing/modifying simple solids, and becoming familiar with the standard views of 3D objects. Once you've completed this chapter, you will have a good working foundation for 3D drawing. Typically, the AutoCAD drawing file should be saved prior to working on it. However, because this chapter is meant to be interactive, there's no need to save the file.

The 3D Modeling Workspace

In order to begin drawing objects in 3D, you must set the workspace to the 3D Modeling Workspace. To begin, start by launching AutoCAD 2010 as you normally do. The 2D Drafting and Annotation Workspace will most likely launch as the current workspace. To make the 3D Modeling Workspace current, do the following:

1. Position the cursor over the Workspaces pulldown arrow located in the bottom-right of the model space interface on the Status toolbar and right-click.

   This action will launch a menu of workspaces from which to choose.

2. Position the cursor over the 3D Modeling Workspace option and left-click.

This action will launch the 3D Modeling Workspace (Figure 5.1). This workspace is very similar in appearance to the 2D Drafting and Annotation Workspace. Some of the major differences include:

- 3D tabs added to the Ribbon
- The 3D UCS icon
- The View Cube
- 3D toolbars added to some of the tabs

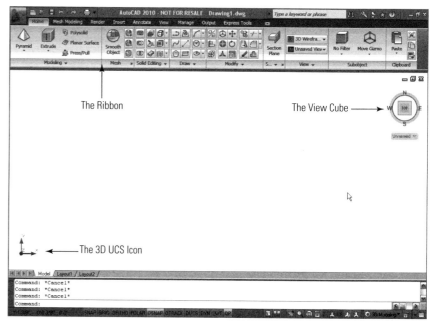

▶ **FIGURE 5.1:** The 3D Modeling Workspace (model space)

Prior to drawing any 3D objects, we will review this workspace.

The 3D Modeling Workspace Ribbon

As previously mentioned, the 3D Modeling Workspace Ribbon features additional 3D tabs with 3D toolbars:

- The Mesh Modeling tab
- The Render tab

The Home tab and the View tab are slightly different from what you are used to, but the rest of the tabs are the same. The Home tab houses the toolbars used to draw, modify, and edit 3D solids. (See Figure 5.2.)

▶**FIGURE 5.2:** The 3D Modeling Workspace Ribbon's Home tab

The Mesh Modeling tab (Figure 5.3) houses the toolbars used to create mesh primitives, as well as modify and edit them. Mesh modeling allows you to model items in greater detail and with enhanced capabilities. This chapter will not explain mesh modeling in great detail.

▶**FIGURE 5.3:** The 3D Modeling Workspace Ribbon's Mesh Modeling tab

The Render tab (Figure 5.4) houses the toolbars used to render 3D solids. As previously mentioned, this chapter will not explain any of the Rendering tools.

▶**FIGURE 5.4:** The 3D Modeling Workspace Ribbon's Render tab

The View tab (Figure 5.5) houses the toolbars used to navigate the 3D Modeling Workspace, as well as change the views of 3D solids.

▶**FIGURE 5.5:** The 3D Modeling Workspace Ribbon's View tab

The 3D UCS Icon and the View Cube

When the 3D Modeling Workspace was set as the current workspace, it may not have updated the appearance of the UCS icon or launched the View Cube because the visual style of the workspace was set to a 2D wireframe. There are several visual styles from which to choose. We will review some of the other styles later in this chapter. If the 3D Modeling Workspace did not launch with the 3D UCS icon and the View Cube, set the Home tab on the Ribbon as current and do the following:

1. Refer to the View toolbar located on the Home tab (Figure 5.6).

▶**FIGURE 5.6:** The View toolbar on the 3D Modeling Workspace Ribbon's Home tab

2. Position the cursor over the pulldown arrow of the Visual Styles Shortcut window and left-click.

This action will launch a Visual Styles Option window (Figure 5.7).

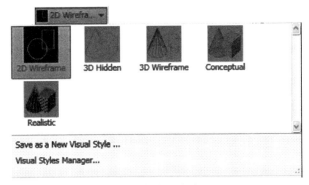

▶**FIGURE 5.7:** The Visual Styles Option window

3. Position the cursor over the 3D Hidden visual style and left-click (Figure 5.8).

▶**FIGURE 5.8:** The 3D Hidden Visual Style icon

This action will set the visual style of the 3D Modeling Workspace to 3D Hidden and update the model space interface. A 3D UCS icon (Figure 5.9) will appear in the lower-left of the interface, and the View Cube will appear in the upper-right of the interface. The 3D UCS icon has three axes: X, Y, and Z. The Z-axis is the vertical axis.

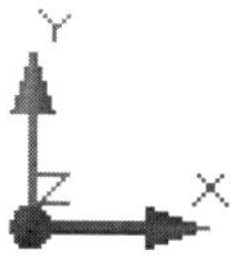

▶ **FIGURE 5.9:** The 3D UCS icon

The View Cube (Figure 5.10) allows you to view the 3D solids you are creating. This icon allows you to view the top, bottom, side, and isometric views of the 3D solid.

▶ **FIGURE 5.10:** The View Cube

When the visual style of the workspace was changed to the 3D Hidden, the View Cube automatically defaulted to the top view. Without drawing anything yet, we will be able to test the View Cube. To change the current view from top view to front view, do the following:

1. Position the cursor over the letter S (or south direction) and left-click.

This action will update the view of the workspace to the front view and update the 3D UCS icon. (See Figures 5.11 and 5.12.)

▶ **FIGURE 5.11:** The View Cube (front view)

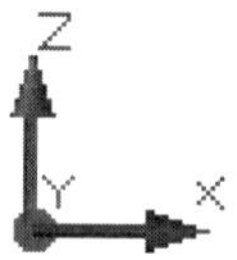

▶ **FIGURE 5.12:** The 3D UCS icon (front view)

Adding Tiled Viewports to the 3D Modeling Workspace

If you have little experience with perspective drawing, 3D drawing can be a bit challenging. One way to make it a bit easier is to split or tile the model space interface display. It is important to watch the axis on which you are drawing. You can add multiple, tiled viewports either vertically or horizontally. This is quite useful in order to set each viewport with a different View Cube or Visual Style setting. This will allow you to draw in one viewport and simultaneously view the results in both viewports.

In the next exercise, you will add two vertically tiled viewports to the 3D Modeling Workspace of the drawing. Both will have the 3D Hidden visual style set as the current visual style. The left viewport will have the View Cube set to the top view, and the right viewport will have a View Cube setting set to southwest isometric view. (Additional views will be discussed later in this chapter.) The New Viewport command is located on the Viewports toolbar of the View tab on the Ribbon. Set the current tab of the Ribbon to the View tab and refer to the Viewports toolbar (Figure 5.13).

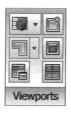

▶ **FIGURE 5.13:** The Viewports toolbar on the 3D Modeling Workspace Ribbon's View tab

The New Viewports Command

To begin, do the following:

1. Position the cursor over the New Viewports icon (Figure 5.14) on the Viewports toolbar of the Ribbon's View tab and left-click.

▶ **FIGURE 5.14:** The New Viewports icon

This action will launch a Viewports window (Figure 5.15).

2. Position the cursor over the Two: Vertical option in the Standard viewports category and left-click. Then click the OK button and left-click to close the window.

This action will result in two vertically tiled viewports in the 3D Modeling Workspace with a 3D Hidden Visual Style set. (See Figure 5.16.)

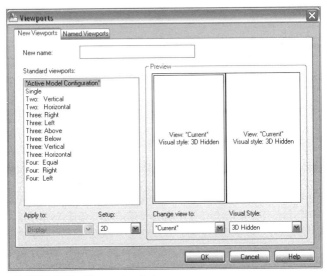

▶ **FIGURE 5.15:** The Viewports window

The View Cube is already set to the front view in the left viewport. To update the View Cube in the right viewport to a southwest view, do the following:

1. Position the cursor in the right viewport and left-click to make it active.

2. Hover the cursor over the View Cube to highlight it (Figure 5.17).

▶ **FIGURE 5.17:** The View Cube in the right viewport (highlighted)

This action will highlight the View Cube, and a House icon will appear in the upper-left corner of the View Cube. To update the view, do the following:

3. Hover the cursor over the House icon and left-click.

This action will update the view to a southwest view in that viewport. (See Figures 5.18 and 5.19.)

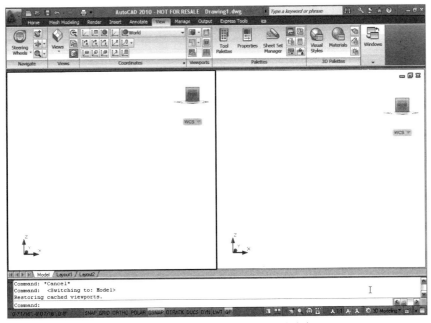

▶ **FIGURE 5.16:** The 3D Modeling Workspace with two vertically tiled viewports

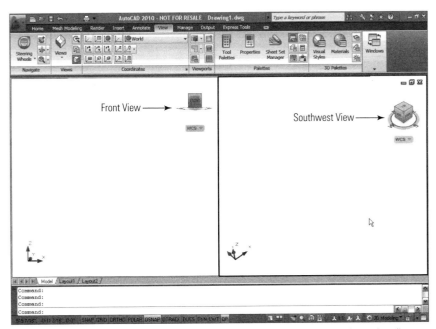

▶ **FIGURE 5.18:** The 3D Modeling Workspace with two vertically tiled viewports (completed)

▶ **FIGURE 5.19:** The View Cube in the right viewport is set to a southwest view.

The 3D Modeling Workspace Ribbon

In this section, you will learn how to work with the 3D toolbars. To begin, do the following:

1. Update the Drawing Units for your drawing to Architectural.

2. Set the Ribbon to the Home tab.

3. Verify that the current Visual Style is set to 3D Hidden.

4. Verify that the current setting of the View Cube for the left viewport is set to the front view.

5. Verify that the current setting of the View Cube for the right viewport is set to the southwest view.

The Modeling Toolbar

The Modeling toolbar (Figure 5.20) houses the icons used to draw 3D solids. These shapes are referred to as *primitive shapes*. These shapes are preloaded to the 3D Modeling Workspace and are the basic shapes used to create 3D objects. When these shapes are combined, they are referred to as *composite shapes*.

The icons used to create surfaces by using 2D objects to manipulate a 3D solid are also located on this toolbar.

▶ **FIGURE 5.20:** The Modeling toolbar on the 3D Modeling Workspace Ribbon's Home tab

Drawing Primitive Shapes

To launch the 3D Primitive Shapes flyout menu, do the following:

1. Position the cursor over the pulldown arrow under the Box icon and left-click.

The available 3D primitive shapes will appear (Figure 5.21).

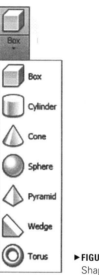

▶ **FIGURE 5.21:** The 3D Primitive Shapes flyout menu

Next, you will begin drawing a solid box primitive shape.

The 3D Solid Box Command

To draw a solid box that is 2″ long × 2″ wide × 2″ high, do the following:

1. Position the cursor over the Solid Box icon (Figure 5.22) on the Modeling toolbar of the Ribbon's Home tab and left-click.

▶ **FIGURE 5.22:** The 3D Solid Box icon

The following prompt appears on the command line:
```
Command: _box
Specify first corner or [Center]:
```

2. Type **0,0** and press the Enter key.

   The following prompt appears on the command line:
   `Specify other corner or [Cube/Length]:`

3. Type **l** and press the Enter key.

   The following prompt appears on the command line:
   `Specify length <0'-0">:`

4. Type **2** and press the Enter key.

   The following prompt appears on the command line:
   `Specify width <0'-0">:`

5. Type **2** and press the Enter key.

   The following prompt appears on the command line:
   `Specify height or [2Point]:`

6. Type **2** and press the Enter key to end the command. (See Figure 5.23.)

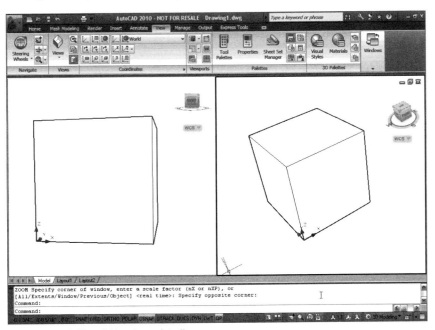

▶**FIGURE 5.23:** A 3D solid box (completed)

The 3D Solid Cylinder Command

Now you will draw a solid cylinder with a radius of 1″ and a height of 2″. To select the 3D Cylinder icon (Figure 5.24) on the Modeling toolbar, do the following:

1. Position the cursor over the pulldown arrow of the Solid Primitive icon currently visible on the Modeling toolbar of the Ribbon's Home tab and left-click. Then hover the cursor over the 3D Solid Cylinder option and left-click.

▶**FIGURE 5.24:** The 3D Solid Cylinder icon

This action will execute and highlight the 3D Solid Cylinder command on the Modeling toolbar as the current primitive shape.

   The following prompt appears on the command line:
   `Command: _cylinder`
   `Specify center point of base or [3P/2P/Ttr/Elliptical]:`

2. Select a point anywhere in model space and left-click.

   The following prompt appears on the command line:
   `Specify base radius or[Diameter]:`

3. Type **1** and press the Enter key.

   The following prompt appears on the command line:
   `Specify height or [2Point/Axis endpoint] <0'-0">:`

4. Type **2** and press the Enter key to end the command. (See Figure 5.25.)

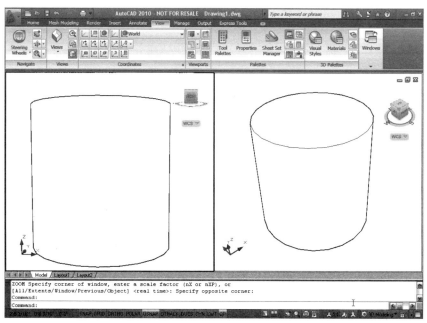

►**FIGURE 5.25:** The 3D solid cylinder (completed)

The 3D Solid Cone Command

Next, you will draw a solid cone with a radius of 1″ and a height of 2″. To select the 3D Cone icon (Figure 5.26) on the Modeling toolbar, do the following:

1. Position the cursor over the pulldown arrow of the Solid Primitive icon currently visible on the Modeling toolbar of the Ribbon's Home tab and left-click. Then hover the cursor over the 3D Solid Cone option and left-click.

►**FIGURE 5.26:** The 3D Solid Cone icon

This action will start and highlight the 3D Solid Cone icon on the Modeling toolbar as the current primitive shape.

The following prompt appears on the command line:
Command: _cone

Specify center point of base or [3P/2P/Ttr/Elliptical]:

2. Select a point anywhere in model space and left-click.

The following prompt appears on the command line:
Specify base radius or[Diameter]:

3. Type **1** and press the Enter key.

The following prompt appears on the command line:
Specify height or [2Point/Axis endpoint/Top radius] <0'-0">:

4. Type **2** and press the Enter key to end the command. (See Figure 5.27.)

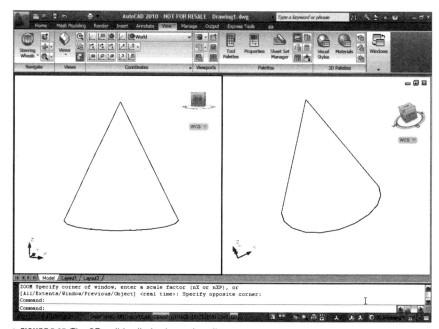

►**FIGURE 5.27:** The 3D solid cylinder (completed)

The 3D Solid Sphere Command

Next, you will draw a solid sphere with a radius of 1″. To select the 3D Sphere icon on the Modeling toolbar, do the following:

1. Position the cursor over the pulldown arrow of the Solid Primitive icon (Figure 5.28) currently visible on the Modeling toolbar of the Ribbon's Home tab and left-click. Then hover the cursor over the 3D Solid Sphere option and left-click.

►**FIGURE 5.28:** The 3D Solid Sphere icon

This action will start and highlight the 3D Solid Sphere icon on the Modeling toolbar as the current primitive shape.

The following prompt appears on the command line:
```
Command: _cone
Specify center point or [3P/2P/Ttr]:
```

2. Select a point anywhere in model space and left-click.

The following prompt appears on the command line:
```
Specify radius or[Diameter]:
```

3. Type **1** and press the Enter key to end the command. (See Figure 5.29.)

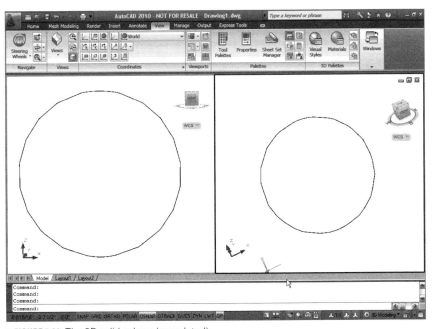

►**FIGURE 5.29:** The 3D solid sphere (completed)

The 3D Solid Pyramid Command

Now, draw a solid pyramid with a radius of 1″ and a height of 2″. To select the 3D Pyramid icon (Figure 5.30) on the Modeling toolbar, do the following:

1. Position the cursor over the pulldown arrow of the Solid Primitive icon currently visible on the Modeling toolbar of the Ribbon's Home tab and left-click. Then hover the cursor over the 3D Solid Pyramid option and left-click.

►**FIGURE 5.30:** The 3D Solid Pyramid icon

This action will start and highlight the 3D Solid Pyramid icon on the Modeling toolbar as the current primitive shape.

The following prompt appears on the command line:
```
Command: _pyramid
4 sides Circumscribed
Specify center point of base or [Edge/Sides]:
```

2. Select a point anywhere in model space and left-click.

The following prompt appears on the command line:
```
Specify base radius or[Inscribed]: <0'-0">:
```

3. Type **1** and press the Enter key.

The following prompt appears on the command line:
```
Specify height or [2Point/Axis endpoint/Top radius] <0'-0">:
```

4. Type **2** and press Enter to end the command. (See Figure 5.31.)

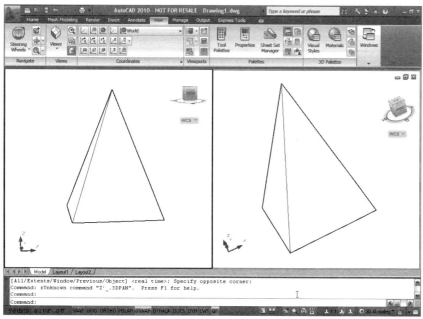

▶ **FIGURE 5.31:** The 3D Solid Pyramid (Completed)

The 3D Solid Wedge Command

Next, draw a solid wedge 2″ long × 2″ wide × 2″ high. To select the 3D Solid Wedge icon (Figure 5.32) on the Modeling toolbar, do the following:

1. Position the cursor over the pulldown arrow of the Solid Primitive icon currently visible on the Modeling toolbar of the Ribbon's Home tab and left-click. Then hover the cursor over the 3D Solid Wedge option and left-click.

▶ **FIGURE 5.32:** The 3D Solid Wedge icon

This action will activate and highlight the 3D Solid Wedge icon on the Modeling toolbar, setting it as the current primitive shape.

The following prompt appears on the command line:
```
Command: _wedge
Specify first corner or [Center]:
```

2. Select a point anywhere in model space and left-click.

The following prompt appears on the command line:
```
Specify other corner or [Cube/Length]:
```

3. Type **l** and press the Enter key.

The following prompt appears on the command line:
```
Specify length <0'-0">:
```

4. Type **2** and press the Enter key.

The following prompt appears on the command line:
```
Specify width <0'-0">:
```

5. Type **2** and press Enter to end the command. (See Figure 5.33.)

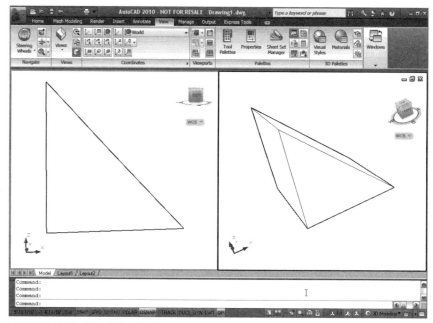

▶ **FIGURE 5.33:** The 3D solid wedge (completed)

The 3D Solid Torus Command

Next, draw a solid torus with a 1″ exterior radius and a ½″ interior tube radius. To select the 3D Solid Torus icon (Figure 5.34) on the Modeling toolbar, do the following:

1. Position the cursor over the pulldown arrow of the Solid Primitive icon currently visible on the Modeling toolbar of the Ribbon's Home tab and left-click. Then hover the cursor over the 3D Solid Torus option and left-click.

Torus

►**FIGURE 5.34:** The 3D Solid Torus icon

This action will start and highlight the 3D Solid Torus icon on the Modeling toolbar, setting it as the current primitive shape.

The following prompt appears on the command line:
```
Command: _torus
Specify center point or [2P/3P/Ttr]:
```

2. Select a point anywhere in model space and left-click.

The following prompt appears on the command line:
```
Specify radius or [Diameter]: <0'-0">:
```

3. Type **1** and press the Enter key.

The following prompt appears on the command line:
```
Specify tube radius or [2Point/Diameter] <0'-0">:
```

4. Type ½ and press the Enter key to end the command. (See Figures 5.35 and 5.36.)

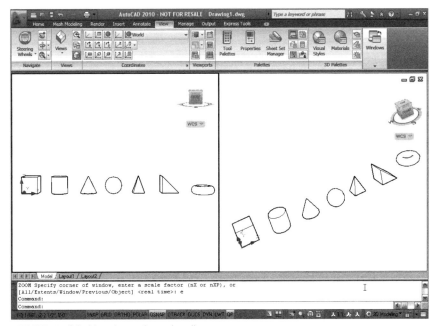

►**FIGURE 5.36:** Primitive shapes (completed)

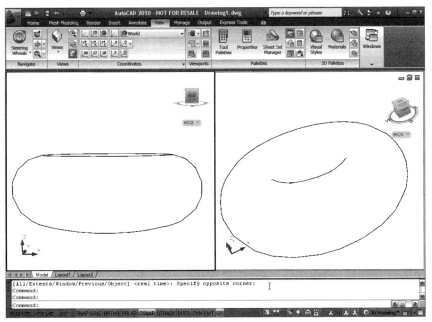

►**FIGURE 5.35:** A 3D solid torus (completed)

Navigating the 3D Modeling Workspace

Now that you have drawn some objects, you may want to look at them more closely. Although the standard commands used when drawing in the 2D Drawing and Annotation Workspace (such as Pan and Zoom) still work, you have one more option for viewing objects that you create in the 3D Modeling Workspace. In addition to the View Cube, you have the tool called the Steering Wheel.

The Full-Navigation Steering Wheel

The Full-Navigation Steering Wheel allows you to orbit, zoom, pan, and walk around a 3D object. This tool is located on the Navigate toolbar on the View tab of the Ribbon. (See Figures 5.37 and 5.38.)

Steering Wheels

►**FIGURE 5.37:** The Navigate toolbar in the 3D Modeling Workspace Ribbon's View tab

▶ **FIGURE 5.38:** The Full-Navigation
Steering Wheels icon

To launch the Full-Navigation Steering Wheel, do the following:

1. Position the cursor over the Full-Navigation Steering Wheels icon on the Navigate toolbar of the Ribbon's View tab and left-click.

This action will launch a Full-Navigation Steering Wheel (Figure 5.39).

▶ **FIGURE 5.39:** The Full-Navigation
Steering Wheel

2. Position the cursor in the active viewport and left-click.

This action will position the Steering Wheel in the selected viewport. Notice that there are several options on the Steering Wheel. By simply positioning the cursor over any option and left-clicking, you will launch the selected option. To launch the Orbit tool, do the following:

3. Position the cursor over the Orbit option, left-click and hold down the left mouse button.

This action will activate the Orbit tool (Figure 5.40). To orbit an object or the current viewport, simply move your cursor in any direction.

To deactivate the Orbit tool, simply lift the left mouse button.

To activate the Zoom tool, do the following:

4. Position the cursor over the Zoom option, left-click and hold down the left mouse button.

This action will activate the Zoom tool (Figure 5.41). To zoom an object or the current viewport, simply move your cursor in any direction and zoom in or out.

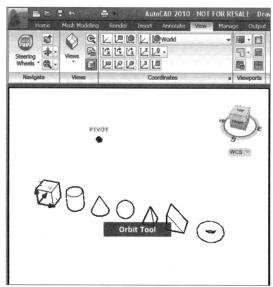

▶ **FIGURE 5.40:** The Full-Navigation Steering Wheel – Orbit tool
(activated)

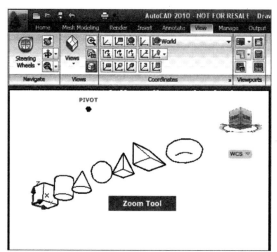

▶ **FIGURE 5.41:** The Full-Navigation Steering Wheel – Zoom tool
(activated)

To deactivate the Zoom tool, simply lift the left mouse button.

To activate the Pan tool, do the following:

5. Position the cursor over the Pan option, left-click and hold down the left mouse button.

This action will activate the Pan tool (Figure 5.42). To pan the current viewport, simply move your cursor in any direction.

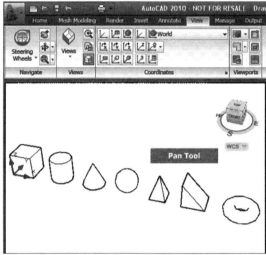

▶ **FIGURE 5.42:** The Full-Navigation Steering Wheel – Pan tool (activated)

To deactivate the Pan tool, simply lift the left mouse button.

To activate the Rewind tool (Figure 5.43), do the following:

6. Position the cursor over the Rewind option, left-click and hold down the left mouse button.

This action will activate the Rewind tool. This will rewind through the previously viewed options that have already been completed. To view a past view, do the following:

7. Position the cursor over any slide view to view that action.

To deactivate the Rewind tool, simply lift the left mouse button.

To activate the Center tool (Figure 5.44), do the following:

8. Position the cursor over the Center option, left-click and hold down the left mouse button.

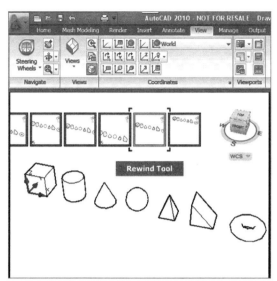

▶ **FIGURE 5.43:** The Full-Navigation Steering Wheel – Rewind tool (activated)

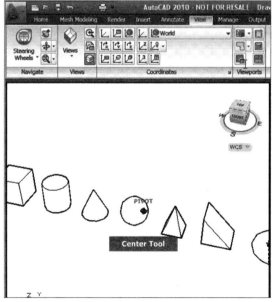

▶ **FIGURE 5.44:** The Full-Navigation Steering Wheel – Center tool (activated)

This action will activate the Center tool. This will center the model at the pivot point you specify. To select a center pivot point, do the following:

9. Position the cursor anywhere within the model and left-click.

This action will reevaluate the center point of your model. To deactivate the Center tool, simply lift the left mouse button.
To activate the Walk tool (Figure 5.45), do the following:

10. Position the cursor over the Walk option, left-click and hold down the left mouse button.

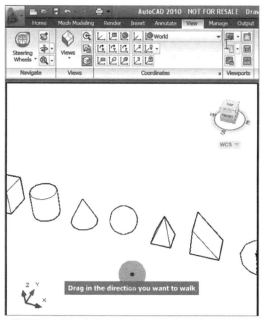

▶**FIGURE 5.45:** The Full-Navigation Steering Wheel – Walk tool (activated)

This action will activate the Walk tool. This will allow you to walk in any direction within the model. To walk in the north direction, do the following:

11. Position the cursor anywhere in the model and left-click. Then move the cursor in the north direction.

This action will move your model in the north direction. To deactivate the Walk tool, simply lift the left mouse button.
To activate the Up/Down tool (Figure 5.46), do the following:

12. Position the cursor over the Up/Down option, left-click and hold down the left mouse button.

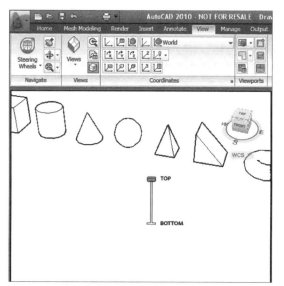

▶**FIGURE 5.46:** The Full-Navigation Steering Wheel – Up/Down tool (activated)

This action will activate the Up/Down tool. This will allow you to move the model either up or down. To move the model down, do the following:

13. Position the cursor on the Sliding Scale icon from the top of the icon and left-click. Then move the cursor in the south direction.

This action will move your model in the south direction or to the bottom. To deactivate the Up/Down tool, simply lift the left mouse button.
To activate the Look tool, do the following:

14. Position the cursor anywhere in the model and left-click. Then move the cursor in the north direction.

This action will move your model in the north direction. To deactivate the Walk tool, simply lift the left mouse button.

To activate the Look tool (Figure 5.47), do the following:

15. Position the cursor over the Look option, left-click and hold down the left mouse button.

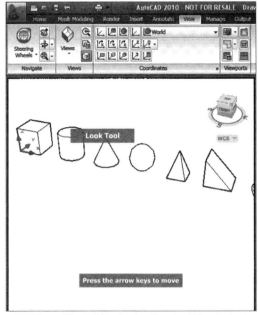

▶ **FIGURE 5.47:** The Full-Navigation Steering Wheel – Look tool (activated)

This action will activate the Look tool. This will allow you to look at the model in any direction. To move the model down, do the following:

16. Move the cursor in any direction.

To deactivate the Look tool, simply lift the left mouse button. Once you are finished navigating the 3D Modeling Workspace, simply left-click the X in the top-right of the Steering Wheel.

Now that you have explored the many options on the Steering Wheel, it is up to you to decide which ones are redundant and which ones are useful to you.

Creating Solids and Surfaces

The icons used to create solids and surfaces by manipulating objects are housed on the flyout menu adjacent to the Modeling toolbar of the Home tab of the Ribbon. To launch the 3D Primitive Shapes flyout menu, do the following:

1. Position the cursor over the pulldown arrow under the Extrude icon and left-click.

This action will launch the flyout menu with the available options to create solids and surfaces (Figure 5.48).

▶ **FIGURE 5.48:** The 3D icons used to create solids and surfaces

Next, you will draw and manipulate a solid with the Extrude command. Before you begin, do the following:

1. Set the Ribbon to the Home tab.

2. Verify that the current Visual Style is set to 3D Hidden.

3. Verify that the current setting of the View Cube for the left viewport is set to the top view.

4. Verify that the current setting of the View Cube for the right viewport is set to the southwest view.

The Extrude Command

The Extrude command will allow you to project the height of a closed polyline. To practice using the Extrude command, do the following:

1. Position the cursor in the left viewport and zoom to a blank area of the viewport.

2. Position the cursor over the Polyline icon located on the Draw toolbar on the Home tab of the Ribbon and left-click.

3. Draw a closed shape. (See Figures 5.49 and 5.50.)

▶ **FIGURE 5.49:** The Extrude icon

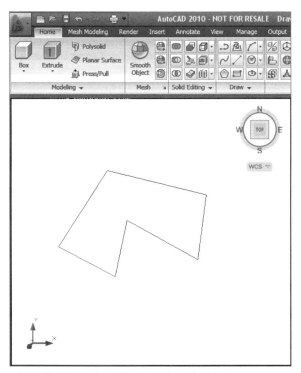

▶ **FIGURE 5.50:** Closed polyline shape (top view)

4. Position the cursor over the View Cube in the left viewport, and left-click the S (or south direction) to change to the front view. Then hold down the middle mouse button to reposition the view, and left-click a Zoom window around the closed polyline. (See Figure 5.51.)

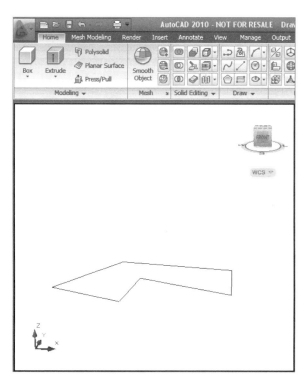

▶ **FIGURE 5.51:** Closed polyline shape (front view)

Now, to extrude this polyline, do the following:

5. Position the cursor over the Extrude icon located on the Modeling toolbar on the Home tab of the Ribbon and left-click.

   The following prompt appears on the command line:
   ```
   Command: _extrude
   Current wireframe density: ISOLINES=4
   Select objects to extrude:
   ```

6. Position the cursor over the closed polyline and left-click.

   The following prompt appears on the command line:
   ```
   Select objects to extrude:
   ```

7. Press the Enter key.

   The following prompt appears on the command line:
   ```
   Specify height of extrusion or [Direction/Path/Taper angle] <0'-0">:
   ```

8. Type **2** and press the Enter key.

This action will extrude the closed polyline to a height of 2″ and end the command. (See Figure 5.52.)

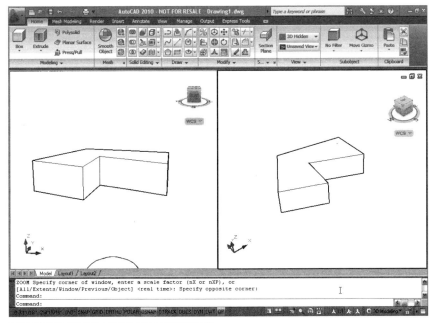

▶**FIGURE 5.52:** Closed polyline shape (extruded)

The Loft Command

The Loft command will allow you to create a solid surface using a series of closed polylines. In this exercise, you will create a funnel shape from a series of circles. The funnel will have a bottom radius of 2″ that will taper off to a top radius of 1″. The overall height of the funnel will be 2″. (See Figure 5.53.)

▶**FIGURE 5.53:** The Loft icon

To demonstrate the Loft command, do the following:

1. Position the cursor in the left viewport and zoom to a blank area. Set the current view to top view on the View Cube.

2. Position the cursor over the Circle icon located on the Draw toolbar on the Home tab of the Ribbon and left-click.

3. Draw a circle with a radius of 2″. Then draw another circle with a radius of 1″ at the center point of the first circle. Then draw the last circle with a radius of ½″ at the center point of the previously drawn circles. Then press the Enter key to end the command.

Next, you will need to move the series of circles to the appropriate heights in order to create the funnel-like object. To continue, do the following:

4. Position the cursor over the View Cube in the left viewport, and left-click the S (or south direction) to change to front view. Then hold down the middle mouse button to reposition the view, and left-click a Zoom window around the series of circles.

5. Position the cursor over the Move icon located on the Modify toolbar of the Home tab of the Ribbon and left-click. Then select the second circle drawn and move it along the Z-axis or in the north direction at a distance of 1″. Then do the same thing for the smallest circle drawn at a distance of 2″. (See Figure 5.54.)

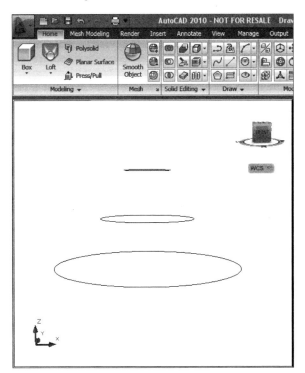

▶**FIGURE 5.54:** Aligned circles (front view)

To create the funnel-like object, do the following:

6. Position the cursor over the pulldown arrow of the 3D icon used to create solids and surfaces (it is currently visible on the Modeling toolbar of the Ribbon's Home tab) and left-click. Then hover the cursor over the Loft option and left-click.

This action will start and highlight the Loft icon on the Modeling toolbar, setting it as the current 3D icon to create solids and surfaces.

> ***The following prompt appears on the command line:***
> Command: _loft
> Select cross sections in lofting order:
> Select objects to extrude:

7. Position the cursor over the bottom circle, and left-click the circles in order from top to bottom. Then press the Enter key.

> ***The following prompt appears on the command line:***
> Enter an option[Guides/Path/Cross sections only]: <cross sections only>:

8. Press the Enter key.

This action will launch a Loft Settings window (Figure 5.55).

▶ **FIGURE 5.55:** The Loft Settings window

The Smooth Fit option will be highlighted in the Surface control of the Cross Sections category. To accept this setting, do the following:

9. Position the cursor over the OK button and left-click.

This action will create the funnel-like object and end the command. (See Figure 5.56.)

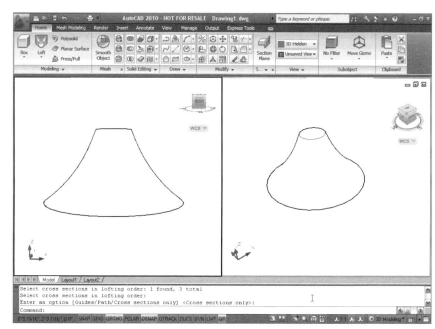

▶ **FIGURE 5.56:** Funnel-like object (lofted)

The Revolve Command

The Revolve command enables you to create a solid circular shape by simply creating half of an object's profile. In this example, you will create a knob shape from a two-dimensional, closed stepped polyline. The knob shape will be 1″ high × 1″ wide, with two steps equally distanced at ½″ high × ½″ deep. (See Figure 5.57.)

▶ **FIGURE 5.57:** The Revolve icon

To demonstrate the Revolve command, do the following:

1. Position the cursor in the left viewport and zoom to a blank area. Set the current view to top view on the View Cube.

   Make sure the Ortho and Osnap functions are On.

2. Position the cursor over the Polyline icon located on the Draw toolbar on the Home tab of the Ribbon and left-click.

3. Draw a vertical polyline at a distance of 1″. Continue in the east direction at ½″, in the south direction at a distance of ½″, in the east ½″, and then in the south direction at a distance of ½″. Then type **C** to end the command. (See Figure 5.58.)

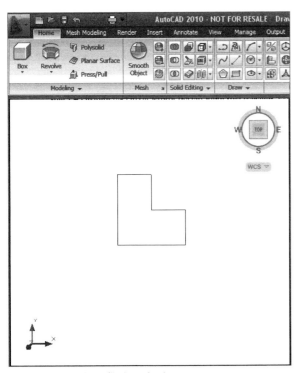

▶**FIGURE 5.58:** Knob profile (top view)

To revolve the knob-shaped profile object, do the following:

4. Position the cursor over the pulldown arrow of the 3D icon used to create solids and surfaces, which is currently visible on the Modeling toolbar of the Ribbon's Home tab, and left-click. Then hover the cursor over the Revolve option and left-click.

This action will start and highlight the Revolve icon on the Modeling toolbar, setting the current 3D icon to Create Solids and Surfaces.

The following prompt appears on the command line:
```
Command: _revolve
Wire frame density: ISOLINES=4
Select objects to revolve:
```

5. Position the cursor over the knob-shaped closed polyline and left-click. Then press the Enter key.

The following prompt appears on the command line:
```
Specify axis start point or define axis by [Object/X/Y/Z] <Object>:
```

6. Left-click a point on the left side of the object.

The following prompt appears on the command line:
```
Specify axis endpoint
```

7. Left-click a vertical point on the left side of the object.

The following prompt appears on the command line:
```
Specify angle of revolution or [Start angle] <360>:
```

8. Press the Enter key.

This action will create a round knob object and end the command (Figure 5.59).

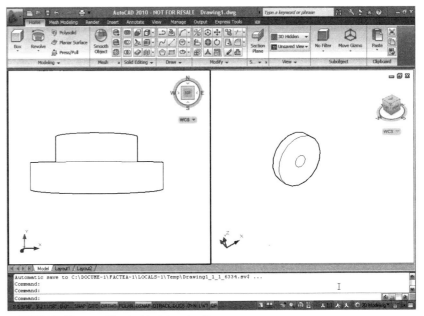

▶**FIGURE 5.59:** The round knob object (revolved)

The Sweep Command

The Sweep command allows you to create a solid object by guiding it across a path. In this exercise, you will create a solid, bent, circular section of tubing. The tubing thickness will be 1" thick. (See Figure 5.60.)

▶ **FIGURE 5.60:** The Sweep icon

To practice using the Revolve command, do the following:

1. Position the cursor in the left viewport and zoom to a blank area. Set the current view to top view on the View Cube.

2. Position the cursor over the Polyline icon located on the Draw toolbar on the Home tab of the Ribbon and left-click.

3. Draw four segments of an angled polyline. Press the Enter key to end the command.

4. Draw a ½"-radius circle to the right of the polyline. Press the Enter key to end the command. (See Figure 5.61.)

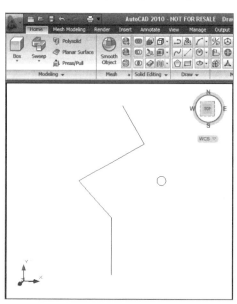

▶ **FIGURE 5.61:** Tubing path (top view)

To sweep the circle along the angled polyline, do the following:

5. Position the cursor over the pulldown arrow of the 3D icon used to create solids and surfaces, which is currently visible on the Modeling toolbar of the Ribbon's Home tab, and left-click. Hover the cursor over the Sweep option and left-click.

This action will start and highlight the Sweep icon on the Modeling toolbar, setting the current 3D icon to Create Solids and Surfaces.

The following prompt appears on the command line:
```
Command: _sweep
Wire frame density: ISOLINES=4
Select objects to sweep:
```

6. Position the cursor over the circle and left-click. Then press the Enter key.

The following prompt appears on the command line:
```
Select sweep path or [Alignment/Base point/Scale/Twist]:
```

7. Click the polyline on the left side of the circle.

This action will create a bent section of 1" circular tubing and end the command (Figure 5.62).

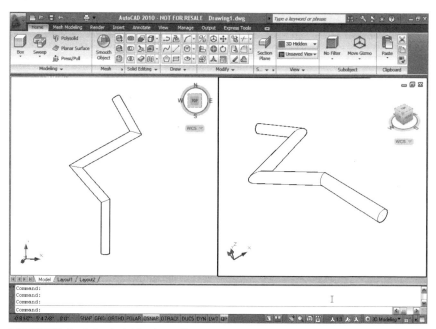

▶ **FIGURE 5.62:** Bent circular tubing (swept)

The Polysolid Command

The Polysolid command allows you to make solid, rectangular objects that are connected. This tool is useful when creating a wall thickness within a 3D model. In this example, you will create a 90-degree angled section of wall with a thickness of 5″ and a height of 3′. (See Figure 5.63.)

▶**FIGURE 5.63:** The Polysolid icon

To demonstrate the Polysolid command, do the following:

1. Position the cursor in the left viewport and zoom to a blank area. Set the current view to top view on the View Cube.

2. Position the cursor over the Polysolid icon located on the Modeling toolbar of the Home tab on the Ribbon and left-click.

   The following prompt appears on the command line:
   ```
   Command: _Polysolid Height=0'-4",Width=0'-¼", Justification=Center
   Specify start point or [Object/Height/Width/Justify] <object>:
   ```

   To update the height, do the following:

3. Type **h** and press the Enter key.

   The following prompt appears on the command line:
   ```
   Specify height:
   ```

4. Type **36** and press the Enter key.

   The following prompt appears on the command line:
   ```
   Height=3'-0",Width=0'-¼", Justification=Center
   Specify start point or [Object/Height/Width/Justify] <object>:
   ```

   To update the width, do the following:

5. Type **w** and press the Enter key.

   The following prompt appears on the command line:
   ```
   Specify width: <0'-¼">
   ```

6. Type **5** and press the Enter key.

   The following prompt appears on the command line:
   ```
   Height=3'-0",Width=5", Justification=Center
   Specify start point or [Object/Height/Width/Justify] <object>:
   ```

   Make sure the Ortho function is On.

7. Select a point and left-click.

   The following prompt appears on the command line:
   ```
   Specify next point or [Arc/Undo]:
   ```

8. Pull the cursor in the south direction and left-click.

   The following prompt appears on the command line:
   ```
   Specify next point or [Arc/Undo]:
   ```

9. Pull the cursor in the east direction and left-click.

   The following prompt appears on the command line:
   ```
   Specify next point or [Arc/Close/Undo]:
   ```

10. Press the Enter key.

This action will create a 90-degree section of wall that is 3′ high × 5″ thick and end the command (Figure 5.64).

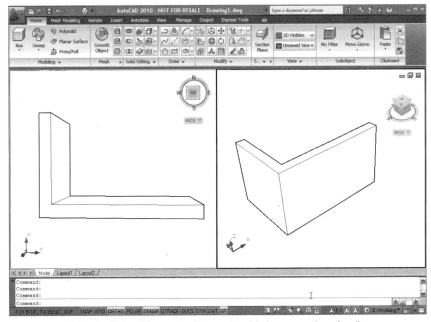

▶**FIGURE 5.64:** Using the Polysolid command to create a 90-degree section of wall

The Planar Surface Command

The Planar Surface command allows you to make solid boxes or rectangles by selecting points. It works similarly to how a rectangle or square is drawn with the Rectangle command. This tool is useful when creating floor planes within a 3D model. (See Figure 5.65.)

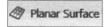

▶**FIGURE 5.65:** The Planar Surface icon

To demonstrate the Planar Surface command, do the following:

1. Position the cursor in the left viewport and zoom to a blank area. Set the current view to top view on the View Cube.

   Ensure that the Ortho function is On.

2. Position the cursor over the Planar Surface icon located on the Modeling toolbar of the Ribbon's Home tab and left-click.

   The following prompt appears on the command line:
   ```
   Command: _Planesurf
   Specify first corner or [Object] <object>:
   ```

3. Select the first point by left-clicking it.

   The following prompt appears on the command line:
   ```
   Specify other corner:
   ```

4. Move the cursor in a diagonal fashion and left-click.

   This action will create a rectangular block and end the command (Figure 5.66).

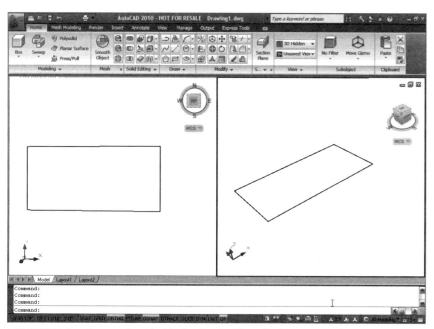

▶**FIGURE 5.66:** Creating a rectangular block using the Planar Surface command

The Solid Editing Toolbar

The Solid Editing toolbar (Figure 5.67) houses the commands used to edit solids and surfaces of 3D objects. This toolbar is located on the Home tab of the Ribbon. We will review a couple of them.

▶**FIGURE 5.67:** The Solid Editing toolbar

The 3D Union Command

The 3D Union command allows you to join two or more like 3D solids. Using this command is very similar to creating a block. When drawing a 3D object, it is referred to a *composite*. (See Figure 5.68.)

▶**FIGURE 5.68:** The 3D Union icon

To demonstrate the 3D Union command, do the following:

1. Position the cursor in the left viewport and zoom to a blank area. Set the current view to top view on the View Cube.

2. Create two spheres using the Sphere icon located on the Modeling toolbar and overlap them slightly (Figure 5.69).

3. Position the cursor over the 3D Union icon located on the Solid Editing toolbar of the Home tab on the Ribbon and left-click.

   The following prompt appears on the command line:
   ```
   Command: _union
   Select objects:
   ```

4. Select both spheres by left-clicking them.

   The following prompt appears on the command line:
   ```
   Select objects:
   ```

5. Press the Enter key.

   This action will join, or union, both spheres and end the command (Figure 5.70).

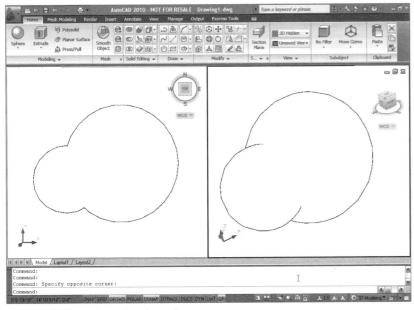

► **FIGURE 5.69**: Two spheres (overlapped)

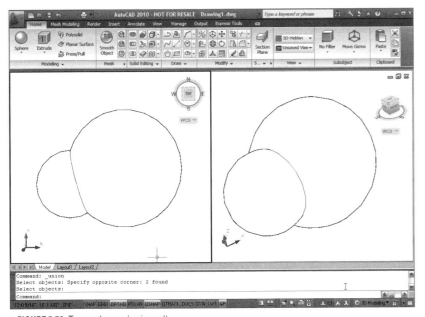

► **FIGURE 5.70**: Two spheres (unioned)

The 3D Subtract Command

The 3D Subtract command allows you to subtract (remove) a portion of a solid by using another solid to do so. (See Figure 5.71.)

► **FIGURE 5.71**: The 3D Subtract icon

To practice using the 3D Subtract command, do the following:

1. Position the cursor in the left viewport and zoom to a blank area. Set the current view to front view on the View Cube.

2. Using the Cone icon located on the Modeling toolbar, create two cones and overlap them slightly at their bases (Figure 5.72).

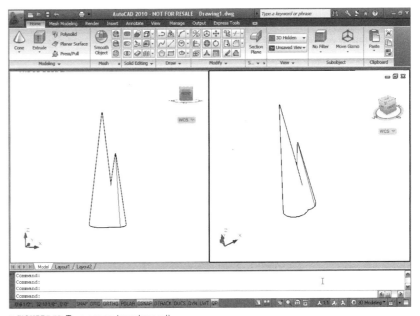

► **FIGURE 5.72**: Two cones (overlapped)

3. Position the cursor over the 3D Subtract icon located on the Solid Editing tool-bar of the Home tab on the Ribbon and left-click.

   The following prompt appears on the command line:
   ```
   Command: _subtract Select solids, surfaces, and regions to subtract
   from ...
   Select objects:
   ```

4. Select the cone on the left side by left-clicking it.

   The following prompt appears on the command line:
   ```
   Command: _subtract Select solids, surfaces, and regions to subtract
   from ...
   Select objects:
   ```

5. Select the cone on the right side by left-clicking it.

   The following prompt appears on the command line:
   ```
   Command: _subtract Select solids, surfaces, and regions to subtract
   from ...
   Select objects:
   ```

6. Press the Enter key.

This action will subtract the cone on the right side from the cone on the left hand side and end the command. (See Figures 5.73 and 5.74.)

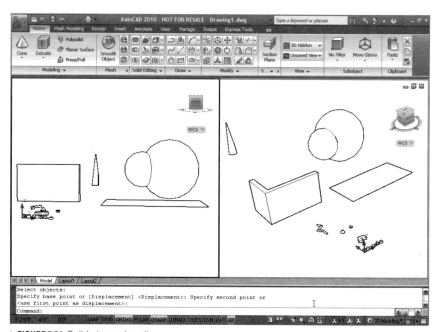

▶**FIGURE 5.74:** Solids (completed)

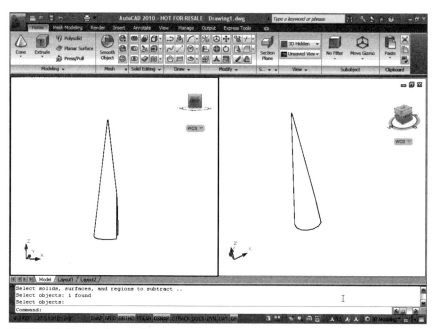

▶**FIGURE 5.73:** Cone (subtracted)

CHAPTER 6

The Commercial Office Space

AFTER COMPLETING THIS CHAPTER, YOU WILL BE FAMILIAR WITH:

▶ Commercial office space

▶ Existing-conditions floor plans

▶ The Layer list

▶ Advanced Layer tools

▶ The drawing template to complete the millwork detail drawings

Now that you've been exposed to some advanced drawing tools, it is time to discuss a project that will help apply what you've learned thus far. This chapter will review the detail drawings of millwork construction for a small commercial office space. This same space will be used in subsequent chapters to compile a full set of millwork drawings.

The tenant space is a project that actually occurred. The millwork component was only a portion of the overall project.

The Commercial Office Space

The space is approximately 2,700 square feet of class "A" office space. It houses a small boutique-style law firm that has occupied the space for over 10 years, and it required renovation (Figure 6.1).

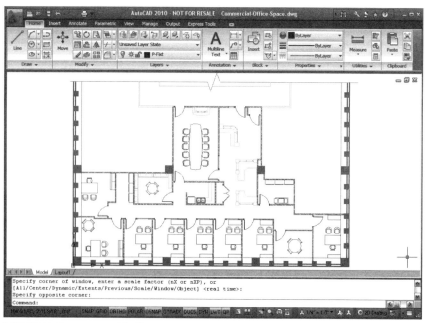

▶ **FIGURE 6.1:** The commercial office space

As previously mentioned, the project encompassed a full remodel that helped to rebrand the client. A large part of the project was the design and development of the millwork for the space. This millwork was designed for the common areas of the law firm, as well as the areas that would have the most impact. These areas included the reception area, main conference room, and the law library.

The millwork items included:

- A reception desk (Figure 6.2)
- A two-person administrative workstation (Figure 6.3)
- A conference room cabinet with bookshelf (Figure 6.4)
- Wood shelves and matching wall-support standards (Figure 6.5)
- A wood wall base

▶ **FIGURE 6.2:** The reception desk (front view)

▶ **FIGURE 6.3:** The workstation (side view)

▶ **FIGURE 6.4:** The conference room cabinet with bookshelf

▶ **FIGURE 6.5:** Wood shelves and matching wall-support standards

The Existing-Conditions Floor Plan

The existing-conditions floor plan (Figure 6.6) is included on the DVD that accompanies this text, and it details the location of the new millwork. This AutoCAD drawing file is located in the chapter drawing file for this chapter on the DVD. The drawing's name is `Commercial-Office-Space.dwg`. This file also includes:

- Floor plan blocks
- Floor plan annotative tags and symbols
- Annotative text and dimension styles
- Floor plan layers
- Titleblock inserted into layout space

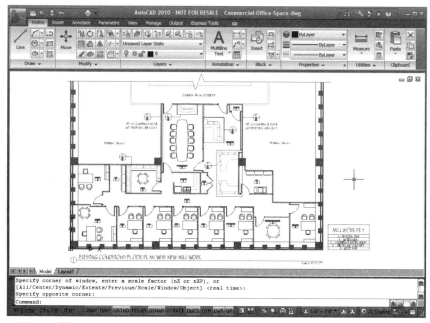

▶**FIGURE 6.6:** The existing-conditions floor plan for the commercial office space

This drawing file should be used as a base drawing file to include with the complete set of millwork drawings. Because the callout bubble tags are annotative, you can use this file to update the detail callout bubble tags that identify the page location for each millwork item. You can also use this drawing file to prepare additional floor plan drawings if you like. Other floor plan drawings could include floor/carpet pattern options or a finished plan.

The millwork will be fully detailed in Chapter 7, "Starting the Millwork Detail Drawings," and Chapter 8, "Continuing the Millwork Detail Drawings." What follows are the plan locations for each piece of millwork.

The reception desk is located in the reception area closest to the main entry (Figure 6.7).

The workstation is located in the reception area adjacent to the reception desk (Figure 6.8).

The conference room cabinet with bookshelf is located in the conference room closest to the second means of egress (Figure 6.9).

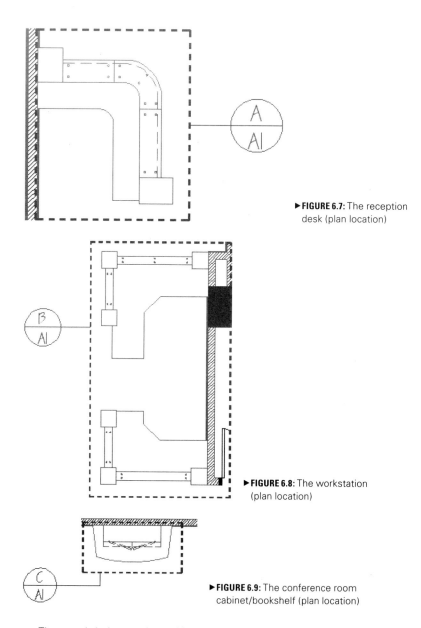

▶**FIGURE 6.7:** The reception desk (plan location)

▶**FIGURE 6.8:** The workstation (plan location)

▶**FIGURE 6.9:** The conference room cabinet/bookshelf (plan location)

The wood shelves and matching wall-support standards are located in the law library (Figure 6.10).

The wood wall base is located along the walls in the reception area and the conference room (Figure 6.11).

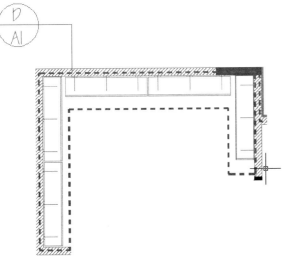

▶ **FIGURE 6.10:** The wood shelves and matching wall-support standards (plan location)

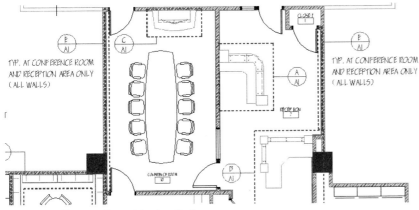

▶ **FIGURE 6.11:** The wood base (plan location)

The Existing-Conditions Layer List

The layers that appear in the Layer Properties Manager of the `Commercial-Office-Space.dwg` closely follow the American Institute of Architects (AIA) standards for naming layers. Figure 6.12 lists and explains the layers added to the existing-conditions floor plan.

DRAWING LAYER LIST				
LAYER NAME	DESCRIPTION	COLOR	LINETYPE	LINEWEIGHT
FLOOR PLAN - EXISTING CONDITIONS LAYERS				
A-COL	BASE COLUMNS	GREEN	CONTINUOUS	DEFAULT
A-DIMS	DIMENSIONS	WHITE	CONTINUOUS	DEFAULT
A-DOORS	DOORS	RED	CONTINUOUS	DEFAULT
A-FL-CSWRK	BUILT IN CASEWORK	YELLOW	CONTINUOUS	DEFAULT
A-FURN	FURNITURE	MAGENTA	CONTINUOUS	DEFAULT
A-MILLWRK-NEW	NEW BUILT IN CASEWORK	RED	CONTINUOUS	DEFAULT
A-PLAN-HATCH	PLAN HATCH	RED	CONTINUOUS	DEFAULT
A-RM NAMES	ROOM NAMES	CYAN	CONTINUOUS	DEFAULT
A-SYMS	PLAN SYMBOLS	CYAN	CONTINUOUS	DEFAULT
A-TAGS	PLAN TAGS	CYAN	CONTINUOUS	DEFAULT
A-TEXT	PLAN TEXT	CYAN	CONTINUOUS	DEFAULT
A-WALL-EXT	EXTERIOR WALLS	GREEN	CONTINUOUS	0.50MM
A-WALL-INT	INTERIOR WALLS	YELLOW	CONTINUOUS	DEFAULT
A-WDWS-EXT	EXTERIOR WINDOWS	MAGENTA	CONTINUOUS	DEFAULT
A-WDWS-INT	INTERIOR WINDOWS	MAGENTA	CONTINUOUS	DEFAULT
P-FIXT	PLUMBING FIXTURES	BLUE	CONTINUOUS	DEFAULT

▶ **FIGURE 6.12:** The Drawing Layer list for the existing-conditions floor plan

Advanced Layer Tools

The Layers toolbar is located on the Home tab of the Ribbon. This toolbar allows access to the Layer Properties Manager as well as various other layer functions available to you, such as the function to isolate a layer or to set a layer current. As a recently added feature, the Layers toolbar allows layers to be faded within model space and active viewports within layout tabs.

As previously mentioned, reducing the visual complexity in a drawing is referred to as *fading layers*. This can be done to keep certain layers On for reference, in order to add additional information to the drawing.

Another useful layer tool is the Layer Walk tool. This tool allows you to verify the layers in a drawing and visually identify the items that are on any particular layer. This tool is especially helpful when a drawing file is received from an outside source. It is good practice to verify any file prior to working on it. Both of these layer features will be reviewed utilizing the `Commercial-Office-Space.dwg`. To begin, do the following:

1. Open the companion DVD and refer to the chapter drawing file for Chapter 6.

2. Download and save the drawing titled `Commercial-Office-Space.dwg`.

3. Make sure the 2D Drafting and Annotation Workspace is current.

4. Set the Home tab to be current.

5. Pin the Layers toolbar (Figure 6.13).

You are now ready to begin.

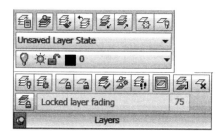

▶ **FIGURE 6.13:** The Layers toolbar (pinned)

The Locked Layer Fading Command

A layer must first be locked before it can be faded. To fade the furniture on the plan, do the following:

1. Access the shortcut pulldown window of the Layer Properties Manager on the Layers toolbar. Position the cursor over the A-Furn layer and click on the Lock icon with the left mouse button. (See Figures 6.14 and 6.15.)

▶ **FIGURE 6.14:** The Locked Layer Fading icon

▶ **FIGURE 6.15:** The A-Furn layer (locked)

This action will lock that layer. To fade that layer, do the following:

2. Position the cursor over the Layer Locked Fading icon in the Layers toolbar and click on it with the left mouse button.

This action will automatically fade any layer within the drawing that is currently locked. The fade setting is automatically defaulted to Fade Layers by 75 Percent. (See Figures 6.16 and 6.17.)

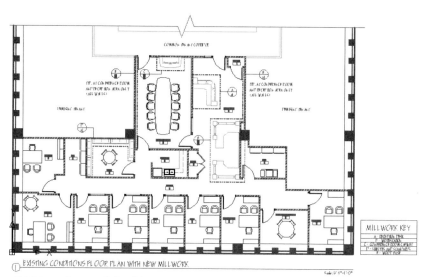

▶ **FIGURE 6.16:** `Commercial-Office-Space.dwg` (prior to fading)

▶ **FIGURE 6.17:** Commercial-Office-Space.dwg (after fading to 75 percent)

This display state allows you to use visible geometry in order to utilize osnaps. Additionally, the fade can be adjusted.

The Layer Walk Command

The Layer Walk tool allows you to view a list of layers in the drawing, and it will isolate the items on any particular layer in order to visually verify them. To use this tool, do the following:

1. Click the Layer Walk icon (Figure 6.18) with the left mouse button.

The action will launch a Layer Walk window (Figure 6.19).

▶ **FIGURE 6.18:** The Layer Walk icon

▶ **FIGURE 6.19:** The Layer Walk window

This window lists all of the layers in the drawing file. In order to isolate a layer, do the following:

2. Left click the A-Col layer (Figure 6.20) in the Layer Walk window.

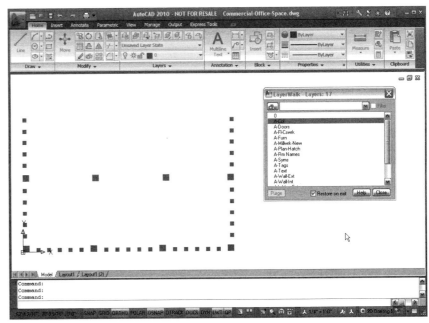

▶ **FIGURE 6.20:** The A-Col layer (Isolated)

This action will automatically isolate the A-Col layer in the drawing, thereby allowing you to visually verify the items on that layer. Try verifying other layers in the drawing. In order to close this command, do the following:

3. Click the Close button in the Layer Walk window with the left mouse button.

The Millwork Detail Drawing Template

Chapters 7 and 8 will detail the millwork items that were briefly explained in this chapter. A drawing template has already been prepared for you. This AutoCAD drawing template file is located in the chapter drawing file for Chapter 7 on the companion DVD. The drawing name is `Millwork-Details.dwt`. This file includes the following:

- Millwork plan blocks
- Annotative tags and symbols
- Annotative text and dimension styles
- Millwork layers
- Titleblock inserted into layout space with several viewports

The Millwork-Details Drawing Template Layer List

The layers that appear in the Layer Properties Manager of the `Millwork-Details.dwt` also closely follow the AIA standards for naming layers. Figure 6.21 details and explains the layers added to this drawing template.

The drawing template will be downloaded in the following chapter.

DRAWING LAYER LIST				
LAYER NAME	DESCRIPTION	COLOR	LINETYPE	LINEWEIGHT
MILLWORK DETAIL LAYERS				
A-MILLWRK-DIMS	DIMENSIONS	WHITE	CONTINUOUS	DEFAULT
A-MILLWRK-DSHD	DASHED LINES	RED	DASHED	DEFAULT
A-MILLWRK-H	HEAVY LINES	GREEN	CONTINUOUS	0.50MM
A-MILLWRK-HATCH	HATCH	RED	CONTINUOUS	DEFAULT
A-MILLWRK-HATCH-LT	LIGHT HATCH	GRAY	CONTINUOUS	DEFAULT
A-MILLWRK-L	LIGHT LINES	MAGENTA	CONTINUOUS	DEFAULT
A-MILLWRK-M	MEDIUM LINES	YELLOW	CONTINUOUS	0.40MM
A-MILLWRK-SYMS	SYMBOLS	CYAN	CONTINUOUS	DEFAULT
A-MILLWRK-TAGS	TAGS	CYAN	CONTINUOUS	DEFAULT
A-MILLWRK-TEXT	TEXT	CYAN	CONTINUOUS	DEFAULT
A-MILLWRK-VL	VERY LIGHT LINES	GRAY	CONTINUOUS	0.15MM

▶ **FIGURE 6.21:** The Drawing Layer list for the Millwork-Details template

CHAPTER 7

Starting the Millwork Detail Drawings

AFTER COMPLETING THIS CHAPTER, YOU WILL BE ABLE TO:

▶ Download and save a drawing template

▶ Draw millwork details for the wood base

▶ Draw millwork details for the wood shelves and matching wall-support standards

▶ Attach and clip an external reference

▶ Modify dynamic blocks

▶ Arrange the details in the viewports in layout space

Millwork is commonly referred to as any carpentry that is produced by a mill. This includes built-in or freestanding casework, shelving, wall bases, and crown moldings. Typically, an interior designer designs a piece of millwork, creates the construction documents, and submits them to a millwork shop to be fabricated. Prior to fabrication, the millwork shop prepares its own drawings based on the drawings that were submitted by the interior designer. Once those drawings are completed, they are returned to the interior designer for review.

The drawings that are submitted back to the interior designer are referred to as *shop drawings*. These drawings are based on the design intent of the item. The unit of measure is inches, and the millworker verifies that the details are based on the Architectural Woodwork Institute (AWI) standards. Once the shop drawings are reviewed by the interior designer, they are returned as approved and production begins.

This chapter will begin the process to prepare the millwork detail drawings for the following:

- The wood base
- The wood shelves and matching wall-support standards

It is important to prepare as many details as necessary in order for the design intent to be realized. Therefore, there is no set number of detail drawings that need to be drawn per item. In other words, you should draw only enough sections and details for someone else to understand and ultimately construct it.

Note that the instructions that follow will be fairly streamlined because the user is assumed to have had some experience using AutoCAD.

The Millwork Drawing Template

To reiterate from Chapter 6, "The Commercial Office Space," the AutoCAD drawing template file is located in the chapter drawing file for this chapter on the accompanying DVD. The drawing's name is `Millwork-Details.dwt`. To begin, do the following:

1. Open the DVD that accompanies this text and refer to the chapter drawing file for this chapter.
2. Download and open the drawing titled `Millwork-Details.dwt`.
3. Save the drawing template file as `MW-1.dwg`.
4. Make sure that the 2D Drafting and Annotation Workspace is current.
5. Set the Home tab current.

You are now ready to begin.

Note that this drawing template should be used every time a new millwork drawing is started.

The Wood Base Millwork Detail

The scale of the drawing is dependent on the size of a particular piece of millwork. Typically, casework would be drawn at a scale of ¾″ = 1′-0″ or ½″ = 1′-0″, with sections drawn at scale of 1½″ = 1′-0″ in order to show enough detail. However, the scale for the wood base (Figure 7.1) should be drawn at full scale or a scale of 1:1. The wood base will be 4″ high × 1″ thick. The detail will consist of:

- A vertical section

▶ **FIGURE 7.1:** The Wood Base section

The Wood Base Section Detail

To begin drawing the wood base, do the following:

1. Insert the Wood Base block into the drawing file.
2. Set the Annotation Scale of the drawing to 1:1.

3. Set the current layer to A-Millwrk-Text.

4. Position the cursor over the Multileader icon on the Annotation toolbar and click it with the left mouse button.

5. Position the cursor near the (midway point) right side of the Wood Base block, and click on it with the left mouse button to begin the leader arrow.

6. Move the cursor to the right at an angle and left-click.

This action will launch a multitext window. Make sure the keyboard's Caps Lock is turned On and do the following:

7. Type **1″ x 4″ CHERRY WOOD BASE**.

8. Set the current layer to A-Millwrk-Dims.

9. Dimension the Wood Base block at the top and the left (vertical) side.

When dimensioning, make sure to dimension the outermost overall dimension first, leaving ample room for additional dimensions on the same plane.

10. Dimension the top and left (vertical) side of the Wood Base block, and detail the smaller nuances of the wood base.

These dimensions should comfortably fit between the previously entered dimensions.

11. Set the current layer to A-Millwrk-Hatch.

12. Position the cursor over the Hatch icon located on the Draw toolbar and left-click.

13. Select the AR-RROOF hatch pattern.

14. In the Angle and Scale category, position the cursor over the pulldown arrow of the Angle field and left-click 45.

15. Select the inside portion of the Wood Base block to fill it, and end the command.

16. Add a drawing title to complete the detail. Set the current layer to A-Millwrk-Tags.

Next, set the Ribbon to the Insert tab, refer to the Block toolbar (Figure 7.2), and then do the following:

►**FIGURE 7.2:** The Block toolbar

17. Position the cursor over the Insert Block icon located on the Block toolbar and left-click.

This action will launch an Insert window (Figure 7.3).

18. Scroll through the list of blocks, and left-click on the Drawing Title – Imperial block, and insert it below the Wood Base detail.

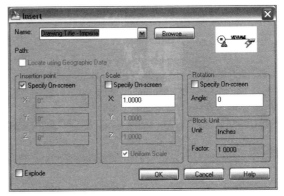

►**FIGURE 7.3:** The Insert window

This tag is an annotative tag with editable attributes so that the tag fields can be updated. Because this is the first drawing tag that will be added to the drawing, the only attribute that will need to be updated is the view title. To update the view title, do the following:

19. Position the cursor over the View Title attribute in the drawing tag and double left-click.

This action will launch an Enhanced Attribute Editor window (Figure 7.4), and the VIEWNAME field will be highlighted. (See Figure 7.5.) To update this field, make sure the Caps Lock key is toggled On and do the following:

20. Type **WOOD BASE DETAIL** and left-click the OK button.

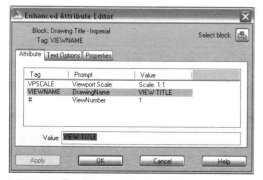

▶ **FIGURE 7.4:** The Enhanced Attribute Editor window

▶ **FIGURE 7.5:** The Wood Base drawing tag

This action will update the DrawingName field and end the command. Note that the drawing name is longer than the title line. To update the title line length to accommodate the title of the drawing, do the following:

21. Position the cursor over the drawing name tag (Figure 7.6) and left-click.

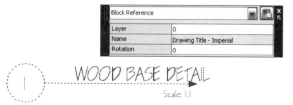

▶ **FIGURE 7.6:** The drawing name tag (highlighted)

This action will highlight the drawing name tag. Note that the title line is highlighted with an arrowhead. In order to stretch the length of the title line, make sure that the Ortho function is On, and do the following:

22. Position the cursor over the arrowhead and left-click. Then stretch the title line to accommodate the title and left-click.

This action will stretch the length of the title line along with the Scale field.

23. Press the Esc key to end the command. (See Figure 7.7.)

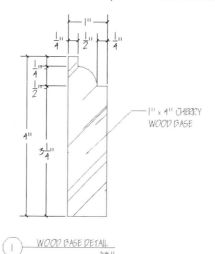

▶ **FIGURE 7.7:** The Wood Base section (completed)

The Wood Shelves and Matching Wall-Support Standards Millwork Details

The wood shelves and matching wall-support standards will be used at the library. The scale for the wall-support standards should be drawn at full scale or a scale of 1:1, and the scale for the wood shelves should be drawn at ¾″ = 1′-0″.

The Wall-Support Standards

The wall-support standards (Figure 7.8) will be 3½″ wide × 1″ thick.
   The detail will consist of:

- A horizontal section

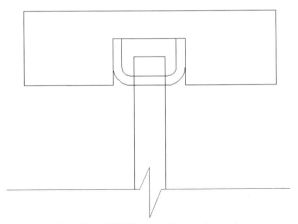

▶ **FIGURE 7.8**: The Wood Wall-Support Standards section

The Wall-Support Standards Section Detail

To begin drawing the wood wall-support standard using the same drawing (MW-1. dwg), do the following:

1. Insert the Wood Wall-Support Standard block into the drawing file.

2. Set the Annotation Scale of the drawing to 1:1.

3. Set the current layer to A-Millwrk-Text.

4. Position the cursor over the Multileader icon on the Annotation toolbar and click it with the left mouse button.

5. To begin the leader arrow, position the cursor near the bracket and standard of the Wood Wall Support block and click on it with the left mouse button.

6. Move the cursor to the right and left-click.

    Verify that the Caps Lock on the keyboard is set to On, and do the following:

7. Type **MILLWORKER SHALL PROVIDE METAL STANDARD AND BRACKET** and then close the Text Editor.

8. Start the Multileader command again.

9. Position the cursor on the Wood Wall Support block and click on it with the left mouse button to begin the leader arrow.

10. Move the cursor to the right and left-click.

Ensure that the Caps Lock key is toggled On and do the following:

11. Type **3½″ x 1″ CHERRY WOOD**, and then close the Text Editor.

12. Set the current layer to A-Millwrk-Dims.

13. Dimension the Wood Wall Support block at the top-left (vertical) side.

    Make sure you dimension the outermost overall dimension first, leaving ample room for additional dimensions on the same plane.

14. Dimension the top-left and right (vertical) side of the Wood Wall Support block that details the smaller nuances of the wood block.

    These dimensions should comfortably fit between the previously entered dimensions.

15. Set the current layer to A-Millwrk-Tags.

    Next, set the Ribbon to the Insert tab and refer to the Block toolbar. Then do the following:

16. Position the cursor over the Insert Block icon located on the Block toolbar and left-click. Insert the Drawing Title – Imperial block below the Wood Wall-Support detail.

17. Position the cursor over the drawing number in the drawing tag and double left-click.

18. Type **2**.

19. Position the cursor over the Drawing Name field in the Enhanced Attribute Editor, left-click in the Value field, and clear the contents.

20. Type **Wood Wall Support Standard Detail** and left-click the OK button.

    To update the title line length to accommodate the title of the drawing, do the following:

21. Position the cursor over the drawing name tag and click.

22. Position the cursor over the arrowhead and left-click. Then stretch the title line length to accommodate the title and left-click.

23. Press the Esc key to end the command.

24. Set the current layer to A-Millwrk-Hatch.

25. Position the cursor over the Hatch icon located on the Draw toolbar and left-click.

26. Select the AR-RROOF hatch pattern.

27. Within the Angle and Scale category, position the cursor over the pulldown arrow of the Angle field and left-click 45.

28. Select the inside portion of the Wood Wall Support block to be filled and end the command. (See Figure 7.9.)

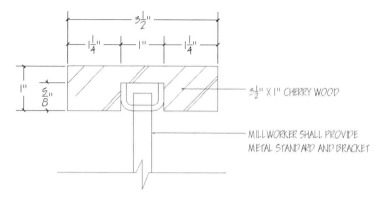

▶**FIGURE 7.9:** The Wood Wall-Support section (completed)

The Wood Shelves

The wood shelves will be ¾″ thick × 4′-6″ wide × 1′-0″ deep, with a ¾″ thick × 1″ high cherry-wood drop edge (included as part of the overall 1′-0″ depth of the shelf). The wood shelves that will be used directly adjacent to the entry of the library will have a ¾″-thick × 1″-high cherry-wood drop edge applied to the right edge in addition to the front face.

The details will consist of:

- A plan location
- Three interior elevations
- A vertical section

Clipping an External Reference (Xref)

Because it has already been drawn, adding the Commercial-Office-Space.dwg drawing as an external reference is the easiest way to create the plan location detail for the wood shelves and matching wood wall-support standards. All you need to do is add the text, dimensions, and tags.

Once an external reference has been attached to a drawing, clipping boundaries can be established to show only the portion of the external reference that is needed. This is helpful because the clipping boundary can be removed and a new boundary can be assigned. To begin, first attach the Commercial-Office-Space.dwg (Figure 7.10) as an Xref to the current drawing (MW-1.dwg). Make sure the current layer is set to layer 0, insert the plan at 0,0, and turn off the following layers:

- Commercial-Office-Space/A-Furn
- Commercial-Office-Space/A-Rm-Names
- Commercial-Office-Space/A-Rm-Syms
- Commercial-Office-Space/A-Tags
- Commercial-Office-Space/A-Text

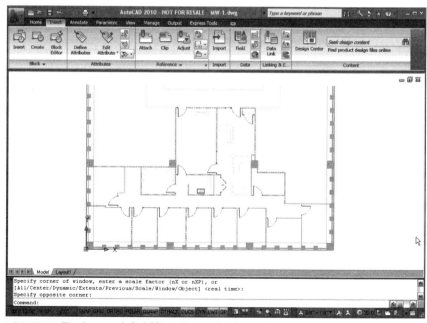

▶**FIGURE 7.10:** The Commercial-Office-Space.dwg inserted as an Xref

Note that the Xref is slightly shaded. In order to clip an Xref, set the Ribbon to the Insert tab and refer to the Reference toolbar. (See Figures 7.11 and 7.12.)

▶**FIGURE 7.11:** The Ribbon's Insert tab

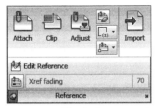

▶**FIGURE 7.12:** The Reference toolbar (pinned)

Next, to clip a boundary around the Library area of the plan, do the following:

1. Position the cursor over the Clip Xref icon (Figure 7.13) and click on it with the left mouse button.

▶**FIGURE 7.13:** The Clip Xref icon

The following prompt appears on the command line:
```
Command: _clip Select Object to clip:
```

2. Left-click the Xref (Commercial-Office-Space.dwg).

The following prompt appears on the command line:
```
Enter clipping option
[ON/OFF/Clipdepth/Delete/generate Polyline/Newboundary] <New>:
```

3. Press the Enter key.

The following prompt appears on the command line:
```
Outside mode - Objects outside boundary will be hidden
Specify clipping boundary or select invert option:
[Select polyline/Polygonal/Rectangular/Invert Clip] <Rectangular>:
```

4. Press the Enter key.

The following prompt appears on the command line:
```
Specify first corner:
```

5. Position the cursor at the upper-left corner of the library and left-click.

The following prompt appears on the command line:
```
Specify opposite corner:
```

6. Position the cursor at the lower-right corner of the library and left-click.

This action will clip a boundary around that portion of the plan and end the command (Figure 7.14).

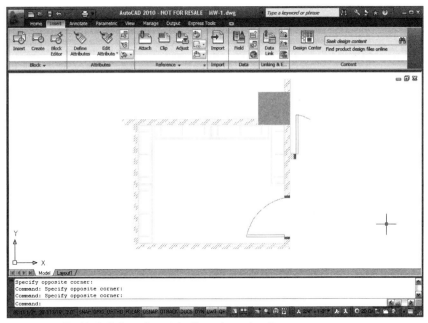

▶**FIGURE 7.14:** The Xref clip boundary of the library (completed)

Turning Off the Fade Option of an External Reference (Xref)

As previously mentioned, the Xref appears faded once it has been inserted into the drawing. This is helpful because it identifies the object as an Xref. However, it can also be a distraction and should not be faded if the Xref is to be used as part of a drawing as an underlay. Turning off the Fade option is quite simple. To turn off the Fade option of the inserted Xref, do the following:

1. Position the cursor over the Xref Fading icon (Figure 7.15) and click on it with the left mouse button.

▶ **FIGURE 7.15:** The Xref Fading icon

The following prompt appears on the command line:
```
Command: XDWGFADECTL
Enter new value for XDWGFADECTL <-70>: 70
```

This action will turn off the Fade option and end the command (Figure 7.16).

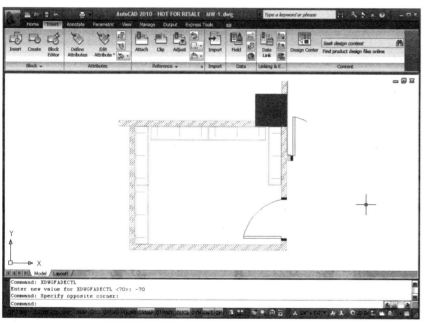

▶ **FIGURE 7.16:** The Xref Clip boundary of the library (completed without fade)

The Wood Shelves Plan Location Detail

Multiple annotation scales will be used to compile the millwork details in this drawing file. Utilizing annotative text, dimensions, and object tag styles will allow you to easily update the annotation scale so they will appear at the appropriate size.

To begin drawing the Wood Shelves Plan Location detail, do the following:

1. Refer to the clipped Xref of the library.

2. Set the Annotation Scale of the drawing to ¾" = 1'-0".

3. Set the current layer to A-Millwrk-Text.

4. Position the cursor over the Multileader icon on the Annotation toolbar and click it with the left mouse button.

5. Position the cursor over the shelf at the lower-left of the room and click on it with the left mouse button to begin the leader arrow.

6. Move the cursor to the right and left-click.

Make sure Caps Lock is turned On and do the following:

7. Type **¾" BLACK MELAMINE ADJUSTABLE SHELVES W/¾" × 1½" CHERRY WOOD DROP EDGE TYP. (AT FRONT FACE ONLY U.N.O.)**, and then close the Text Editor.

8. Start the Multileader command again.

9. Position the cursor over the shelf adjacent to the door, and click on it with the left mouse button to begin the leader arrow.

10. Move the cursor to the left and left-click.

Make sure Caps Lock is turned On and do the following:

11. Type **¾" BLACK MELAMINE ADJUSTABLE SHELVES W/¾" × 1½" CHERRY WOOD DROP EDGE AT FRONT FACE AND RIGHT SIDE FACE (THIS ELEVATION ONLY)**, and then close the Text Editor. (See Figure 7.17.)

12. Set the current layer to A-Millwrk-Dims.

13. Dimension the Overall inside corners of the north wall (top wall), and do the same for the west wall.

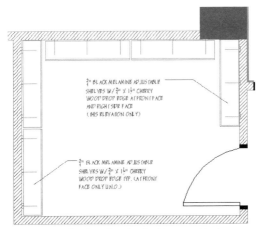

▶ **FIGURE 7.17:** Plan location detail with text added

Leave ample room for additional dimensions on the same plane. For the next dimension string, which will identify the centerline placement of the wood wall-support standards, do the following:

14. Dimension from the top-left corner of the room, both vertically and horizontally, to the centerline of the first wood wall-support standard. Then also dimension the distance between the centerlines of the subsequent wood wall-support standards.

These dimensions should fit comfortably between the previously entered dimensions. The dimensions that detail the distance between the wood wall-support standards are typical. Therefore, it is prudent to update or override the dimension instead of dimensioning each location. To override the text of the dimension between the centerlines of the wood wall-support standards, do the following:

15. Position the cursor over the previous dimension and double-right-click on it.

This action will launch the Properties Manager window for that particular dimension.

16. Scroll through the available fields in the Text category. In the Override field, type **1'-9" TYP** and close the window.

Do the same for the other instance.

17. Dimension the distance between the centerlines of the third and fourth wood wall-support standards, both vertically and horizontally.

18. Dimension one of the wood shelves and override the dimension to show them as typical dimensions.

19. Dimension the distance from the right side of the door frame to the edge of the shelf at that elevation, the distance to the centerline of the first wood wall-support standard, and end with the dimension between the centerline of the next. (See Figure 7.18.)

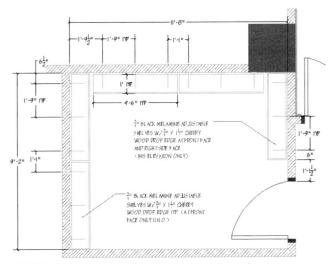

▶ **FIGURE 7.18:** Plan Location detail with text and dimensions

The last task is to add drawing tags to this drawing. The drawing tags reference another drawing within the set of drawings for additional information. The following tags should be added to the drawing:

- Detail tag
- Section tag
- Elevation tags
- Drawing name tag

To add a detail tag that will call out the wood wall-support standard, do the following:

20. Set the current layer to A-Millwrk-Tags.

21. Draw a rectangular, dashed polyline around the instance of one of the wood wall-support standards.

22. Insert the Callout Bubble – Imperial block from the list of blocks already loaded to the drawing, and place it adjacent to the previously drawn polyline.

23. Double-left-click the Callout Bubble – Imperial block to update the attributes.

This action will launch an Enhanced Attribute Editor window. The wood wall-support standard is the second drawing that was added to this drawing file; therefore, the attributes should be updated as follows:

24. For the View Number, type **2** in the Value field. For the Sheet Number, type **MW-1** in the Value field. Close the window. Then draw a line connecting both the Callout Bubble – Imperial block and the dashed polyline.

One section will be drawn. To add a section tag, do the following:

25. Insert the Section Callout – Imperial block from the list of blocks already loaded to the drawing, and place it adjacent to the detail tag.

To update this tag, do the following:

26. Double-left-click the Section Callout – Imperial block to update the attributes.

27. For the View Number, type **7** in the Value field. For the Sheet Number, type **MW-1** in the Value field. Close the window.

Three elevations will be drawn. To add elevation tags, do the following:

28. Insert the Elevation – Imperial block from the list of blocks already loaded to the drawing, and place three of them into the center of the drawing.

Using Dynamic Blocks

The Elevation – Imperial block is a *dynamic block*. This basically means that a *behavior* was added to this block when it was created. These behaviors can be modified once the block is inserted into the drawing without affecting other

instances of the block. In this exercise, you will use the Elevation – Imperial block to demonstrate how dynamic blocks are used. Refer to the three blocks that were previously inserted into the drawing (Figure 7.19).

▶ **FIGURE 7.19:** The three Elevation – Imperial blocks (prior to modification)

All three tags are shown with the arrowheads pointing in the west direction. The left-hand tag can remain as-is. The arrowhead on the middle tag should be rotated in the north direction, and the arrowhead on the right-hand tag should be rotated in the east direction. To rotate the arrowhead on the middle tag, do the following:

29. Left-click on the Middle Elevation – Imperial block.

This action will highlight the tag. At the tip of the arrowhead is a Symbol Rotation Point icon (a blue, circular icon). To continue, do the following:

30. Left-click on the Symbol Rotation Point icon (Figure 7.20), move the cursor to the north position, and left-click. Then press the Esc key to end the command.

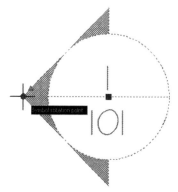

▶ **FIGURE 7.20:** The Symbol Rotation Point icon

To rotate the arrowhead on the right-hand tag, do the following:

31. Left-click on the Middle Elevation – Imperial block. (See Figures 7.21 and 7.22.)

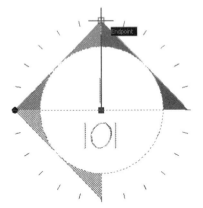

▶ **FIGURE 7.21:** Arrowhead rotation

▶ **FIGURE 7.22:** Elevation – Imperial block (modified in the north direction)

This action will highlight the tag. At the bottom portion of the arrow is a Flip the Symbol Direction icon (a blue arrow). To continue, do the following:

32. Left-click the Flip the Symbol Direction icon (Figure 7.23) and press the Esc key to end the command. (See Figure 7.24.)

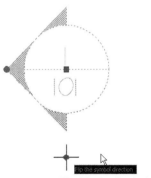

▶ **FIGURE 7.23:** The Flip the Symbol Direction icon

▶ **FIGURE 7.24:** Elevation – Imperial Block (modified in the east direction)

To update these tags, do the following:

33. Double-left-click the left-hand Elevation – Imperial block to update the attributes for the west elevation.

34. For the View Number, type **4** in the Value field. For the Sheet Number, type **MW-1** in the Value field. Close the window.

38. Double-left-click the middle Elevation – Imperial block to update the attributes for the north elevation.

36. For the View Number, type **5** in the Value field. For the Sheet Number, type **MW-1** in the Value field. Close the window.

37. Double-left-click the right-hand Elevation – Imperial block to update the attributes for the east elevation.

38. For the View Number, type **6** in the Value field. For the Sheet Number, type **MW-1** in the Value field. Close the window. (See Figure 7.25.)

▶**FIGURE 7.25**: Three Elevation – Imperial blocks (modified)

To insert the drawing title tag into the drawing, do the following:

39. Position the cursor over the Insert Block icon located on the Block toolbar, and left-click and insert the Drawing Title – Imperial block below the Wood Shelves Plan Location detail.

40. Position the cursor over the drawing number in the drawing tag and double-left-click.

41. Type **3**.

42. Position the cursor over the Drawing Name field in the Enhanced Attribute Editor and left-click. Then left-click in the Value field and clear the contents.

43. Type **Wood Shelves Plan Location Detail**.

44. Position the cursor over the Viewport Scale field within the Enhanced Attribute Editor and left-click. Then left-click in the Value field and clear the contents.

45. Type **¾″=1′-0** and left-click the OK button.

To update the title line length to accommodate the title of the drawing, do the following:

46. Position the cursor over the drawing name tag and click.

47. Position the cursor over the arrowhead and click. Then stretch the title line length to accommodate the title and left-click.

48. Press the Esc key to end the command. (See Figure 7.26.)

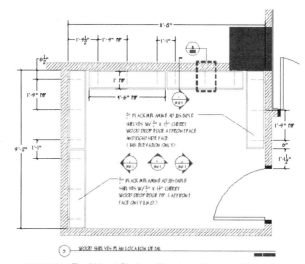

▶**FIGURE 7.26**: The Wood Shelves Plan Location detail (completed)

The Wood Shelves Elevation Details

As previously mentioned, the wood shelves and matching wall-support standards will be used at the library. Although you have already laid out the components in the plan, you still need to prepare the three elevations where these items will be installed. The interior ceiling height of the space is 8′-6″ Above the Finished Floor (AFF). There is an existing 4″ wall base. The wall support standards are 7′-10″ high, and they will be installed inline directly above the 4″ wall base. The first wood shelf will be installed at 1′-4″ AFF. Each subsequent shelf will be installed at a distance of

1'-4" from the top edge of the previous shelf to the top edge of the next shelf, for a total of five shelves at each elevation.

To begin drawing these elevations, do the following:

1. Copy the clipped Xref of the library.

This instance of the copied Xref will be erased after the elevations are completed.

2. Set the Annotation Scale of the drawing to ¾" = 1'-0".

3. Set the current layer to A-Millwrk-H.

4 Begin projecting lines in the north direction from the innermost boundaries of the north elevation of the library.

5. Set the current layer to A-Millwrk-M.

6. Continue projecting lines in the north direction from the corners of each shelf at that elevation.

7. Set the current layer to A-Millwrk-L.

8. Project lines in the north direction from the outermost and innermost corners of each wall-support standard at that elevation.

9. Trim all of the extraneous lines. (See Figure 7.27.)

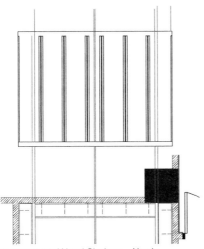

▶ **FIGURE 7.27:** Wood Shelves – North Elevation (progress)

10. Offset the floor line in the north direction at a distance of 1'-4'. Do this five times.

These lines designate the top edge of each shelf. Now, to designate the ¾" × 1½" cherry-wood edge at the front face of each shelf, do the following:

11. Offset each line in the south direction at a distance of 1½".

Because these lines represent the front and side profiles for each wood shelf, they should reside on the A-Millwrk-M layer.

12. Manage/move the Wood Shelf lines to the A-Millwrk-M layer and trim their boundaries.

To delineate the side profile of the wood shelves and metal brackets on the left side of the elevation, do the following:

13. Offset each vertical front edge line of the wood shelf in the west direction at a distance of ¾".

14. Offset each horizontal bottom line of the wood shelf in the north direction at a distance of ¾".

15. Trim the intersections. (See Figure 7.28.)

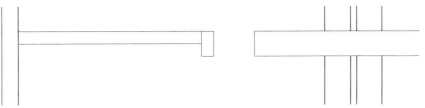

▶ **FIGURE 7.28:** The Wood Shelf profile

Next, you will need to add the metal brackets. Each bracket is approximately ½" high × 10½" long. To add the metal brackets on the left side of the elevation, do the following:

16. Offset the vertical left-hand line of the wall-support standard in the east direction at a distance of 10½"

17. Offset the bottom line of the ¾″ wood shelf in the south direction at a distance of ½″.

18. Trim the intersections.

19. Manage/move the Wood Shelf and Metal Bracket lines to layer A-Millwrk-M. (See Figure 7.29.)

▶ **FIGURE 7.29:** Profile of a wood shelf with metal bracket

Update all of the other wood shelves with metal brackets for this elevation.

20. Set the current layer to A-Millwrk-Dims.

21. Dimension the overall width and height of the elevation.

22. Dimension the overall height of the wood wall-support standard on the left side of the elevation.

23. Dimension the distance from the top face of one wood shelf to the top face of the next wood shelf on the right side of the elevation.

24. Dimension the overall width of one wood shelf and override the dimension as 4′-6″ TYP.

Be careful and make sure you organize all of the dimensions correctly. (See Figure 7.30.)

To add a detail tag that will call out the Wood Shelves and Wall-Support Standard Section detail, do the following:

25. Set the current layer to A-Millwrk-Tags.

26. Insert the Section Callout – Imperial block from the list of blocks already loaded to the drawing, and place it within the elevation.

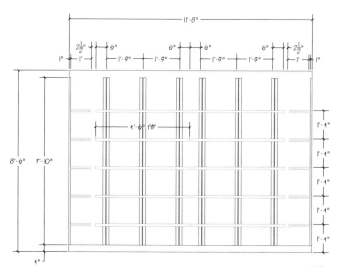

▶ **FIGURE 7.30:** North elevation (dimensioned)

27. Double-click the Section Callout – Imperial block to update the attributes.

28. For the View Number, type **7** in the Value field. For the Sheet Number, type **MW-1** in the Value field. Close the window.

To insert the drawing title tag into the drawing, do the following:

29. Position the cursor over the Insert Block icon located on the Block toolbar and left-click. Insert the Drawing Title – Imperial block below the Wood Shelves North Elevation detail.

30. Position the cursor over the drawing number in the drawing tag and double-left-click.

31. Type **5**.

32. Position the cursor over the Drawing Name field in the Enhanced Attribute Editor and left-click, then left-click in the Value field and clear the contents.

33. Type **Wood Shelves – North Elevation**.

34. Position the cursor over the Viewport Scale field within the Enhanced Attribute Editor and left-click. Then left-click in the Value field and clear the contents.

35. Type **¾"=1'-0"** and left-click the OK button.

To update the title line length to accommodate the title of the drawing, do the following:

36. Position the cursor over the drawing name tag and left-click.

37. Position the cursor over the arrowhead and left-click. Then stretch the title line length to accommodate the title and left-click.

38. Press the Esc key to end the command. (See Figure 7.31.)

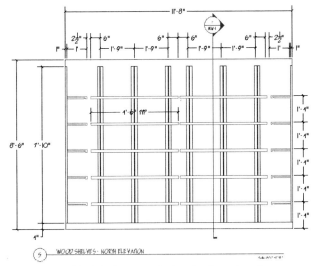

▶ **FIGURE 7.31:** Wood shelves – north elevation (completed)

Utilizing what has already been drawn, draw the west and east elevations (Figures 7.32 and 7.33.).

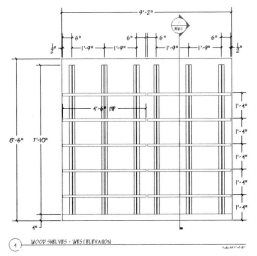

▶ **FIGURE 7.32:** Wood shelves – west elevation (completed)

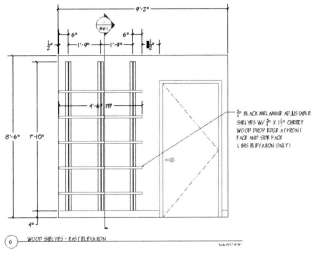

▶ **FIGURE 7.33:** Wood shelves – east elevation (completed)

The Wood Shelves Section Detail

Using the previously drawn north elevation, begin drawing the Wood Shelves section orthogonally. Base the interior wall thickness at 5" TYP.

To begin drawing this section, do the following:

1. Set the Annotation Scale of the drawing to 1" = 1'-0".

2. Set the current layer to A-Millwrk-H.

3. Refer to the left side of the copy of the north elevation and erase the extraneous information not associated with the section. (See Figure 7.34.)

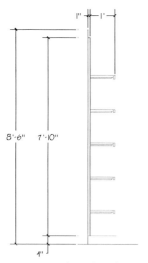

►**FIGURE 7.34:** A section of the wood shelves (in progress)

4. Offset the line of the wall in the west direction at a distance of 5". You will need to show the thickness of the metal standard at the wood wall support. Metal standards are typically ⅝".

5. Offset the line of the wood wall support in the west direction at a distance of ⅝". (See Figure 7.35.)

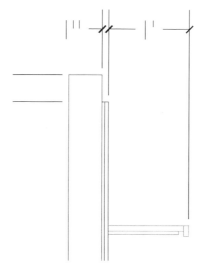

►**FIGURE 7.35:** A section of the wood shelves (wall thickness shown)

When you are specifying shelves that will ultimately carry a heavy load, you should specify that *wood blocking* be installed at each elevation. Wood blocking can be an entire sheet of plywood sheathing at ½" thickness, or it can be 2" × 4" wood studs. For this section, you will add wood studs as the method of blocking.

6. Set the current layer to A-Millwrk-M.

7. Draw a 2" × 4" rectangle with diagonal lines, the first from the top-left corner to the bottom-right corner. Then do the same for the opposite corner.

8. Insert the 2" × 4" block in the wall cavity beginning at the bottom of the Wood Wall Support and space them 1' on center in the north direction.

9. Set the current layer to A-Millwrk-Hatch.

10. Hatch the wall section with the ANSI31 hatch pattern and a Hatch Pattern Scale of 12.

11. Hatch the ¾" × 1½" Cherry Wood block at the edge of each shelf with the AR-RROOF hatch pattern, a Hatch Pattern Scale of ½", and a Hatch Pattern Angle of 45.

12. Hatch the black melamine portion of each shelf with the AR-Conc hatch pattern and a Hatch Pattern Scale of ¼".

13. Set the current layer to A-Millwrk-Dims.

14. Dimension one wood shelf from its top edge to the top edge of the nearest wood shelf and override the dimension as 1'-4" TYP.

15. Dimension the top portion of the Cherry Wood block at the second wood shelf from the bottom of the finished floor and override the dimension as ¾" TYP.

16. Dimension the side portion of the Cherry Wood block at the second wood shelf from the bottom of the finished floor and override the dimension as 1½" TYP.

17. Offset the floor line in the north direction at a distance of 1'-4". Do this five times. (See Figure 7.36.)

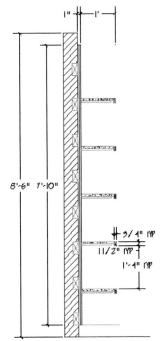

▶ **FIGURE 7.36:** A section of the wood shelves (dimensioned and hatched)

Now you need to add the notes. When you add notes to a drawing, make sure you enter them so that the drawing reads clearly. These notes will be inserted into the right side of the drawing. To insert these notes, do the following:

18. Set the current layer to A-Millwrk-Text.

19. Start the Multileader command.

Ensure that the Caps Lock key is toggled On, and do the following:

20. Position the cursor at the top portion of the Wood Support block and type **1" × 3" CHERRY WOOD BLOCK**.

21. Start the Multileader command and position the cursor at the top shelf. Type **5 ADJUSTABLE SHELVES: BLACK MELAMINE ON ¾" PARTICLE BOARD W/ ¾" × 1½" CHERRY WOOD DROP EDGE (AT FRONT FACE ONLY U.N.O.)**.

22. Start the Multileader command, position the cursor at a 2" × 4" Wood block, and type **2" × 4" WOOD BLOCKING**.

23. Start the Multileader command, position the cursor at a metal bracket, and type **MILLWORKER SHALL PROVIDE METAL BRACKETS AND STANDARDS**.

To insert the drawing title tag into the drawing, do the following:

24. Position the cursor over the Insert Block icon located on the Block toolbar and left-click. Insert the Drawing Title – Imperial block below the Wood Shelves – Section detail.

25. Position the cursor over the drawing number in the drawing tag and double-left-click.

26. Type **7**.

27. Position the cursor over the Drawing Name field in the Enhanced Attribute Editor and left-click. Then left-click in the Value field and clear the contents.

28. Type **Wood Shelves – Section**.

29. Position the cursor over the Viewport Scale field in the Enhanced Attribute Editor and left-click. Then left-click in the Value field and clear the contents.

30. Type **1"=1'-0** and left-click the OK button.

To update the title line length to accommodate the title of the drawing, do the following:

31. Position the cursor over the drawing name tag and left-click.

32. Position the cursor over the arrowhead and left-click. Then stretch the title line length to accommodate the title and left-click.

33. Press the Esc key to end the command. (See Figure 7.37.)

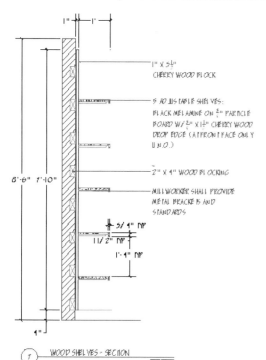

▶ **FIGURE 7.37:** The Wood Shelves section (completed)

Arranging the Details in Layout Space

The `Millwork-Details.dwt` drawing template that was used to create this drawing also had several viewports and a generic titleblock inserted into the Layout 1 tab. Now that the detail drawings for MW-1 have been completed, you need to organize all of your drawings to fit within the viewports.

You may need to modify some of the notes or dimensions that were added to the drawing. Be sure to arrange the detail drawings in some sort of order. Take special care in aligning your drawing titles, etc. All of the detail drawings for MW-1 are assembled within the Layout 1 tab in the example shown in Figure 7.38.

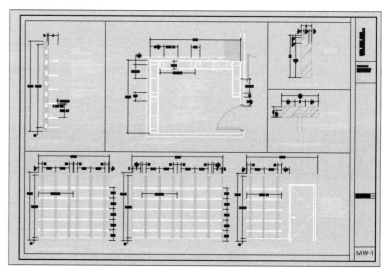

▶ **FIGURE 7.38:** The Layout 1 tab – MW-1 (assembled)

CHAPTER 8

Continuing the Millwork Detail Drawings

AFTER COMPLETING THIS CHAPTER, YOU WILL BE ABLE TO:

▶ Download and save the Millwork drawing template

▶ Draw millwork details for the conference room cabinet/bookshelf

▶ Modify dynamic blocks

▶ Arrange the details in the viewports in layout space

An AutoCAD drawing template file has already been prepared. It is located on the companion DVD in the chapter drawing file for this chapter. The drawing's name is `Millwork-Details.dwt`. This drawing template is primarily the same as the one used in Chapter 7, "Starting the Millwork Detail Drawings." The only differences are the viewports inserted into the Layout 1 tab.

Again, the following instructions will be fairly streamlined because the user is assumed to have some AutoCAD experience.

In this chapter, you will continue preparing the millwork detail drawings for the conference room's cabinet with bookshelf. To begin, do the following:

1. Open the DVD that accompanies this text, and refer to the chapter drawing file for Chapter 8.

2. Download and open the drawing titled `Millwork-Details.dwt`.

3. Save the drawing template file as `MW-2.dwg`.

4. Make sure that the 2D Drafting and Annotation Workspace is current.

5. Set the Home tab current.

You are now ready.

The Conference Room's Cabinet/Bookshelf Millwork Detail

Although the conference room cabinet with bookshelf is actually two pieces of millwork, those pieces will combine to form one uniform built-in unit. This piece of millwork will feature an open adjustable bookshelf that is 5'-6" high × 4' wide × 1'-2" deep. It rests on a 3¼" bowed-wood countertop on a closed storage cabinet that is 3' high × 4' wide × 1'-7" deep. The overall height of the unit is 8'-6", and the overall width of the unit is 5'-6". The unit will be constructed of wood. (See Figure 8.1.)

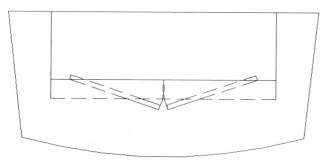

▶ **FIGURE 8.1:** The Conference Room's Cabinet/Bookshelf plan detail

The details will consist of:

- A plan/horizontal section of the lower cabinet
- A plan/horizontal section of the upper cabinet
- A front elevation
- A side elevation
- A vertical section

The Conference Room's Lower-Cabinet Plan Detail

To begin drawing the conference room's lower cabinet, do the following:

1. Insert the Conference Room block into the drawing file.

2. Set the Annotation Scale of the drawing to 1" = 1'-0".

To draw the plan view of the lower cabinet, you need to explode the Conference Room Cabinet block for clarity.

3. Explode the Conference Room Cabinet block.

4. Erase the front horizontal, continuous line that designates the bookshelf above and erase the dashed lines.

5. Update the linetype of the bowed counter to a dashed linetype.

6. Move all of the lines to the A-Millwrk-H layer.

7. Set the current layer to A-Millwrk-M. (See Figure 8.2.)

▶ **FIGURE 8.2:** The Conference Room Lower Cabinet plan detail (managed)

The cabinet sides will be constructed of ¾" wood. The actual interior of the cabinet will be 3'-2½" wide/clear. To begin drawing them, do the following:

8. Offset the outside lines of the cabinet to the inside by a distance of ¾".

9. Offset those lines to the inside by a distance of 3¼".

10. Offset those lines to the inside by a distance of ¾".

11. Offset the horizontal line of the front of the cabinet to the inside by a distance of ¾".

12. Trim the middle horizontal lines of the front of the cabinet.

This action will form the 4" outside supports of the lower cabinet at either side (Figure 8.3).

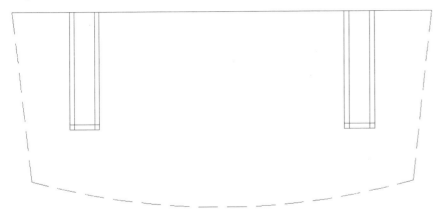

▶ **FIGURE 8.3:** The lower-cabinet side supports

13. Trim the front corner intersections.

14. Offset the front horizontal lines of the side supports on either side to the inside by a distance of 3".

15. Refer to the left-hand side support.

16. Offset the second, right-hand vertical line in the west direction by a distance of ¾".

17. Extend both of those lines to the horizontal front line of the side support.

18. Trim all of the intersecting lines on the right-hand side of the side support.

19. Draw diagonal lines at the front corners of the side support.

This action will create a shape similar to a backward letter "J." The diagonal lines are necessary to join (*miter*) the wood pieces. Repeat the same procedure for the opposite side support.

20. Draw a horizontal line from the inside outermost corners of the side supports.

21. Offset that line to the inside of the cabinet at a distance of 1".

22: Refer to the left side support. (See Figure 8.4.)

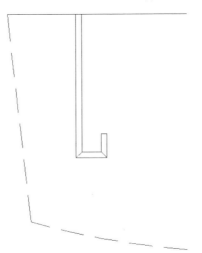

▶ **FIGURE 8.4:** Closeup of the left side support (front)

23. Extend the outermost right-hand vertical line to the back of the cabinet and offset it in the east direction at a distance of ¾".

24. Trim all of the intersecting lines.

This will complete a 3¼" cavity with a 1" jog for the cabinet doors to recess (Figure 8.5.). Do the same for the opposite side support.

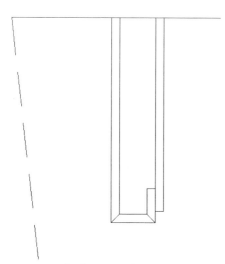

▶ **FIGURE 8.5:** Cavity in the left side support (progress)

To add wood support blocking to the rear of the side support cavity, do the following:

25. Offset the horizontal line of the back of the cabinet to the inside at a distance of ¾″.

26. At the rear of each side support, draw a diagonal line from the top-left corner of the cavity to the lower-right corner of the cavity, and then repeat in the opposite direction.

27. Trim the intersecting lines for each side support.

To add a piece of wood for the back of the cabinet, do the following:

28. Offset the rear horizontal line of the cabinet to the inside at a distance of ½″.

29. Trim the intersecting lines for each side support.

30. Refer to the left-hand side support.

31. Offset the right-hand vertical line closest to the wood blocking in the east direction at a distance of ⅜″.

Joining the wood in this way is the easiest method for the backside of the cabinet.

32. Extend the horizontal line at the rear of the cabinet that was previously offset to the recently offset vertical line, and trim the intersections. (See Figure 8.6.)

Repeat the same procedure for the opposite side support.

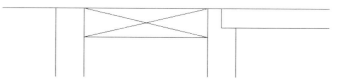

▶ **FIGURE 8.6:** Cavity in the left side support (rear)

Next, draw the cabinet doors. They will be ⅞″ thick, and there will be a reveal of ⅛″ between the doors at the center of the unit and on either side at the side supports (Figure 8.7). To draw the doors, do the following:

33. Draw a horizontal line at the front of the cabinet, where the side supports are located.

34. Offset that line in the south direction at a distance of ⅛″.

35. Offset the inner vertical lines of each side support at a distance of ⅛″.

36. Offset that line in the south direction at a distance of ⅛″.

37. Trim the intersecting lines.

38. Draw a vertical line in the south direction at the midpoint of the horizontal line that was previously offset.

39. Offset that vertical line to the right and left at a distance of 1⁄16″.

40. Offset the horizontal line that designates the back of the door in the south direction at a distance of ⅞″.

41. Trim the intersection lines.

▶ **FIGURE 8.7:** The lower cabinet with doors

To add hatch to the horizontal areas of the side supports and the rear of the cabinet, do the following:

42. Set the current layer to A-Millwrk-Hatch.

43. Start the Hatch command and select the Dolmit hatch pattern.

44. Select the inside horizontal areas at the front of each side support and the backside of the cabinet.

45. Start the Hatch command and select the Dolmit hatch pattern with a Hatch Angle of 90.

46. Select the inside vertical areas at each side support.

47. Start the Hatch command and select the AR-SAND hatch pattern with a Hatch Angle of 90 and a Hatch Scale of ¼".

48. Select the inside areas at each door. (See Figure 8.8.)

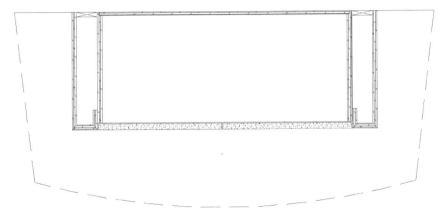

▶ **FIGURE 8.8:** The lower cabinet with hatch

To add dimensions, do the following:

49. Set the current layer to A-Millwrk-Dims.

50. Dimension the rear and side of the cabinet.

Make sure you pull these dimensions far enough away from the item that you can add additional dimensions.

51. Dimension the doors of the cabinet. Arrange these dimensions so they clear the front edge of the wood top. Then override the dimension as EQ.

Next, dimension the smaller details.

52. Dimension the thickness of the doors and the ⅛" reveals.

53. Dimension one of the jogs at the side support and the backside thickness of the cabinet.

54. Dimension the thickness of one side and override the dimension as ¾" TYP. (See Figure 8.9.)

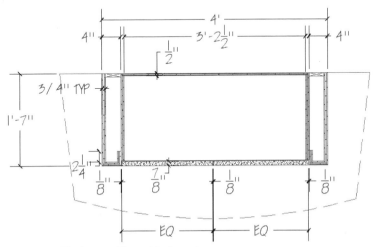

▶ **FIGURE 8.9:** The lower cabinet with dimensions

To add text, do the following:

55. Set the current layer to A-Millwrk-Text.

56. Start the Multileader command and add pertinent notes.

To add the drawing name tag, do the following:

57. Set the current layer to A-Millwrk-Tags.

58. Insert the Drawing Title – Imperial block below the Conference Room Lower Cabinet detail.

59. Position the cursor over the drawing number in the drawing tag and double-left-click.

60. Type **1**.

61. Position the cursor over the Drawing Name field within the Enhanced Attribute Editor, left-click in the Value field, and clear the contents.

62. Type **Conference Room Lower Cabinet Plan** and left-click the OK button.

63. Position the cursor over the Viewport Scale field within the Enhanced Attribute Editor, left-click in the Value field, and clear the contents.

64. Type **Scale: 1" = 1'-0"** and left-click the OK button.

To update the title line length to accommodate the title of the drawing, do the following:

65. Position the cursor over the drawing name tag and left-click.

66. Position the cursor over the arrowhead and left-click. Then stretch the title line length to accommodate the title and left-click.

67. Press the Esc key to end the command. (See Figure 8.10.)

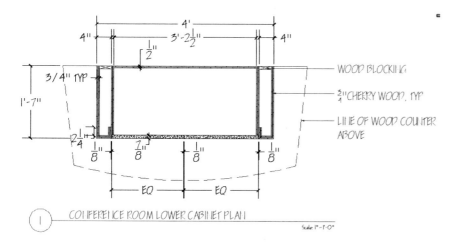

▶**FIGURE 8.10:** The Lower Cabinet plan (completed)

The Conference Room's Upper-Cabinet Plan Detail

To begin drawing the conference room's upper cabinet, do the following:

1. Insert the Conference Room block into the drawing file.

2. Set the Annotation Scale of the drawing to 1" = 1'-0".

In order to draw the plan view of the upper cabinet, you will need to explode the Conference Room Cabinet block for clarity.

3. Explode the Conference Room Cabinet block.

4. Move all of the lines to the layer A-Millwrk-H.

5. Set the current layer to A-Millwrk-M.

This bookshelf sides will be constructed of ¾" wood. The actual interior of the cabinet will be 3'-10" wide/clear. To begin drawing this, do the following:

6. Offset the outside lines of the side of the bookshelf to the inside by a distance of ¼".

7. Offset those lines to the inside by a distance of ¾".

The front face of the bookshelf will be finished with a solid block of cherry wood. This block is ¾" thick × 1¼" wide. To draw this, do the following:

8. Draw a ¾" × 1¼" block, copy it and place one on either side at the front of the bookshelf limit.

9. Erase the outermost vertical lines of the sides of the bookshelf.

10. Trim the intersecting lines.

To add a piece of wood for the back of the cabinet, do the following:

11. Offset the rear horizontal line of the bookshelf to the inside at a distance of ½".

12. Trim the intersecting lines for each side support.

13. Refer to the left-hand side at the rear of the bookshelf.

14. Offset the right-hand side vertical in the west direction at a distance of ⅜".

15. Extend the horizontal line at the rear of the cabinet that was previously offset to the recently offset vertical line, and trim the intersections.

Repeat the same procedure for the opposite side support. (See Figure 8.11.)

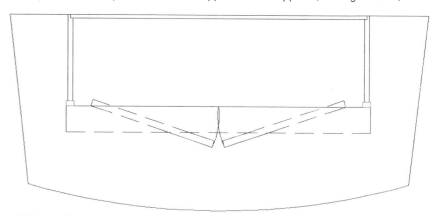

▶**FIGURE 8.11:** The upper cabinet (progress)

To add hatch to the back side of the bookshelf, do the following:

16. Set the current layer to A-Millwrk-Hatch.

17. Start the Hatch command and select the Dolmit hatch pattern.

18. Select the inside horizontal areas on the back side of the bookshelf.

To add hatch to the sides of the bookshelf, do the following:

19. Start the Hatch command and select the Dolmit hatch pattern with a Hatch Angle of 90.

20. Select the inside vertical areas on each side.

To add hatch to the wood blocks at the front of the bookshelf, do the following:

21. Start the Hatch command, and select the AR-RROOF hatch pattern with a Hatch Angle of 45 and a Hatch Scale of ½".

22. Select the inside areas of each block. (See Figure 8.12.)

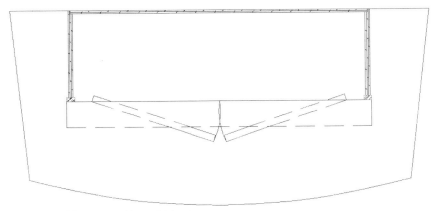

▶**FIGURE 8.12:** The upper cabinet with hatch

To add dimensions, do the following:

23. Set the current layer to A-Millwrk-Dims.

24. Dimension the rear, front, and side of the bookshelf and the wood counter.

Make sure you pull these dimensions far enough away from the item that you can add more dimensions later.

25. Dimension the radius of the front edge of the wood counter.

Next, dimension the smaller details.

26. Dimension the front wood blocks and the ¼" offset of the sides of the bookshelf. (See Figure 8.13.)

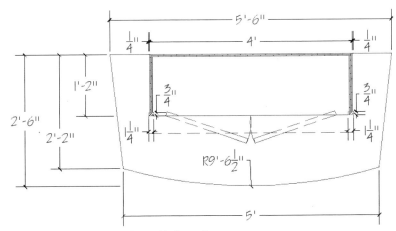

▶**FIGURE 8.13:** The upper cabinet with dimensions

To add text, do the following:

27. Set the current layer to A-Millwrk-Text.

28. Start the Multileader command and add pertinent notes.

To add the drawing name tag, do the following:

29. Set the current layer to A-Millwrk-Tags.

30. Insert the Drawing Title – Imperial block below the Conference Room Upper Cabinet detail.

31. Position the cursor over the drawing number within the drawing tag and double-left-click.

32. Type **2**.

33. Position the cursor over the Drawing Name field within the Enhanced Attribute Editor, left-click in the Value field, and clear the contents.

34. Type **Conference Room Upper Cabinet Plan** and left-click the OK button.

35. Position the cursor over the Viewport Scale field within the Enhanced Attribute Editor, left-click in the Value field, and clear the contents.

36. Type **Scale: 1″ = 1′-0″** and left-click the OK button.

To update the title line length to accommodate the title of the drawing, do the following:

37. Position the cursor over the drawing name tag and left-click.

38. Position the cursor over the arrowhead and left-click. Then stretch the title line to accommodate the title and left-click.

39. Press the Esc key to end the command. (See Figure 8.14.)

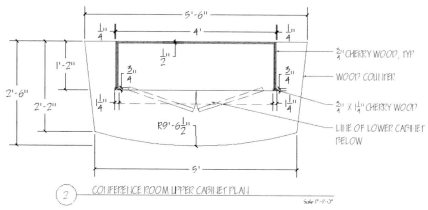

▶ **FIGURE 8.14:** The Upper Cabinet plan (completed)

The Conference Room's Cabinet/Bookshelf Front Elevation Detail

As previously mentioned, the conference room's cabinet/bookshelf will look like it is built into the conference room. The overall height of the unit will be 8'-6". The upper bookshelf will have four adjustable wood shelves, and the lower cabinet will have one adjustable wood shelf.

To begin drawing the cabinet/bookshelf's front elevation, do the following:

1. Insert the Conference Room block into the drawing file.

2. Set the Annotation Scale of the drawing to ¾" = 1'-0".

3. Set the current layer to A-Millwrk-H.

4. From the boundaries of the back edges of the wood counter and the bookshelf, begin projecting lines in the north direction.

5. Offset the horizontal floor line in the north direction by a distance of 3'.

6. Offset that line in the south direction by a distance of 3¼".

7. Trim all of the intersecting lines that were just offset, and do the same for the lines above and beneath that point. (See Figure 8.15.)

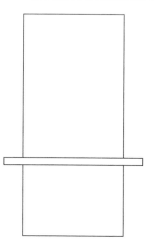

▶ **FIGURE 8.15:** The conference room's Cabinet/ Bookshelf front elevation (delineated)

To continue building the unit, do the following:

8. Set the current layer to A-Millwrk-M.

9. Offset the upper cabinet's vertical lines on either side to the inside at a distance of 1¼".

10. Offset the lower cabinet's vertical lines to the inside at a distance of 4".

To identify the front edge of the bowed wood counter, do the following:

11. Project a vertical line from the front edge of the wood counter from the plan to the elevation on either side. Then trim the lines.

The doors on the lower cabinet will feature a segmented horizontal design. The top opening of the lower cabinet will have a 1¼" solid block of wood, and the lower portion of the cabinet will be in line with the 4" wood wall base. The design front of each door will feature a 10" segment at the top and bottom, with a ⅛" reveal between. To begin drawing this, do the following:

12. Offset the bottom horizontal line of the cabinet in the north direction at a distance of 4".

13. Offset the bottom horizontal line of the wood counter in the south direction at a distance of 1¼".

14. Trim the intersecting lines.

15. Offset the bottom horizontal line of the 1¼" wood block in the south direction at a distance of 10". Then offset that line again in the same direction at a distance of ⅛".

16. Offset the bottom horizontal line of the lower cabinet in the north direction at a distance of 10". Then offset that line again in the same direction at a distance of ⅛".

17. Manage/move all of these lines to layer A-Millwrk-M.

18. Draw a vertical line from the midpoint of the bottom horizontal line of the 1¹⁄₁₄" wood block to the midpoint of the bottom horizontal line of the lower cabinet.

To draw the direction lines for the hinge points of the doors and the ¾" adjustable shelf on the lower cabinet, do the following:

19. Set the current layer to A-Millwrk-L.

20. Draw a line from the midpoint of the bottom horizontal line of the 1¼" wood block to the midpoint of the left-hand side of the door. Then continue that line to the bottom horizontal line of the lower cabinet.

    Do the same for the opposite door.

21. Offset the bottom horizontal line of the lower cabinet in the north direction at a distance of 1'. Then offset that line again in the north direction at a distance of ¾".

22. Manage those lines to the layer A-Millwrk-L.

23. Update all of these lines to a dashed linetype.

24. Set the current layer to A-Millwrk-M.

The door pulls will appear as generic door pulls. Draw a rectangle that is ⅜" wide × 4½" long for each door pull. Then place the pulls 2" from the top and side of the door.

25. Place the door pulls on the door fronts. (See Figure 8.16.)

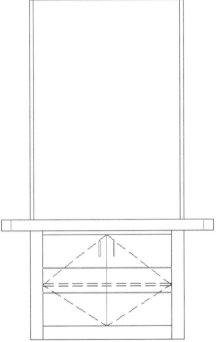

▶ **FIGURE 8.16:** The Cabinet/Bookshelf front elevation (lower cabinet's progress)

Next, you will need to add crown molding to the top of the built-in. This crown molding is fairly simple (Figure 8.17). It extends horizontally 2¾" beyond both sides of the bookshelf at the top and it extends ¹⁵⁄₁₆" horizontally beyond the bottom. The overall height of the molding is 2-⅜". To draw the crown molding, do the following:

26. Extend the top horizontal line of the upper cabinet by 2¾" on both sides.

27. Offset the top horizontal line of the upper cabinet in the south direction at a distance of ½". Next, offset that line in the south direction at a distance of 1-⅝". Then offset that line in the south direction at a distance of ¼".

28. Trim the intersections.

29. Offset the outermost vertical lines of the upper cabinet on either side to the outside at a distance of $^{15}/_{16}$".

30. Then extend those lines on either side in the north direction to the limit of the lower portion of the crown molding.

31. Draw a diagonal line on either side from the endpoint of the extended line to the endpoint of the lower line on the top portion of the crown molding.

32. Continue that line on either side in the north direction to the endpoint of the top of the crown molding.

33. Trim the vertical line below the crown molding and manage the previously drawn lines to layer A-Millwrk-H.

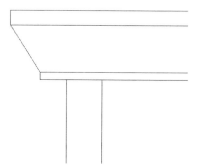

▶**FIGURE 8.17:** The crown molding (close-up)

Similar to the top portion of the lower cabinet, the top portion of the bookshelf will be constructed with a 1¼" wood block. To show this, do the following:

34. Offset the lower horizontal line of the crown molding in the south direction at a distance of 1¼", and trim the intersecting lines.

The bookshelf contains four 1¼" adjustable wood shelves. These shelves should be spaced equidistantly. To do this, do the following:

35. Draw a vertical line from the bottom midpoint of the lower line of the 1¼" wood block at the top of the bookshelf to the midpoint of the horizontal line at the top of the wood counter.

The easiest way to space the four adjustable wood shelves is to use the Divide command. Because there are four shelves, the previously drawn vertical line should be divided into five segments.

36. Start the Divide command and divide the previously drawn vertical line into five segments.

37. Draw a horizontal line from each node (division) of the previously divided line across the top portion of the cabinet.

Each shelf is 1¼" thick; to draw the thickness of each shelf, do the following:

38. Offset each of these lines in the north and south directions at a distance of ⅝".

When you are done, erase all of the guidelines. (See Figure 8.18.)

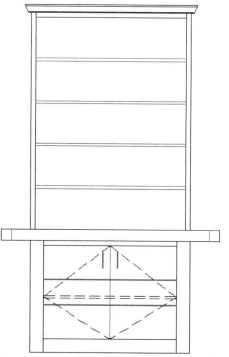

▶**FIGURE 8.18:** The Cabinet/Bookshelf front elevation (upper/lower cabinet progress)

To add dimensions, do the following:

39. Set the current layer to A-Millwrk-Dims.

40. Dimension the top, bottom, and side of the overall unit.

41. Dimension the crown molding and adjustable shelves. Then dimension the smaller elements of the lower cabinet. (See Figure 8.19.)

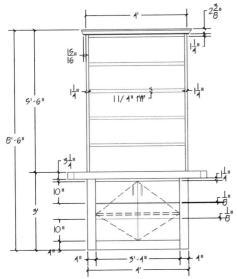

▶ **FIGURE 8.19:** The Cabinet/Bookshelf front elevation with dimensions

To add text, do the following:

42. Set the current layer to A-Millwrk-Text.

43. Start the Multileader command and add any pertinent notes.

Don't forget to add the detail markers for the two horizontal sections and the vertical section that is yet to be drawn. Refer back to Chapter 7 for directions for modifying dynamic blocks if needed. Remember that you should strive for clarity in your drawings. Therefore, make sure the tags and notes do not overlap or conflict with one another. To add the section detail marker for the lower cabinet, do the following:

44. Set the current layer to A-Millwrk-Tags.

45. Insert the Section Callout – Imperial block into the drawing.

This tag will enter your drawing in a vertical position. Remember, this tag is a dynamic block. It has a parameter set to it that allows it to rotate the arrowhead and attributes. You will need to double-click this tag in order to access the parameter you want to change. Simply rotating the entire tag will not accomplish the correct outcome.

46. Rotate this tag, update it, and place it horizontally in the drawing to key the Conference Room Lower Cabinet plan.

Next, to add the section detail marker for the horizontal section for the upper cabinet, you can either insert another tag or copy the previously inserted tag.

47. Rotate this tag, update it, and place it horizontally in the drawing to key the Conference Room Upper Cabinet plan.

You will need to insert another section detail marker to key the vertical section that is yet to be drawn. This vertical section will be the last drawing detail for drawing MW-2. To continue, do the following:

48. Insert another Section Callout – Imperial block into the drawing.

49. Stretch the tag accordingly, and place it midway on the drawing to identify the vertical section.

50. Position the cursor over the View Number field within the Enhanced Attribute Editor, left-click in the Value field, and clear the contents.

51. Type **5**.

52. Position the cursor over the Sheet Number field within the Enhanced Attribute Editor, left-click in the Value field, and clear the contents.

53. Type **MW-2** and left-click the OK button.

54. Insert the Drawing Title – Imperial block below the Conference Room Cabinet/ Bookshelf Front Elevation detail.

55. Position the cursor over the drawing number within the drawing tag and double-left-click.

56. Type **3**.

57. Position the cursor over the Drawing Name field within the Enhanced Attribute Editor, left-click in the Value field, and clear the contents.

58. Type **Conference Room Cabinet/Bookshelf Front Elevation** and left-click the OK button.

59. Position the cursor over the Viewport Scale field within the Enhanced Attribute Editor, left-click in the Value field, and clear the contents.

60. Type **Scale: ¾″ = 1′-0″** and left-click the OK button.

To update the title line length to accommodate the title of the drawing, do the following:

61. Position the cursor over the drawing name tag and left-click.

62. Position the cursor over the arrowhead and left-click. Then stretch the title line to accommodate the title and left-click.

63. Press the Esc key to end the command. (See Figure 8.20.)

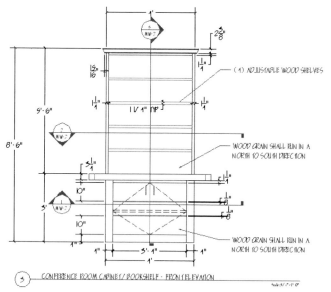

▶ **FIGURE 8.20:** The Cabinet/Bookshelf front elevation (completed)

The Conference Room's Cabinet/Bookshelf Side Elevation Detail

Using the previously drawn front elevation, begin drawing the conference room's Cabinet/Bookshelf side elevation orthogonally. Base the interior wall thickness at 5″ TYP.

To begin drawing this elevation, do the following:

1. Set the Annotation Scale of the drawing to ¾″ = 1′-0″.

2. Set the current layer to A-Millwrk-H.

3. Refer to previously drawn front elevation, and project the horizontal lines from the right-hand side.

For this drawing, you will not need to show the interior elements of the unit. This drawing is meant to identify only the side face of the unit.

4. Draw a vertical line to identify the backside of the unit.

The crown molding extends 2¾″ beyond the bookshelf. To draw it, do the following:

5. Offset the previously drawn vertical line in the east direction at a distance of 1′-4¾″.

6. Offset that line in the west direction at a distance of 2¾″.

7. Trim the intersecting lines.

8. Offset that line in the east direction at a distance of $^{15}/_{16}$″.

9. Extend that line in the north direction to the upper limit of the lower portion of the crown molding.

10. Draw a diagonal line from the endpoint of the extended line to the endpoint of the lower line of the top portion of the crown molding.

11. Continue that line in the north direction to the endpoint of the top of the crown molding.

12. Trim the lines beyond the crown molding.

13. Offset the front vertical line of the bookshelf in the west direction at a distance of ¾″ and trim the line below.

To delineate the front of the wood counter and the point at which it bows, do the following:

14. Offset the backside vertical line of the unit in the east direction at a distance of 2′-6″. Then offset that line in the west direction at a distance of 4″.

15. Trim all intersecting lines.

The side view of the lower cabinet has many nuances. You must take into consideration the following:

- The overall depth including the doors is 1'-7".
- There is a 1¼" gap directly between the wood countertop and the top of the door.
- The metal door pull projects 1" from the face of the door.
- There are two instances of a ⅛"-deep reveal on the door front.
- There is a 4" high × 3" deep toekick.
- The thickness of the door is ⅞" with a ⅛" gap between the cabinet and the backside of the door.

To begin drawing the side elevation elements of the lower cabinet, do the following:

16. Offset the backside vertical line of the unit in the east direction at a distance of 1'-9", and trim and erase any extraneous lines.

17. Offset that line in the west direction at a distance of 1".

18. Offset the lower horizontal line of the wood counter in the south direction at a distance of 1¼" and trim any intersecting lines.

19. Offset the lower horizontal line of the unit in the north direction at a distance of 4", and trim any intersecting lines.

20. Offset the vertical line of the front of the door in the west direction at a distance of ⅞". Then trim any intersecting lines.

This action will delineate the overall dimensions of the door. Now, to draw the depth of the toekick, do the following:

21. Offset the backside vertical line of the unit in the east direction at a distance of 1'-6", and trim any intersecting lines.

Now to draw the reveals on the door front, do the following:

22. Offset the top horizontal line of the door in the south direction at a distance of 10". Then offset that line in the south direction at a distance of ⅛".

23. Offset the outside vertical line of the door in the west direction at a distance of ⅛", and trim any intersecting lines.

Repeat the same procedure for the bottom of the door. Finally, draw the metal door pull. A typical door pull might have the following dimensions:

- ⅜" thick
- 4½" high
- Protrude from face of door at a distance of 1"

Draw a typical door pull and place it 2" from the top of the door at the door front. (See Figure 8.21.)

▶ **FIGURE 8.21:** The conference room's Cabinet/Bookshelf side elevation (delineated)

To add dimensions, do the following:

24. Set the current layer to A-Millwrk-Dims.

25. Dimension the top, bottom, and side of the overall unit.

26. Dimension the crown molding and then dimension the smaller elements of the lower cabinet. (See Figure 8.22.)

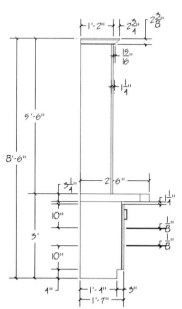

▶ **FIGURE 8.22:** The Cabinet/Bookshelf side elevation with dimensions

To add text, do the following:

27. Set the current layer to A-Millwrk-Text.

28. Start the Multileader command and add any pertinent notes.

To insert the drawing title tag into the drawing, do the following:

29. Position the cursor over the Insert Block Icon located on the Block toolbar and left-click and insert the Drawing Title – Imperial block below the Conference Room Cabinet/Bookshelf Side Elevation detail.

30. Position the cursor over the drawing number within the drawing tag and double-left-click.

31. Type **4**.

32. Position the cursor over the Drawing Name field within the Enhanced Attribute Editor and left-click. Then left-click in the Value field and clear the contents.

33. Type **Conference Room Cabinet/Bookshelf Side Elevation**.

34. Position the cursor over the Viewport Scale field within the Enhanced Attribute Editor and left-click. Then left-click in the Value field and clear the contents.

35. Type ¾″ = 1′-0″ and left-click the OK button.

To update the title line length to accommodate the title of the drawing, do the following:

36. Position the cursor over the drawing name tag and left-click.

37. Position the cursor over the arrowhead and left-click. Then stretch the title line to accommodate the title and left-click.

38. Press the Esc key to end the command. (See Figure 8.23.)

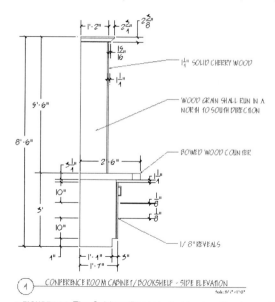

▶ **FIGURE 8.23:** The Cabinet/Bookshelf side elevation (completed)

The Conference Room's Cabinet/Bookshelf Section Detail

Using the previously drawn side elevation, begin drawing the conference room's Cabinet/Bookshelf section orthogonally. Base the interior wall thickness at 5″ TYP.

To begin drawing this section, do the following:

1. Set the Annotation Scale of the drawing to 1″ = 1′-0″.

2. Set the current layer to A-Millwrk-H.

3. Offset the line of the wall in the west direction at a distance of 5″.

Wood blocking should be included at the counter and upper cabinet. The 2″ × 6″ wood studs will be installed at this elevation, placed 1′-6″ on center, with the first wood stud flush with the top of the unit. Create the wood stud and insert it in the cavity of the wall.

4. Extend the outermost right-hand vertical line at the crown molding, all the way in the north direction, and trim the intersection of the lower horizontal line of the crown molding. Then erase the other horizontal lines of the crown molding.

5. Erase the second vertical line in front of the bookshelf.

6. Offset the vertical backside line of the unit in the east direction at a distance of ½″, and trim any intersecting lines.

Do not include this thickness at the wood countertop.

7. Offset the outermost right-hand vertical line of the upper cabinet in the west direction at a distance of ¾″, and trim any intersecting lines.

8. Refer to the upper-left corner of the unit and offset the top horizontal line in the south direction at a distance of ⅜″. Then trim the intersecting lines to form a notch. (See Figure 8.24.)

▶ **FIGURE 8.24:** The upper cabinet (close-up)

Now you need to draw the four adjustable wood shelves for the upper cabinet. All of these shelves have a solid wood block at the front face that is 1¼″ high × ¾″ thick. The rest of the shelf is made from ¾″-thick wood. To draw these shelves, do the following:

9. Draw a vertical line from the midpoint of the horizontal line at the top of the bookshelf to the bottom horizontal line at the bottom of the bookshelf.

10. Start the Divide command and divide the previously drawn vertical line into five segments.

11. Draw a horizontal line from each node (division) of the previously divided line across the top portion of the cabinet.

12. Offset each of those lines in the north and south direction at a distance of ⅜″.

13. Erase the middle line from every shelf.

To accommodate the ¾″-thick × 1¼″-high wood block at the front face of the shelf, do the following:

14. Draw a rectangle that is ¾″ wide × 1¼″ long, and then insert the upper-right corner of the rectangle at the endpoint of the vertical lines that were previously offset to represent the front face of the shelves.

The wood counter will consist of two pieces of ¾″ wood at the top and bottom plane. They will be supported and secured by several pieces of wood blocking within the cavity. To draw this, do the following:

15. Offset the top and bottom horizontal lines of the wood counter to the inside area at a distance of ¾″. Then trim the area in front of the wood counter where the item bows.

16. Offset the vertical line at the rear of the wood counter twice in the east direction at a distance of ¾″.

17. Offset the vertical line at the front of the wood counter where it bows three times in the west direction at a distance of ¾″.

18. Trim and erase the lines beyond the wood counter cavity.

These lines represent the wood blocking to secure and support the countertop. Draw an X at each instance. (See Figure 8.25.)

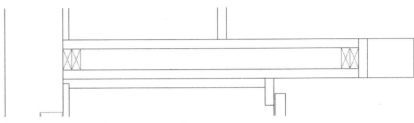

▶ **FIGURE 8.25:** The wood counter (close-up)

To draw the elements of the lower cabinet, do the following:

19. Extend the horizontal line that represents the bottom of the interior cabinet in the west direction.

20. Offset the bottom horizontal line of the wood counter in the south direction at a distance of ¾". Then offset that line in the south direction at a distance of 1½".

21. Offset the outermost vertical line of the front of the lower cabinet in the west direction at a distance of ¾". Trim any intersecting lines in order to form a ¾" × 2¼" block.

22. Offset the rear vertical line of the inside of the lower cabinet in the east direction at a distance of ½".

23. Offset the bottom horizontal line of the lower cabinet in the north direction at a distance of ¾".

24. Refer to the upper-left corner of the lower cabinet, and offset the top horizontal line in the south direction at a distance of ⅜". Then trim the intersecting lines to form a notch. Repeat the same procedure at the bottom-left of the lower cabinet.

The lower cabinet calls for a 1'-5"-deep × ¾"-thick adjustable wood shelf. This shelf will be adjustable with movable pegs (Figure 8.26). Peg holes need to be drilled into both sides of the lower cabinet. The specifications for the placement of these holes are as follows:

- Each hole is ¼" in diameter.

- The vertical placement of the holes at the front and rear of the lower cabinet from the edge of each side is 1-⅜" on center of the ¼" circle.

- The first circles will be placed at approximately 3" from the upper portion at the inside of the cabinet, with the balance of the ¼" diameter circles placed 1¼" on center to approximately 3" from the bottom portion of the inside of the cabinet.

25. Offset the rear and front vertical lines of the lower cabinet to the inside at a distance of 1-⅜". Then offset the top vertical line of the lower cabinet to the inside at a distance of 3".

26. Draw a ¼" diameter circle at both intersections that were just created from the lines that were previously offset.

27. Offset the horizontal line eighteen times in the south direction at a distance of 1¼". Then copy the previously created circles and place them at the intersections created. Erase the guidelines when you are done.

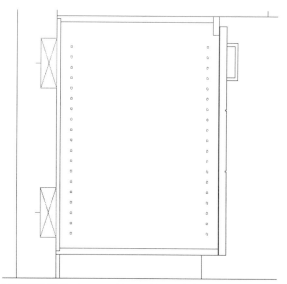

▶ **FIGURE 8.26:** The lower cabinet with peg holes

To create the 1'-5"-deep × ¾"-thick wood shelf, do the following:

28. Draw a horizontal line from the midpoint of the vertical backside line of the lower cabinet in the east direction at a distance of 1'-5". Offset that line in the south direction at a distance of ¾". Then draw a vertical line at the opposite ends connecting the endpoints of the lines previously drawn. Ideally, this shelf should appear somewhere midway in the lower cabinet and cover the corresponding peg holes. If it does not, move the shelf accordingly.

The lower cabinet doors will have two concealed hinges for each door. One hinge will be placed 3" from the top edge of the door (on the hinge side), and one will be placed 3" from the bottom edge (on the hinge side) to the center line of the door. A new layer (A-Millwrk-Hrdw) and a block (hinge) have been created. To insert these hinges, do the following:

29. Offset the top vertical line of the door in the south direction at a distance of 3".

30. Insert the hinge block into the drawing at the left endpoint of the previously offset line, and erase any peg holes that conflict with its placement.

Repeat this procedure for the lower portion of the door. (See Figure 8.27.)

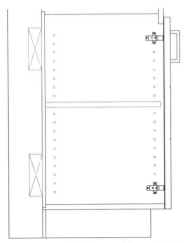

▶ **FIGURE 8.27:** The lower cabinet with hinges and adjustable wood shelf

To draw the base of the base of the lower cabinet, do the following:

31. Offset the front and rear vertical lines and the top horizontal lines of the lower cabinet to the inside at a distance of ¾", and trim only the intersecting horizontal lines.

32. Offset the front and rear vertical lines of the lower cabinet to the inside at a distance of 4", and trim the vertical lines below the intersection and the middle horizontal line. (See Figure 8.28.)

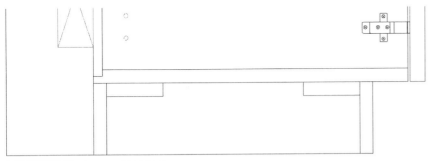

▶ **FIGURE 8.28:** The lower cabinet base

Next, you will need to add hatch. Refer to the upper cabinet first. To add hatch, do the following:

33. Set the current layer to A-Millwrk-Hatch.

34. Hatch the section of crown molding, adjacent vertical wood block, and the wood block fronts of each shelf with the AR-RROOF hatch pattern and a Hatch Pattern Scale of ½" at a Hatch Angle of 45.

35. Hatch the horizontal portion of the top of the cabinet and the horizontal portion of each shelf with the Dolmit hatch pattern and a Hatch Pattern Scale of 1.

36. Hatch the backside vertical portion of the cabinet with the Dolmit hatch pattern and a Hatch Pattern Scale of 1 at a Hatch Angle of 90. (See Figure 8.29.)

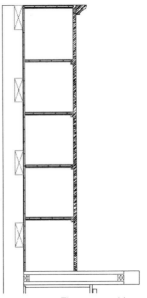

▶ **FIGURE 8.29:** The upper cabinet with hatch

To hatch the elements of the wood counter, do the following:

37. Hatch the top and bottom portions of the wood counter with the AR-SAND hatch pattern and a Hatch Pattern Scale of ¼" at a Hatch Angle of 45. Then do the same to the front portion of the wood counter in the area in front of where the counter bows.

To hatch the elements of the lower cabinet, do the following:

38. Hatch the vertical portion of the door and the vertical portion of the front wood base with the AR-SAND hatch pattern and a Hatch Pattern Scale of ¼" at a Hatch Angle of 45.

39. Hatch the vertical wood block at the top of the cabinet with the AR-RROOF hatch pattern and a Hatch Pattern Scale of ½" at a Hatch Angle of 45.

40. Hatch the horizontal portions of the lower cabinet and base with the Dolmit hatch pattern and a Hatch Pattern Scale of 1.

41. Hatch the vertical portions of the lower cabinet and base with the Dolmit hatch pattern and a Hatch Pattern Scale of 1 at a Hatch Angle of 90.

42. Hatch the interior portion of the wall with the ANSI31 hatch pattern and a Hatch Pattern Scale of 12. (See Figure 8.30.)

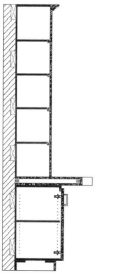

▶ **FIGURE 8.30:** The cabinet/bookshelf with hatch

The dimensions that were used for the side elevation can also be used for the section. It would be prudent to dimension the shelves at the upper cabinet and lower cabinet shelf.

43. Set the current layer to A-Millwrk-Dims.

44. Add more dimensions for the upper cabinet shelves and lower cabinet shelf, and then override the dimensions to display them as TYP. (See Figure 8.31.)

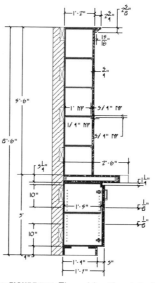

▶ **FIGURE 8.31:** The cabinet/bookshelf with dimensions

Several pertinent notes need to be added. As previously mentioned, when you add notes to a drawing, they should be entered so that the drawing reads clearly. You may need to move some text so that it is clearly visible and organized. So far, we have been adding text to the right side of the drawing. Consider this standard. To insert these notes, do the following:

45. Set the current layer to A-Millwrk-Text.

46. Start the Multileader command.

Make sure the Caps Locks key is toggled On and do the following:

47. Position the cursor at the wood base and type **4" CHERRY WOOD BASE**.

48. Start the Multileader command and position the cursor at the lower hinge. Type **MILLWORKER SHALL PROVIDE HINGES**.

49. Start the Multileader command and position the cursor in front of the door. Type **DOORS: CHERRY WOOD VENEER ON ¾" MDF W/VENEER EDGES. WOOD GRAIN SHALL RUN NORTH TO SOUTH IN DIRECTION.**

50. Start the Multileader command, position the cursor at a 1/8" reveal, and type **⅛" X ⅛" REVEALS**.

51. Start the Multileader command, position the cursor at the door pull, and type **MILLWORKER SHALL PROVIDE METAL DOOR PULLS**.

52. Start the Multileader command, position the cursor at the lower cabinet, and type **CABINET CONSTRUCTION: ¾" CHERRY VENEER PLYWOOD W/ VENEER EDGES. ½" CHERRY VENEER PLYWOOD AT BACK PANEL. WOOD GRAIN SHALL RUN IN A NORTH TO SOUTH DIRECTION**.

53. Start the Multileader command, position the cursor at the wood counter, and type **COUNTER CONSTRUCTION: ¾" CHERRY VENEER ON MDF W/ VENEER EDGES. WOOD GRAIN SHALL RUN IN A NORTH TO SOUTH DIRECTION**.

54. Start the Multileader command, position the cursor at a wood shelf, and type **(4) ADJUSTABLE WOOD SHELVES: ¾" CHERRY VENEER PLYWOOD W/ ¾" X 1¼" CHERRY WOOD EDGE**.

55. Start the Multileader command, position the cursor at a 2" × 6" piece of wood blocking, and type **2" X 6" WOOD BLOCKING, SPACED 1'-6" ON CENTER, TYP.**

56. Start the Multileader command, position the cursor at the upper cabinet, and type **CABINET CONSTRUCTION: ¾" CHERRY VENEER PLYWOOD W/ VENEER EDGES. ½" CHERRY VENEER PLYWOOD AT BACK PANEL. WOOD GRAIN SHALL RUN IN A NORTH TO SOUTH DIRECTION**.

57. Start the Multileader command, position the cursor at the crown molding, and type **CHERRY WOOD CROWN**.

To insert the drawing title tag into the drawing, do the following:

58. Set the current layer to A-Millwrk-Tags.

59. Position the cursor over the Insert Block Icon located on the Block toolbar and left-click. Insert the Drawing Title – Imperial block below the Conference Room Cabinet/Bookshelf Section detail.

60. Position the cursor over the drawing number within the drawing tag and double-left-click.

61. Type **5**.

62. Position the cursor over the Drawing Name field within the Enhanced Attribute Editor and left-click. Then left-click in the Value field and clear the contents.

63. Type **Conference Room Cabinet/Bookshelf Section**.

64. Position the cursor over the Viewport Scale field within the Enhanced Attribute Editor and left-click. Then left-click in the Value field and clear the contents.

65. Type **1"=1'-0"** and left-click the OK button.

To update the title line length to accommodate the title of the drawing, do the following:

66. Position the cursor over the drawing name tag and left-click.

67. Position the cursor over the arrowhead and left-click. Then stretch the title line to accommodate the title and left-click.

68. Press the Esc key and end the command. (See Figure 8.32.)

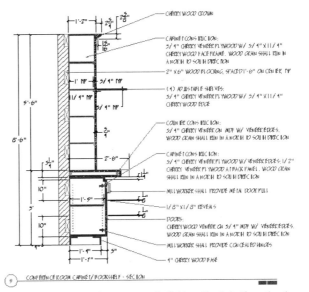

▶**FIGURE 8.32:** The conference room's Cabinet/Bookshelf section (completed)

Arranging the Details in Layout Space

The Millwork-Details.dwt drawing template that was used to create this drawing had several viewports and a generic titleblock inserted into the Layout 1 tab. Now that the detail drawings for MW-2 are completed, you need to organize all of your drawings to fit in the viewports.

You may need to modify some of the notes or dimensions that were added to the drawing. Make sure you arrange the detail drawings in some sort of order. Take special care when aligning your drawing titles, etc. The detail drawings for MW-2 assembled within the Layout 1 tab are shown in the example in Figure 8.33.

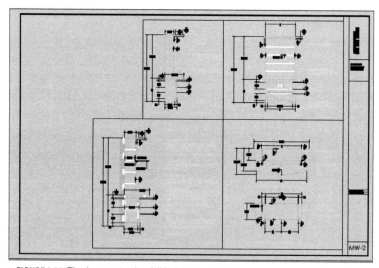

▶**FIGURE 8.33:** The Layout 1 tab – MW-2 (assembled)

CHAPTER 9

Progressing the Millwork Detail Drawings

AFTER COMPLETING THIS CHAPTER, YOU WILL BE ABLE TO:

▶ Download and save the Millwork drawing template

▶ Draw millwork details for the reception desk

▶ Modify dynamic blocks

▶ Arrange viewport details within layout space

An AutoCAD drawing template file has already been prepared. It is located on the accompanying DVD in the chapter drawing file for this chapter. The drawing name is `Millwork-Details.dwt`. This drawing template is primarily the same as the ones used in the previous chapters. The only differences are the viewports inserted into the Layout 1 tab.

Again, the following instructions will be fairly streamlined because the user is assumed to have some experience with AutoCAD. In this chapter, you will finish preparing the millwork detail drawings for the reception desk. To begin, do the following:

1. Open the DVD that accompanies this text and refer to the drawing file for Chapter 9.

2. Download and open the `Millwork-Details.dwt` drawing.

3. Save the drawing template file as `MW-3.dwg`.

4. Make sure that the 2D Drafting and Annotation Workspace is current.

5. Set the Home tab current.

You are now ready.

The Reception Area Millwork

The reception area was not terribly large. In order to accommodate a two-person workstation and a reception desk, the reception desk needed to be somewhat small and the two-person workstation needed to be more rectangular in shape.

Both guidelines were met. The reception desk just needed to be big enough for a receptionist to meet and greet clients, answer phones, and engage in light administrative work. The workstation needed to house only one administrative assistant with space to expand for a possible second administrative assistant or office clerk in the future.

The design of both of these pieces of millwork was to be consistent with the pieces of millwork already designed, and because both of these pieces reside in the same open area, similar designs were key. This was accomplished by easing the front corner of the reception desk with a curved edge, so it was welcoming to the traffic flow from the front door, and by squaring off the boundaries of the two-person workstation for maximum use of space, while incorporating the same wood panels and flanking vertical towers for every piece.

The Reception Desk details will be explained and streamlined a bit in this chapter. The details for the two-person workstation will be significantly scaled back in Chapter 10, "Completing the Millwork Detail Drawings."

The Reception Desk Millwork Detail

Keeping the design consistent, the reception desk will also feature linear, segmented panels similar to the detail on the doors of the conference room's cabinet/bookshelf. These segmented panels will be raised panels applied to the face of the desk.

The plan of this piece of millwork will feature a shape similar to an elongated, lowercase "j," with rectangular towers on both sides and a forward, raised, glass-covered transaction counter. The overall dimensions of this unit will be 6'-2" × 6'-10". The actual desk will be 2'-5" high, with one wood file cabinet. The forward, raised, glass-covered transaction counter will be 1' deep × 2'-10" high, to meet Americans with Disabilities Act (ADA) requirements for Universal Design Guidelines. The rectangular towers that flank the unit will be 1'-2" wide × 1'-6" deep and 3'-6" high. These towers will not be segmented in design. The unit will be constructed of wood.

The details will consist of:

- A plan
- A horizontal section
- Two front-view elevations
- Two inside-view elevations
- Two vertical sections

The Reception Desk Plan Detail

To begin drawing the Reception Desk plan (Figure 9.1), do the following:

1. Insert the Reception Desk block into the drawing file, and rotate it 270 degrees from the lower-right corner of the block.

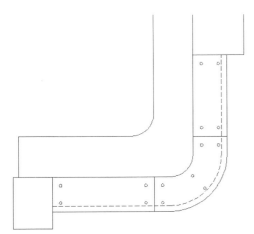

▶ **FIGURE 9.1:** The Reception Desk plan detail

2. Set the Annotation Scale of the drawing to ¾″ = 1′-0″.

In order to draw the plan view of the lower cabinet, you will need to explode the reception desk to see it better.

3. Explode the Reception Desk block.

4. Move all of the lines to the A-Millwrk-H layer.

5. Set the current layer to A-Millwrk-M.

The front of the reception desk will have a 4¾″ curved wall supporting the desk and a wood file cabinet on the lower-left side. The wood file cabinet will set in from the left side of the lower desk, 2″ from the side and 1½″ from the front, and will be 1′-3″ wide. To draw these elements, do the following:

6. Offset the dashed line already drawn to the inside of the desk at a distance of 4¾″. Offset the lower-left vertical line of the desk in the east direction at a distance of 2″; offset that line in the same direction at 1′-3″ and extend it in the south direction to the inside face of the wall. Then offset the front horizontal line of the interior side of the desk in the south direction at a distance of 1½″.

7. Trim all of the intersecting lines and match the properties of those lines for the front wall support only with the dashed lines already drawn in the plan.

8. Offset the vertical lines and horizontal back side of the wood file cabinet to the inside at a distance of ¾″. Then offset the inside dashed line of the front wall support in the north direction at a distance of ¾″.

9. Trim all of the intersecting lines and match the properties of those lines for the wood file cabinet only with the continuous lines already drawn in the plan. (See Figure 9.2.)

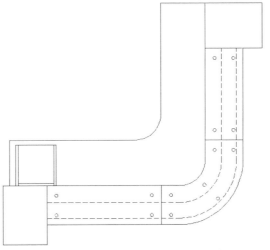

▶ **FIGURE 9.2:** The Reception Desk plan detail with file cabinet and front wall support

Now, add two grommets to the lower portion of the desk. These grommets are holes that the millworker will drill after the millwork has been installed in the field. However, it is a good idea to show them in plan now. These grommets allow electrical cords to be fed from the underside of the desk to the surface of the lower desk. These grommet holes are approximately 2½″ in diameter, and they are set in from the inside face of the wall support at a distance of 2½″ to their centerline. Place one grommet approximately 2′ in from the bottom-left tower and place the other one 6″ in from the upper tower.

10. Offset the right-hand vertical line of the lower-left tower in the east direction at a distance of 2′. Then offset the inside horizontal line of the upper desk in the south direction at a distance of 2½″.

11. Offset the inside vertical line of the upper tower in the east direction at a distance of 2½″. Then offset the horizontal line of the tower in the south direction at a distance of 6″.

12. Draw two circles with a diameter of 2½″ at the intersections of the previously drawn lines and then erase the guidelines.

The upper surface of the transaction desk and the front walls of the reception desk will be drawn in sections, already drawn in plan. These elements will need some sort of support. The lower desk will also need support. A good area to place this support would be at the section of desk that connects the upper portion (in plan) to the curved portion. To show this support, do the following:

13. Offset the horizontal line of the upper counter at the upper portion (in plan) to the curved portion in the north and south directions at a distance of 1″ each. Then offset the dashed vertical line of the wall of the inside face of the wall support in the west direction at a distance of 1′-3″. Then extend the previously offset horizontal lines to the previously offset dashed vertical line.

14. Trim all of the intersecting lines and match the properties of those lines with the dashed lines already drawn in plan.

15. Draw a horizontal line at the upper outside edge of the tower and lower desk. Then match the properties of that line to the properties of the inside vertical line of the lower desk. (See Figure 9.3.)

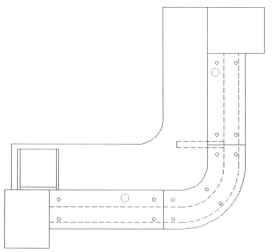

▶ **FIGURE 9.3:** The Reception Desk plan detail with grommets and support

To add dimensions, do the following:

16. Set the current layer to A-Millwrk-Dims.

17. Dimension the outside overall dimensions of the reception desk, and then dimension the smaller elements.

Make sure you pull these dimensions far enough away from the respective items that you'll be able to add additional dimensions.

18. Dimension the radii at the curved portion of the reception desk and the transaction counters. (See Figure 9.4.)

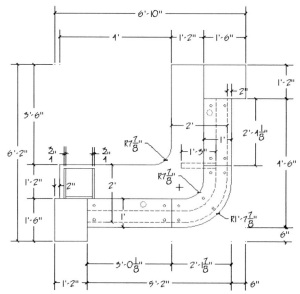

▶ **FIGURE 9.4:** The Reception Desk plan detail (dimensioned)

To add text, do the following:

19. Set the current layer to A-Millwrk-Text.

20. Start the Multileader command and add any pertinent notes.

Ensure that the Caps Lock is set to On and do the following:

21. Position the cursor at the lower desktop and type **PLASTIC LAMINATE DESK WITH CHERRY WOOD EDGE.**

22. Start the Multileader command, position the cursor at the upper tower, and type **CHERRY VENEER TOWER.**

23. Position the cursor at the grommet and type **2½″ GROMMETS, TYP. MILLWORKER SHALL LOCATE IN FIELD.**

24. Start the Multileader command, position the cursor at the support, and type **METAL SUPPORT.**

25. Position the cursor at the standoffs located at the upper transaction counter, and type **MILLWORKER SHALL PROVIDE 1″ METAL STANDOFFS TO SECURE GLASS PANELS.**

26. Start the Multileader command, position the cursor at the glass panel, and type **MILLWORKER SHALL PROVIDE ½″ CLEAR TEMPERED GLASS FOR UPPER COUNTER. ALL EDGES SHALL BE FACTORY POLISHED.**

27. Start the Multileader command, position the cursor at the wood file cabinet, and type **WOOD FILE CABINET.**

Organize the notes so they are clearly legible and they don't clutter your drawing. Then add the elevation tags and the drawing name tag by doing the following:

28. Set the current layer to A-Millwrk-Tags.

29. Insert the Elevation – Imperial block into the drawing; copy and manage these tags accordingly.

As previously mentioned, two front elevations and two inside elevations will be drawn for the reception desk. These drawings will be drawing numbers 3 through 6 on sheet MW-3.

30. Insert the Drawing Title – Imperial block below the Reception Desk plan detail. Copy and manage this tag accordingly.

The Reception Desk plan (Figure 9.5) will be drawing number 1 on sheet MW-3. In the next section, you will draw the horizontal section of the reception desk.

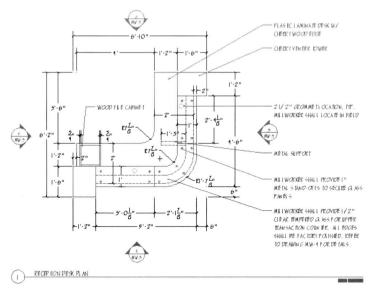

▶**FIGURE 9.5:** The Reception Desk plan (completed)

The Reception Desk Horizontal Section Detail

To begin drawing the reception desk's horizontal detail, do the following:

1. Copy the previously drawn Reception Desk plan to another location.

2. Set the Annotation Scale of the drawing to ¾″ = 1′-0″.

In order to draw the horizontal section, you will need to change some of the linetypes and erase some items in the Reception Desk plan for clarity.

3. Erase the lines of the glass at the transaction top, the grommets, and the metal standoffs.

4. Match the properties of the interior lines of the lower desk and upper transaction counter, the lines of the wood file, and the outside line of the glass with the properties of the dashed lines already drawn in plan.

5. Match the properties of the lines of the front support walls with the properties of the solid lines already drawn in plan. (See Figure 9.6.)

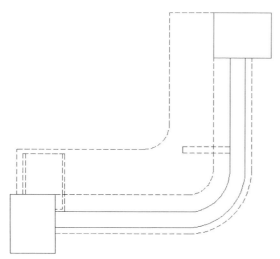

► **FIGURE 9.6:** The reception desk's horizontal section

Now that the horizontal section is managed correctly, you can start to show some detail. The curved front portion of the wall support will be constructed from a rigid flexboard that is used for architectural panels. This flexboard is sometimes referred to as *wacky board*. It is quite useful because it is easy to work with when constructing a curved surface, and it's strong and stable. The thickness of this flexboard is typically ⅜″. Two layers will be used to form the curve, and then it will be covered with cherry-wood veneer for a total thickness of 1½″ (¾″ thick for the front face of the support wall and ¾″ thick for the panel applied to the front face).

The balance of the support wall and front-face panels will be constructed from ¾″ medium-density fiberboard (MDF) covered with cherry-wood veneer. The ¾″ wood blocking will be added at 1′ on center, between the front and back support wall. The towers will also be constructed of ¾″ MDF covered with cherry-wood veneer. The towers will not have segmented panels attached. To continue, do the following:

6. Offset the inside continuous lines of the wall support to the inside at a distance of ¾″, and trim any intersecting lines. Then offset the front continuous line of the wall support to the inside at a distance of ¾″ twice.

7. Offset those lines to the inside by a distance of ¾″.

Now, draw the ¾″ wood blocking at the wall support. Remember, these will be placed 1′ on center from one another.

8. Offset the right-hand vertical line of the lower tower in the east direction at a distance of ¾″. Then offset that line in the same direction at a distance of 11¼″. Then offset that line in the same direction at a distance of ¾″.

9. Add two additional pieces of blocking in this direction.

10. Repeat the same procedure for the upper tower.

You will need to extend and trim the lines at the curve. Then, to add the blocking at the curve, do the following:

11. Set the current layer to A-Millwrk-M.

12. Draw a line from the midpoint of the inside line of the wall support at the curve to the opposite side. Then offset that line in either direction at a distance of ⅜″and erase the center line.

13. Manage the wood blocking to the current layer (Figure 9.7).

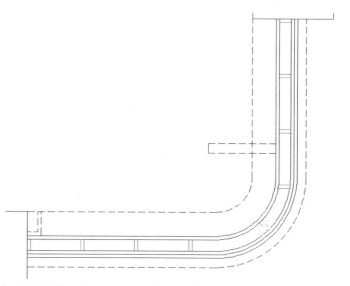

► **FIGURE 9.7:** Wood blocking at a wall support

Now, to add the limits of the flexboard at the curve of the wall support, do the following:

14. Offset the right-hand vertical line of the lower tower in the east direction at a distance of 3'-6", and trim the line, leaving only a vertical line at each layer of the wall support.

15. Offset the lower horizontal line of the upper tower in the south direction at a distance of 2'-10", and trim the line, leaving only vertical line at each layer of the wall support.

Now, draw the wood panels on the front of the reception desk. The wood panels on either side are 1'-10" wide, with a ½" reveal on either side. There are two segments of panels on either side. To draw these wood panels, do the following:

16. Offset the right-hand vertical line of the lower tower in the east direction at a distance of ½". Offset that line in the same direction at a distance of 1'-10". Then repeat both steps again. Trim the lines of the outside layer of the wood panel to form the reveal. Then repeat the same procedure for the panels on the other side.

To add the reveal at the front face of the curve, refer to the last lines that were offset on either side of the curve at the front face. Then do the following:

17. Offset the line at the bottom-left of the curve in the east direction at a distance of ½". Then repeat the same procedure for the line on the opposite side of the curve.

Verify that the Ortho and Osnap functions are On, and do the following:

18. Draw a line from the endpoint of the line that was just offset at the outside panel to the perpendicular point of the line behind. Then repeat the same procedure for the line on the opposite side of the curve.

19. Copy these lines to the endpoint of the lines at the outside panel that were previously offset. (See Figure 9.8.)

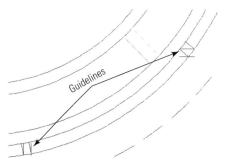

▶FIGURE 9.8: Reveal guidelines at curved front panel

20. Erase the original lines that were offset, trim any intersecting lines, and manage those lines to the same layer of the front face of the wood panel. (See Figure 9.9.)

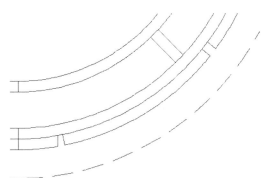

▶FIGURE 9.9: Reveals at the curved front panel

Next, add the thickness of the tower walls.

21. Offset the outer lines of each tower to the inside at a distance of ¾", trim any intersecting lines, and draw a diagonal line to miter each corner.

To add hatch to the MDF panels of the wall support, the walls of the towers, and the wood panels on the front face on either side of the curve, do the following:

22. Set the current layer to A-Millwrk-Hatch.

23. Start the Hatch command, and select the AR-SAND hatch pattern with a Hatch Angle of 90 and a Hatch Scale of ½".

24. Select the inside areas of the MDF panels at the wall support, the walls of the towers, and the wood panels on the front face on either side of the curve. (See Figure 9.10.)

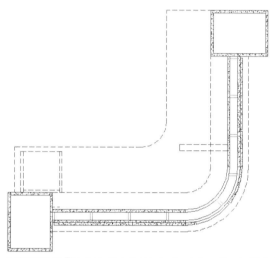

▶ **FIGURE 9.10:** The reception desk's horizontal section (with hatching)

To add dimensions, do the following:

25. Set the current layer to A-Millwrk-Dims.

26. Dimension a reveal and then override it as ½" TYP.

To add text, do the following:

27. Set the current layer to A-Millwrk-Text.

28. Start the Multileader command and add any pertinent notes.

Verify that the Caps Lock key is toggled On and do the following:

29. Position the cursor at the lower desktop, and type **PLASTIC LAMINATE DESK WITH CHERRY WOOD EDGE**.

30. Start the Multileader command, position the cursor at the upper tower, and type **CHERRY VENEER TOWER WITH ¾" MDF**.

31. Start the Multileader command, position the cursor at the wood blocking, and type ¾" **WOOD BLOCKING SPACED 1' ON CENTER, TYP**.

32. Start the Multileader command, position the cursor at the support, and type **METAL SUPPORT**.

33. Position the cursor at the wood panels, and type **CHERRY VENEER PANELS AT BOTH SIDES OF WALL SUPPORT ON ¾" MDF, TYP**.

34. Start the Multileader command, position the cursor at the panels at the curve, and type **CHERRY VENEER PANELS ON (2) LAYERS OF ⅜" FLEXBOARD AT FRONT FACE CURVE**.

35. Start the Multileader command, position the cursor at the ½" reveal cabinet, and type ½" **CHERRY VENEER REVEAL, TYP**.

Organize the notes so they are legible on your drawing. Then, to add the drawing name tag, do the following:

36. Set the current layer to A-Millwrk-Tags.

37. Insert the Drawing Title – Imperial block below the Reception Desk Horizontal Section detail and manage this tag accordingly. (See Figure 9.11.)

The Reception Desk Horizontal section will be drawing number 2 on sheet MW-3. In the next section, you will draw the front elevations.

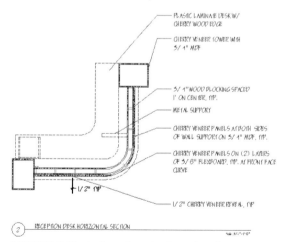

▶ **FIGURE 9.11:** The horizontal section (completed)

The Reception Desk Front-View (Side) Elevation Detail

Because the reception desk is curved to differentiate the views, the portion of the desk that is closest to the opening of the desk will be referred to as the side and the other portion that is considered the "public" side is referred to as the front. The front (side) elevation of the reception desk features rectangular wood panels with a ½" reveal around every corner. The overall height of the desk to the glasstop transaction counter is 2'-10". There will be a 4" wood base. There will be three linear rows of wood panels. The top and bottom wood panels will measure 1'-10" wide × 10" high, and the middle row of wood panels will measure 1'-10" wide × 6" high. The wood countertop will be 1" thick and placed on top of that will be a horizontal piece of ½" clear, tempered glass set off of the woodtop transaction counter by ½". The towers that flank the unit will be 3'-6" high. To begin drawing the elevation that features the wood file cabinet behind it, copy the Reception Desk plan that you have already drawn to a blank area and do the following:

1. Set the Annotation Scale of the drawing to ¾" = 1'-0".

2. Set the current layer to A-Millwrk-H.

3. Begin projecting vertical lines in the north direction from the boundaries of the towers at both locations.

4. Draw a horizontal line to delineate the floor plane. Then offset that line in the north direction at a distance of 2'-10", and offset that line in the same direction at a distance of 8". Trim all of the intersecting lines to delineate the boundaries of the reception desk for that elevation.

To delineate the right side of the reception desk (Figure 9.12), do the following:

5. Draw a vertical line in the north direction from the dashed line of the wall support (in plan) at the upper tower to the uppermost horizontal line of the tower in elevation view.

6. Offset that line in the east direction at a distance of 2". Then extend the top horizontal line of the transaction counter to this line, and trim any intersecting lines to form the profile of the desk.

To form the ½" piece of glass, the 1"-thick wood transaction countertop, and the space between them, do the following:

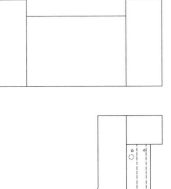

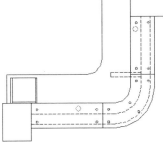

▶ **FIGURE 9.12:** The Reception Desk side elevation (delineated)

7. Offset the top horizontal line of the desk in the south direction at a distance of ½" twice. Then offset the second line in the same direction at a distance of 1". Trim the intersecting lines on the right side.

To form the horizontal lines of the segmented wood panels, do the following:

8. Offset the bottom horizontal line of the transaction top in the south direction at a distance of ½". Next, offset that line in the same direction at a distance of 10" and again by ½".

This will form the horizontal boundary for the top wood panels. To continue, do the following:

9. Offset the previously offset horizontal line in the south direction at a distance of 6". Offset that line in the same direction at a distance of ½". Offset that line in the same direction at a distance of 10" and again by ½". Trim the intersecting lines on the right side.

To form the vertical boundary for the wood panels, do the following:

10. Offset the right-hand line of the tower on the left-hand side of the elevation in the east direction at a distance of ½". Offset that line in the same direction at a distance of 1'-10".

This will form the vertical boundary for the left-hand wood panels. To continue, do the following:

11. Offset the previously offset vertical line in the east direction at a distance of ½". Next, offset that line in the same direction at a distance of 1'-10" and again by ½". Then trim and erase any intersecting or extraneous lines.

To form the profile of the wood panels on the right-hand side of the elevation, do the following:

12. Offset the right-hand vertical line of the desk in the west direction at a distance of ½". Then trim the lines between the panels at the reveals and erase any extraneous lines. (See Figure 9.13.)

▶**FIGURE 9.13:** Reveals in reception desk profile (close-up)

The metal standoffs are the last items to draw. Their overall height is 1-⅜". To draw them, do the following:

13. Project vertical lines in the north direction from the left and right quadrants of each standoff in plan.

14. Offset the top horizontal line of the transaction countertop in the north direction at a distance of 1-⅜". Then trim and erase any intersecting and extraneous lines at each standoff (Figure 9.14).

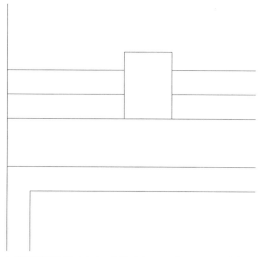

▶**FIGURE 9.14:** Metal standoff at transaction counter (close-up)

The glass panels that will be connected to the transaction top with the metal standoffs will be manufactured in sections. The pilot holes for the metal standoffs for the reception desk will be spaced approximately 3" on center to the inside portion of the glass on either end. The glass panels will have a ¾" space between them. To draw the space between the glass panels for this elevation, do the following:

15. Project a vertical line from the plan that separates the glass panels for this elevation in the north direction to the top horizontal line of the glass panel.

16. Offset this line in the east and west directions at a distance of ⅛", and trim and erase any intersecting or extraneous lines (Figure 9.15).

▶ **FIGURE 9.15:** Separation at glass panel (closeup)

To add dimensions, do the following:

17. Set the current layer to A-Millwrk-Dims.

18. Dimension the top, bottom, and side of the overall unit.

19. Dimension the glass and transaction counter. Then dimension the wood panels and smaller elements. (See Figure 9.16.)

When dimensioning the metal standoff and the ½″ reveal, override the dimensions and add TYP.

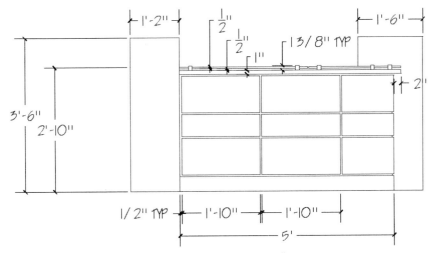

▶ **FIGURE 9.16:** The Reception Desk side elevation (dimensioned)

To add text, do the following:

20. Set the current layer to A-Millwrk-Text.

21. Start the Multileader command and add any pertinent notes.

Make sure the Caps Lock key is toggled On and do the following:

22. Position the cursor at the right-hand tower and type **CHERRY VENEER TOWER**.

23. Start the Multileader command, position the cursor at a metal standoff, and type **1″ DIAMETER BY 1⅜″ HIGH METAL STANDOFFS, TYP**.

24. Start the Multileader command, position the cursor at the glass panel, and type **½″ CLEAR, TEMPERED GLASS**.

25. Start the Multileader command, position the cursor at the transaction counter, and type **1″ CHERRY VENEER TOP**.

26. Start the Multileader command, position the cursor at a wood panel, and type **¾ CHERRY WOOD VENEER PANELS**.

27. Position the cursor at a ½″ reveal of a wood panel and type **½″ CHERRY VENEER REVEALS, TYP**.

28. Position the cursor at a wood panel and type **ALL WOOD GRAIN SHALL RUN IN A NORTH TO SOUTH DIRECTION, TYP**.

29. Start the Multileader command, position the cursor at the wood base, and type **CHERRY VENEER BASE**.

Organize the notes to maintain clarity and legibility on your drawing. Add the section detail markers for the two horizontal sections. If you need to review how to modify dynamic blocks, refer to Chapter 7. Remember to strive for clarity in your drawings. Make sure the tags and notes do not overlap or conflict with one another. To add the section detail markers for the reception desk, do the following:

30. Set the current layer to A-Millwrk-Tags.

31. Insert the Section Callout – Imperial block into the drawing.

Remember, this tag is a dynamic block. It has a parameter set to it that allows it to rotate the arrowhead and attributes. You will need to double-click this tag to access the parameter that you want to change.

32. Position this tag near the lower portion of the reception desk and update the attributes.

This tag denotes the plan drawing of the reception desk. It is drawing 1 on sheet MW-3. Repeat the same procedure and add a section tag for the horizontal section of the reception desk. That is drawing number 2 on sheet MW-3. You can insert another tag or copy the previously inserted tag.

Then, to add the drawing name tag, do the following:

33. Insert the Drawing Title – Imperial block below the Reception Desk Side Elevation – Front View detail and manage this tag accordingly.

The Reception Desk Side Elevation – Front View will be drawing number 3 on sheet MW-3. (See Figure 9.17.) You will draw the front elevation next.

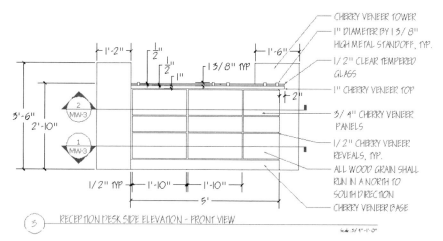

▶**FIGURE 9.17:** The Reception Desk side elevation (front view, completed)

The Reception Desk Front Elevation – Front View Detail

The front-view elevation of the reception desk (Figure 9.18) is nearly identical to the side view. The only difference is that the width of the desk on this elevation is 4'-4". You should be able to mirror the side elevation and modify it quickly.

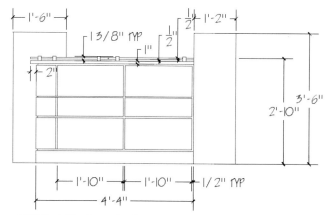

▶**FIGURE 9.18:** The Reception Desk front elevation (front view with dimensions)

This elevation should appear directly adjacent to the side elevation, so they can share the notes that have already been added to that elevation. Add the same section tags and the drawing name tag. This drawing will be drawing number 4 on sheet MW-3. (See Figure 9.19.) You will draw the interior elevations of the reception desk next.

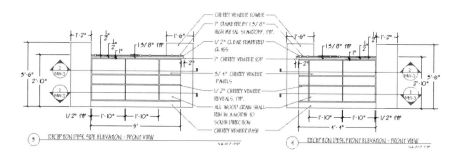

▶**FIGURE 9.19:** The Reception Desk side/front elevations (front view, completed)

The Reception Desk Inside-View Elevation Detail

The inside-front elevations of the reception desk feature the actual desk, metal support, and front and side views of the wood file cabinet. The removable panels should be called out on this side. The removable panels can be useful when a client wants to add any telephone/data hookups, etc. Again, a great deal of these elevations can be duplicated from the dimensions already drawn on the front-view elevations. Therefore, the dimensions we've already reviewed will not be explained in great detail.

The wood file cabinet is 1'-½" deep with ¾" wood drawer fronts. It is 1'-3" wide with a 4" wood base. This file occupies the full height beneath the desk. The thickness of the desk is 1½". The metal support is approximately 1' high × 1' long with a thickness of 1½", and the removable panels are approximately 2' wide × 1'-6" high.

Before you begin drawing the new elements, copy the Reception Desk plan to a blank area of your display. Project vertical lines from the plan view to delineate the towers, transaction counter, glass panels, standoffs, etc. (See Figure 9.20.)

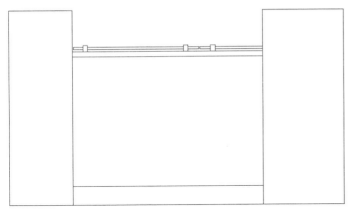

▶ **FIGURE 9.20:** The Reception Desk front elevation (inside view, delineated)

To continue the drawing, do the following:

1. Set the Annotation Scale of the drawing to ¾" = 1'-0".

2. Set the current layer to A-Millwrk-H.

3. Offset the bottom horizontal line of the reception desk in the north direction at a distance of 2'-5". Then offset that line in the south direction at a distance of 1½".

This action will outline the horizontal boundary of the desk height.

4. Project a vertical line from the edge of the counter near the wood file cabinet to the top vertical line that was previously offset. Trim and erase any intersecting or extraneous lines to outline the vertical boundaries of the desk.

Next, you will delineate the side view of the cabinet drawers. The following are some dimensions to note.

- The metal drawer pulls project 1" from the face of the drawer.
- There are three drawers. The top drawer front is 6" high, and the bottom two are 8½" high with a ⅛" gap between them.
- There is a 4" high × 2⅛" deep toekick.
- The thickness of the door is ¾", with a ⅛" gap between the drawer and the backside of the drawer, and below the desk.

5. Offset the vertical line that was just previously offset in the east direction at a distance of 2⅛" and then trim any intersecting lines.

This action will delineate the side view of the file cabinet and outline the profile of the toekick. Next, to draw the drawer fronts, do the following:

6. Offset the vertical line of the side of the file in the west direction at a distance of ⅛", and again in the same direction at a distance of ¾".

7. Offset the bottom horizontal line of the desk in the south direction at ⅛". Then offset that line in the same direction at a distance of 6" to delineate the boundary of the top drawer.

To delineate the bottom two drawer fronts, continue doing the following:

8. Offset the previously offset horizontal line in the south direction at a distance of ⅛", and again in the same direction at a distance of 8½". Then repeat the same procedure to delineate the bottom drawer.

9. Trim and erase any intersecting or extraneous lines.

Now, draw the metal drawer pulls. A typical drawer pull might have the following dimensions:

- ⅜" thick
- 4½" long
- Protrude from face of door at a distance of 1"

Draw a typical door pull and place it at the midpoint on each drawer face.

To draw the removable panel, do the following:

10. Offset the right-hand vertical line of the tower on the left in the east direction at a distance of 2", and again in the same direction at a distance of 2'.

11. Offset the top horizontal line of the wood base in the north direction at a distance of 1'-6", and trim and erase any intersecting or extraneous lines. (See Figure 9.21.)

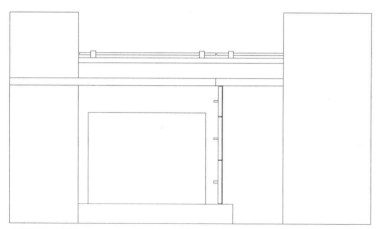

▶ **FIGURE 9.21:** The Reception Desk front elevation (inside view, progress)

To add dimensions, do the following:

12. Set the current layer to A-Millwrk-Dims.

13. Dimension the main elements that were drawn. (See Figure 9.22.)

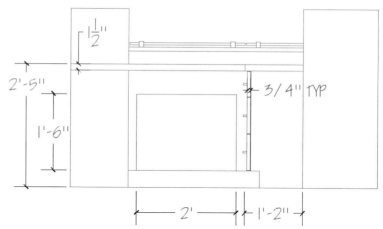

▶ **FIGURE 9.22:** The Reception Desk front elevation (inside view with dimensions)

To add text, do the following:

14. Set the current layer to A-Millwrk-Text.

15. Start the Multileader command and add any pertinent notes.

Make sure the Caps Lock key is toggled On, and do the following:

16. Position the cursor at the desktop and type **PLASTIC LAMINATE DESK WITH CHERRY WOOD EDGE.**

17. Start the Multileader command, position the cursor at the wood file, and type **¾" MDF ON CHERRY VENEER**.

18. Position the cursor at a tower and type **ALL WOOD GRAIN SHALL RUN IN A NORTH TO SOUTH DIRECTION, TYP.**

19. Start the Multileader command, position the cursor at the removable panel, and type **REMOVABLE PANEL**.

Then, to add the elevation and section tags, do the following:

20. Set the current layer to A-Millwrk-Tags.

21. Insert the Section Callout – Imperial block into the drawing.

You will need to insert three instances of this tag. Make sure to call out the horizontal sections as you did with the prior elevations. In addition, call out the vertical section for this portion of the reception desk. This detail will be drawing number 7 on sheet MW-3. To add the drawing name tag, do the following:

22. Insert the Drawing Title – Imperial block below the Reception Desk Front Elevation – Inside View detail, and manage this tag accordingly.

The Reception Desk Front Elevation – Inside View will be drawing number 5 on sheet MW-3. (See Figure 9.23.) We will draw the side elevation of the inside view next.

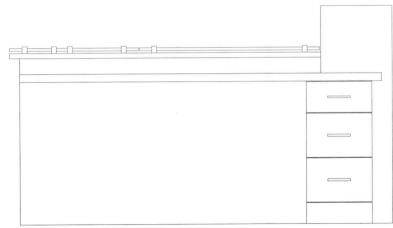

▶**FIGURE 9.24:** The Reception Desk side elevation (inside view, delineated)

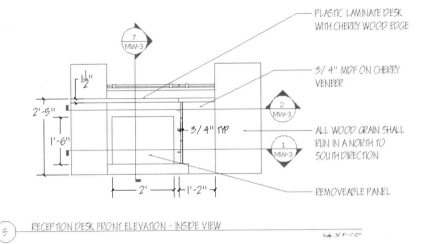

▶**FIGURE 9.23:** The Reception Desk front elevation (inside view, completed)

The Reception Desk Side Elevation – Inside View Detail

This elevation will feature the support wall section, metal support, grommet location, file cabinet front, and additional removable panels.

Before you begin drawing the new elements, copy the Reception Desk plan to a blank area of your display and project vertical lines from the plan view to delineate the tower, transaction counter, glass panels, standoffs, file cabinet, etc. (See Figure 9.24.)

To continue the drawing, do the following:

1. Set the Annotation Scale of the drawing to ¾″ = 1′-0″.

2. Set the current layer to A-Millwrk-H.

To delineate the support wall and wood panels attached to the front face, do the following:

3. Offset the front left-hand vertical line of the reception desk in the east direction at a distance of 4¾″. Then offset that line in the west direction at a distance of ¾″.

4. Offset the front left-hand vertical line of the reception desk twice in the east direction at a distance of ¾″.

Next, to outline the side view of the wood panels on the front face, do the following:

5. Offset the bottom vertical line of the transaction counter in the south direction at a distance of ½″. Then offset that line in the same direction at a distance of 10″. Next, offset that line in the same direction at a distance of ½″.

Continue outlining the wood panels.

6. Offset the previously offset vertical line in the south direction at a distance of 6″. Then do it again in the same direction at a distance of ½″, and again in the same direction at a distance of 10″.

7. Trim and erase any intersecting or extraneous lines to form the ½″ reveals at the front face.

To delineate the wood base and complete the bottom wood panel at the front face, do the following:

8. Offset the bottom horizontal line of the reception desk in the north direction at a distance of 4″, and do it again in the same direction at a distance of ½″. Then trim and erase any intersecting or extraneous lines.

Now, to delineate the toekick profile, do the following:

9. Offset the interior right-hand vertical line of the wall support in the west direction at a distance of 2″. Then offset the bottom horizontal line of the reception desk again in the north direction at a distance of 4″. Trim and erase any intersecting or extraneous lines to form the wood base profile (Figure 9.25).

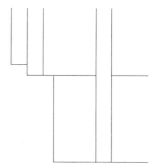

▶**FIGURE 9.25:** The wood base profile (delineated)

10. Offset the top horizontal line of the wood base in the north direction at a distance of ¾″. Then offset that line in the south direction twice at ¾″. Then offset the left-hand vertical wall of the wood base in the east direction at ¾″. Trim and erase any intersecting or extraneous lines.

11. Offset the bottom horizontal line of the transaction counter in the north direction twice at a distance of ¾″. Then trim the lines, leaving only the lines between the wall supports.

To draw the removable panels, do the following:

12. Offset the inside vertical line of the wall support in the east direction at a distance of 2″, and again in the same direction at 2′. Then offset that line again in the same direction at a distance of 4″.

13. Offset the top horizontal line of the wood base in the north direction at a distance of 1′-6″. Then trim and erase any intersecting or extraneous lines. (See Figure 9.26.)

▶**FIGURE 9.26:** The Reception Desk side elevation (inside view in progress)

To draw the metal support, do the following:

14. Offset the inside vertical line of the wall support in the east direction at a distance of 1½″, and again in the same direction at 1′. Then offset the bottom line of the desk in the south direction at a distance of 1½″, and again in the same direction at a distance of 1′. Then trim and erase any intersecting or extraneous lines.

To draw the location of the grommet, do the following:

15. Project a vertical line from the left and right sides of the grommet (in plan) to the desktop. Then offset the horizontal line of the desktop in the north direction at a distance of ¼". Then trim and erase any intersecting or extraneous lines.

To add dimensions, do the following:

16. Set the current layer to A-Millwrk-Dims.

17. Dimension the main elements that were drawn. (See Figure 9.27.)

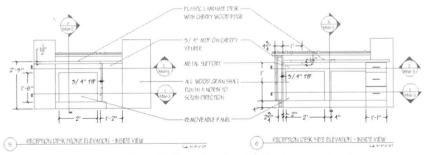

▶ **FIGURE 9.28:** The Reception Desk side/front elevations (inside view, completed)

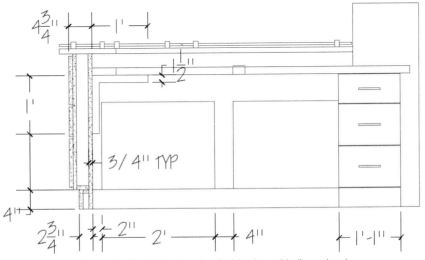

▶ **FIGURE 9.27:** The Reception Desk side elevation (inside view with dimensions)

You should complete this elevation in a similar fashion to the front-view elevations. It should appear directly adjacent to the front elevation's inside view, so they can share the notes that have already been added. Add any additional notes, and use the same section tags and the drawing name tag. This drawing will be drawing number 6 on sheet MW-3 (Figure 9.28). You will draw the vertical sections of the reception desk next.

The Reception Desk Vertical Section Details

These vertical sections will be rather simple to complete because most of the drawing has already been done for the previous elevations. Therefore, you should be able to comfortably delineate a great deal of this section on your own.

The sections will feature more detail for the wood file cabinet and metal support portions of the reception desk.

The Reception Desk's Metal Support Detail

Before you begin drawing the new elements, copy the Reception Desk Side Elevation – Inside View to a blank area of your display and modify the elements to re-create the elevation of the wall support, transaction counter, desk, etc. (See Figure 9.29.)

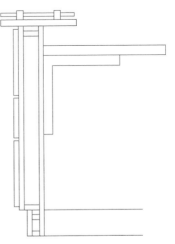

▶ **FIGURE 9.29:** The reception desk's metal-support section (delineated)

To continue drawing, do the following:

1. Set the Annotation Scale of the drawing to 1½″ = 1′-0″.

2. Set the current layer to A-Millwrk-H.

To delineate the ¾″ × 1½″ wood edge and the MDF at the desk, do the following:

3. Offset the top horizontal line of the desk in the south direction at a distance of ¾″. Then offset the front vertical line of the edge of the desk in the west direction at a distance of ¾″, and again in the same direction at a distance of 3″.

4. Trim and erase any intersecting or extraneous lines to show the wood edge and two layers of MDF behind, with the bottom layer of MDF segmented by 3″ at the front (Figure 9.30).

▶ **FIGURE 9.30:** The desk's front edge (close-up)

Now add the hatching.

5. Set the current layer to A-Millwrk-Hatch.

Begin adding hatch to the front edge of the desk.

6. Hatch the front edge of the desk with the AR-RROOF hatch pattern and a Hatch Pattern Scale of ½″ at a Hatch Angle of 45.

7. Hatch the two layers of MDF at the desk with the AR-CONC hatch pattern and a Hatch Pattern Scale of ¼″ at a Hatch Angle of 90.

Now, hatch the wood panels and wall support.

8. Hatch the wood panels at the front face and the wall support with the AR-SAND hatch pattern and a Hatch Pattern Scale of ¼″ at a Hatch Pattern Scale of ¼″.

Hatch the wood blocking at the wall support.

9. Hatch the wood blocking at the wall support with the Dolmit hatch pattern and a Hatch Pattern Scale of ¾″.

Now, add dimensions. You won't need to add very many dimensions because most of the information will be called out with notes. To add dimensions, do the following:

10. Set the current layer to A-Millwrk-Dims.

11. Dimension the overall height of the front face and desk elements. (See Figure 9.31.)

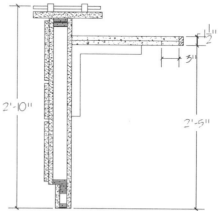

▶ **FIGURE 9.31:** The reception desk's metal-support section (with hatching and dimensions)

Next, add the text.

12. Set the current layer to A-Millwrk-Text.

13. Start the Multileader command.

Make sure the Caps Lock key is toggled to On, and do the following:

14. Position the cursor at the glass panel, and type ½″ **CLEAR, TEMPERED GLASS WITH FACTORY POLISHED EDGES.**

15. Start the Multileader command, position the cursor at the metal standards, and type **1″ DIAMETER METAL STANDOFFS.**

16. Start the Multileader command, position the cursor at the wood top, and type **WOOD TOP: CHERRY VENEER OVER 1″ MDF WITH VENEER EDGES.**

17. Start the Multileader command, position the cursor at the desk, and type **DESK TOP: PLASTIC LAMINATE DESK ON (2) LAYERS OF ¾″ PARTICLE BOARD WITH ¾″ X 1½″ CHERRY WOOD EDGE.**

18. Start the Multileader command, position the cursor at a metal support, and type **1½″ × 1½″ METAL SUPPORT**.

19. Start the Multileader command, position the cursor at a wood panel, and type **ALL GRAIN DIRECTION SHALL RUN IN A NORTH–SOUTH DIRECTION, TYP**.

20. Start the Multileader command, position the cursor at a removable panel, and type **REMOVEABLE PANEL: CHERRY VENEER ON ¾″ MDF**.

To add the drawing name tag, do the following:

21. Set the current layer to A-Millwrk-Tags.

22. Insert the Drawing Title – Imperial block below the Reception Desk – Section at Metal Support detail and manage this tag accordingly.

The Reception Desk – Section at Metal Support detail will be drawing number 7 on sheet MW-3. (See Figure 9.32.)

In the next section, you will draw the last vertical section.

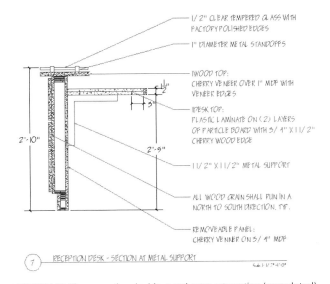

▶**FIGURE 9.32:** The reception desk's metal-support section (completed)

The Reception Desk's File Cabinet Detail

Before you begin drawing the new elements, copy the Reception Desk Front Elevation – Inside View to a blank area of your display and modify the elements to re-create the elevation of the wall support, transaction counter, desk, tower, file drawer fronts, hatching, etc. (See Figure 9.33.)

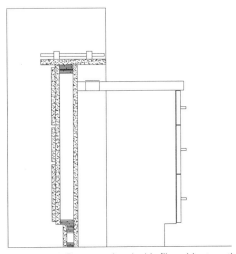

▶**FIGURE 9.33:** The reception desk's file-cabinet section (delineated)

To continue the drawing, do the following:

1. Set the Annotation Scale of the drawing to 1½″ = 1′-0″.

2. Set the current layer to A-Millwrk-H.

To delineate the ¾″ × 1½″ wood edge and the MDF at the desk, do the following:

3. Offset the top horizontal line of the desk in the south direction at a distance of ¾″. Then offset the front vertical line of the edge of the desk in the west direction at a distance of ¾″, and again in the same direction at a distance of 3″.

4. Trim and erase any intersecting or extraneous lines to show the wood edge and two layers of MDF behind with the bottom layer of MDF segmented by 3″ at the front.

At the intersection of the upper-right corner of the file cabinet and the underside of the desk, add a piece of wood blocking that is 4″ long × ¾″ high.

Next, delineate the wood file cabinet.

5. Offset the line of the backside of the file in the east direction at a distance of ¾″.

Before continuing with the wood file cabinet, note the following pertinent dimensions for the drawers:

- The drawer will feature a ⅝″ wood back, a ½″ wood bottom, an overall depth of 10-⅞″, and a drawer slide.
- The top drawer will have an overall height of 4-⅝″ and be centered on the backside of the drawer front.
- The bottom two drawers will have an overall height of 6-⅝″ and be centered on the backside of the drawer front.

To draw the top drawer, do the following:

6. Draw a horizontal line from the midpoint of the backside of the top drawer in the west direction at a distance of 10-⅞″. Then offset that line in the north and south directions at a distance of 2-⁵⁄₁₆″. Then draw a vertical line connecting the two endpoints on the left side and erase the middle horizontal line.

7. Offset the lower horizontal line of the drawer in the north direction at a distance of ¼″. Then offset that line in the same direction at a distance of ½″. Next, offset the vertical backside line of the drawer in the east direction at a distance of ¾″, and trim any intersecting lines in order to form the bottom, backside corner of the drawer.

8. Offset the backside, inside vertical line of the drawer in the west direction at a distance of ¼″, and extend the horizontal lines of the drawer bottom to meet that previously offset vertical line. Then trim any intersecting lines in order to display the joinery. (See Figure 9.34.)

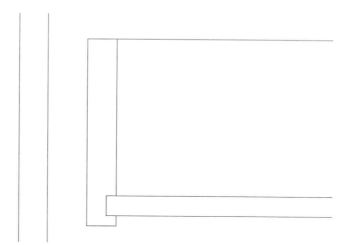

▶ **FIGURE 9.34:** Bottom corner of the file drawer (close-up)

To add the drawer slide, do the following:

9. Offset the back vertical line of the drawer front in the west direction at a distance of ¼″. Then offset the top line of the drawer bottom in the north direction at a distance of ⅝″. Insert the Drawer Slide block into the drawing and place the lower-right corner of the block at the intersection of the previously offset lines. Then erase the guidelines. (See Figure 9.35.)

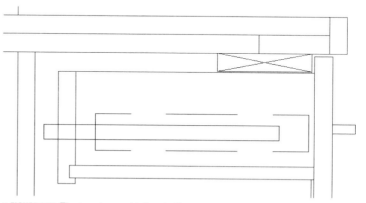

▶ **FIGURE 9.35:** The top drawer (delineated)

Repeat the same procedure to draw the larger bottom drawers.

To add the detail at the wood base, do the following:

10. Extend the horizontal line of the top of the wood base to the backside of the file. Then offset that line in the north direction at a distance of ¾". Then offset the original line in the south direction twice at a distance of ¾". Next, offset the vertical front line of the wood base in the west direction. Trim and erase any intersecting or extraneous lines. (See Figure 9.36.)

▶ **FIGURE 9.36:** The wood base (closeup)

Now add the hatching.

11. Set the current layer to A-Millwrk-Hatch.

Begin adding hatch to the front edge of the desk.

12. Hatch the front edge of the desk with the AR-RROOF pattern and a Hatch Pattern Scale of ½" at a Hatch Angle of 45.

13. Hatch the two layers of MDF at the desk with the AR-CONC hatch pattern and a Hatch Pattern Scale of ¼" at a Hatch Angle of 90.

Hatch the wood base and drawer fronts.

14. Hatch the vertical wood base and drawer fronts with the AR-SAND hatch pattern and a Hatch Pattern Scale of ¼" at a Hatch Pattern Scale of ¼".

Then, hatch the vertical pieces of the wood file.

15. Hatch the vertical pieces of the wood file with the Dolmit hatch pattern and a Hatch Pattern Scale of ¾" at a Hatch Angle of 90.

Hatch the horizontal pieces of the wood file.

16. Hatch the horizontal pieces of the wood file with the Dolmit hatch pattern and a Hatch Pattern Scale of ¾".

Now, add the dimensions. You should call out as many dimensions as possible on at least one of these sections, so the millworker can understand the design intent. To add dimensions, do the following:

17. Set the current layer to A-Millwrk-Dims.

18. Dimension the overall height of the front of the reception desk and the inside face of the desk.

19. Dimension the smaller elements of the front face of the reception desk, wall support, and front face of the wood file. (See Figure 9.37.)

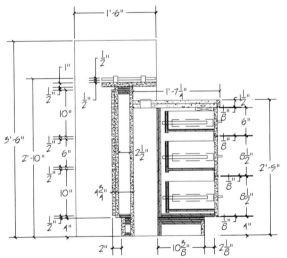

▶ **FIGURE 9.37:** The reception desk's file cabinet section (with hatching and dimensions)

Next, add the text.

20. Set the current layer to A-Millwrk-Text.

21. Start the Multileader command.

Several notes need to be added to the right side of the section. Verify that the Caps Lock key is turned On, and do the following:

22. Position the cursor at the tower, and type **TOWER: CHERRY VENEER ON ¾" MDF.**

23. Position the cursor at the glass panel, and type ½" **CLEAR, TEMPERED GLASS WITH FACTORY POLISHED EDGES.**

24. Start the Multileader command, position the cursor at the metal standards, and type **1" DIAMETER METAL STANDOFFS.**

25. Start the Multileader command, position the cursor at the desk, and type **DESK TOP: PLASTIC LAMINATE DESK ON (2) LAYERS OF ¾" PARTICLE BOARD WITH ¾" X 1½" CHERRY WOOD.EDGE.**

26. Start the Multileader command, position the cursor at a drawer pull, and type **DRAWER PULL.**

27. Start the Multileader command, position the cursor at a drawer, and type **DRAWER: CHERRY VENEER ON ¾" MDF WITH VENEER EDGES, DRAWER FRONT: ¾" CHERRY VENEER (SIDES & BACK), DRAWER BOTTOM: ½" CHERRY VENEER.**

28. Start the Multileader command, position the cursor at the cabinet, and type **CABINET CONSTRUCTION: ¾" CHERRY VENEER.**

29. Start the Multileader command, position the cursor at the wood base, and type **4" CHERRY VENEER BASE.**

The following notes should appear on the left side of the section.

30. Start the Multileader command, position the cursor at the tower, and type **ALL GRAIN DIRECTION SHALL RUN IN A NORTH–SOUTH DIRECTION, TYP.**

31. Start the Multileader command, position the cursor at a reveal, and type **1½" CHERRY VENEER REVEALS, TYP.**

32. Start the Multileader command, position the cursor at a wood panel at the front face, and type **WOOD PANELS: CHERRY VENEER ON ¾" MDF WITH VENEER EDGES (CHERRY VENEER ON TWO LAYERS OF ⅜" FLEXBOARD AT CURVE ONLY).**

To add the drawing name tag, do the following:

33. Set the current layer to A-Millwrk-Tags.

34. Insert the Drawing Title – Imperial block below the Reception Desk – Section at the Wood File Cabinet detail and manage this tag accordingly.

The Reception Desk – Section at Wood File Cabinet will be drawing number 8 on sheet MW-3. (See Figure 9.38)

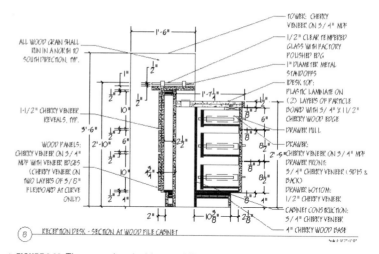

▶ **FIGURE 9.38:** The reception desk's wood file cabinet (completed)

Arranging the Details in Layout Space

The `Millwork-Details.dwt` drawing template used to create this drawing also had several viewports and a generic titleblock inserted into the Layout 1 tab. Now that the detail drawings for MW-3 have been completed, you will need to organize all of your drawings to fit in the viewports.

You may need to modify some of the notes or dimensions that were added to the drawing. Be sure to arrange the detail drawings in some sort of order. Take special care in aligning your drawing titles, etc. Figure 9.39 is an example of all of the detail drawings for MW-3 assembled within the Layout 1 tab.

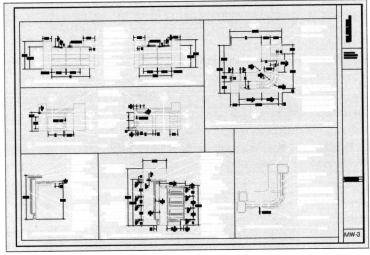

▶ **FIGURE 9.39:** The Layout 1 tab for MW-3 (assembled)

CHAPTER 10

Completing the Millwork Detail Drawings

AFTER COMPLETING THIS CHAPTER, YOU WILL BE ABLE TO:

▶ Download and save the Millwork drawing template

▶ Draw the millwork details for the two-person workstation in the reception area

▶ Modify dynamic blocks

▶ Arrange viewport details in layout space

An AutoCAD drawing template file has already been prepared. It is located in the chapter drawing file for this chapter on the companion DVD. The drawing name is Millwork-Details.dwt. This drawing template is primarily the same as the ones used in the previous chapters. The only difference is the viewports inserted into the Layout 1 tab.

Again, the following instructions will be fairly streamlined because the user is assumed to have had some experience with AutoCAD. This chapter will complete the process to prepare the millwork detail drawings for the two-person workstation. To begin, do the following:

1. Open the companion DVD and refer to the chapter drawing file for Chapter 10.

2. Download and open the drawing titled Millwork-Details.dwt.

3. Save the drawing template file as MW-4.dwg.

4. Make sure that the 2D Drafting and Annotation Workspace is current.

5. Set the Home tab current.

You are now ready.

The Reception Area Workstation Detail

As mentioned in Chapter 9, "Progressing the Millwork Detail Drawings," the intent was to maintain consistency in designing the workstation.

The plan for this piece of millwork is nearly identical to the design of the reception desk, except that it is rectangular. The design calls for the same rectangular towers on both sides and a raised, glass-covered transaction counter. The overall plan dimensions of this unit will be 14'-1¾" long × 6'-8" deep. The desk will be 2'-5" high with a wood file cabinet on both sides. The forward, raised, glass covered transaction counter will be 1' deep × 2'-10" high to meet Americans with Disabilities Act (ADA) requirements for Universal Design Guidelines. The rectangular towers that flank the unit will be 1'-2" wide × 1'-6" deep and 3'-6" high, but they will not be segmented in design. The unit will be constructed of wood.

The details will consist of:

- A plan
- A horizontal section
- One front-view elevation

- One side-view elevation
- One inside-view elevation
- One vertical section

Because a great deal of detail was already covered while you were drawing the details of the reception desk, the detail drawings for the workstation will be significantly scaled back. If you need to refresh your memory, refer back to the appropriate chapter.

The Reception Area Workstation Plan Detail

To begin drawing the Reception Desk plan (Figure 10.1), do the following:

1. Insert the Workstation block into the drawing file, and rotate it 90 degrees from the lower-right corner of the block.

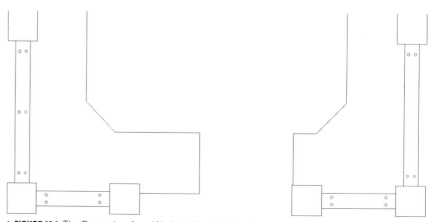

▶**FIGURE 10.1:** The Reception Area Workstation plan detail

2. Set the Annotation Scale of the drawing to ¾" = 1'-0".

In order to draw the plan view of the workstation, you will need to explode the workstation so you can see it clearly.

3. Explode the Workstation block.

4. Move all of the lines to the layer A-Millwrk-H.

5. Set the current layer to A-Millwrk-M.

The workstation will have a 4¾" support wall at the perimeter and a wood file cabinet on the side elevations. These cabinets have an overall depth of 1'-10¼", and they will be recessed 1½" from the front edge of the desk and the rear portion of the workstation. The left-hand work area will feature a return, and the right-hand work area will be slightly smaller. To begin drawing these elements, do the following:

6. Draw a horizontal line at the back of the workstation, connecting the tower to the front edge of the desk on the left-hand side. Then repeat this step for the opposite side.

To form the file cabinets (Figure 10.2), do the following:

7. Offset the previously drawn horizontal lines in the south direction at 1½". Next, offset that line in the same direction at a distance of ¾". Then offset that line in the same direction at a distance of 1'-1½", and offset that line in the same direction at a distance of ¾".

8. Offset the right-hand vertical line of the tower on the left-hand side in the east direction at a distance of ¾", and offset that line in the same direction at a distance of 1'-8-⅝". Trim and erase any intersecting or extraneous lines in order to form the wood file below.

9. Draw a vertical line from the upper-right corner of the file in the north direction at a distance of 1½". Then offset that line in the west direction at a distance of ¾".

10. Offset both of the interior horizontal lines of the file to the outside at a distance of ¼". Extend the inside vertical line of the back of the file to meet those previously offset lines, and then trim and erase any intersecting or extraneous lines for the joinery at the rear.

11. Either repeat the same procedure for the opposite side of the workstation or simply mirror this detail.

Now, show the modesty panel at the entrance on the right-hand side.

12. Offset the vertical line of the right-hand work surface at the entrance in the east direction at a distance of 1". Then offset this line again in the same direction at a distance of ¾". Offset the horizontal line at the edge of the work surface in the south direction at a distance of 1". Then trim any intersecting lines to form the modesty panel.

To show the circular metal post on the opposite side of the entry, do the following:

13. Offset the vertical line of the left-hand work surface at the entrance in the west direction at a distance of 3". Draw a circle at the midpoint of that line with a diameter of 4" and erase the guideline.

To draw the metal support on this side of the workstation, do the following:

14. Offset the left-hand vertical line of the tower in the west direction at a distance of 6". Then offset that line in the same direction at a distance of 2". Offset the horizontal rear line of the transaction counter from the wall support in the north direction at a distance of 1'-6", and trim any intersecting lines to form the metal support.

15. Change the lines of the transaction counter, metal support, the circular support, the files, and the modesty panel to a dashed linetype.

To show the grommet locations on both sides, do the following:

16. Offset the inside vertical line at the lower-left corner of the transaction counter in the east direction at a distance of 6", and offset the inside horizontal line of the transaction counter in that corner to the north direction at a distance of 6". Draw a 2½"-diameter circle at the intersection and erase the guidelines.

17. Repeat the same procedure for the opposite side. (See Figure 10.3.)

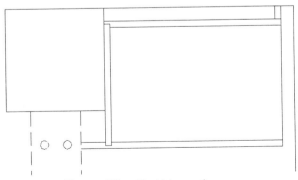

▶ **FIGURE 10.2:** The wood file cabinet (close-up)

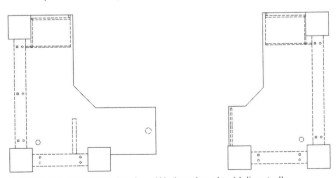

▶ **FIGURE 10.3:** The Reception Area Workstation plan (delineated)

To add dimensions, do the following:

18. Set the current layer to A-Millwrk-Dims.

19. Dimension the outside overall dimensions of the workstation, and then dimension the smaller elements.

Make sure the dimensions are far enough away from the items that you can add more dimensions. (See Figure 10.4.)

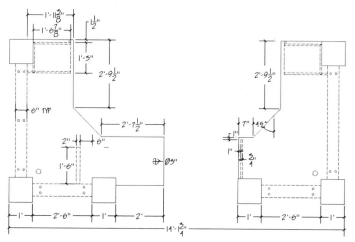

▶**FIGURE 10.4:** The Reception Area Workstation plan detail (dimensioned)

To add text, do the following:

20. Set the current layer to A-Millwrk-Text.

21. Start the Multileader command and add any pertinent notes.

Make sure the Caps Lock key is toggled On, and do the following:

22. Position the cursor at the wood file cabinet, and type **WOOD FILE CABINET**.

23. Start the Multileader command, position the cursor at the tower, and type **CHERRY VENEER TOWER**.

24. Position the cursor on the lower desktop and type **PLASTIC LAMINATE DESK WITH CHERRY WOOD EDGE**.

25. Position the cursor at the standoffs located at the upper transaction counter, and type **MILLWORKER SHALL PROVIDE 1″ METAL STANDOFFS TO SECURE GLASS PANELS**.

26. Start the Multileader command, position the cursor at the glass panel, and type **MILLWORKER SHALL PROVIDE ½″ CLEAR TEMPERED GLASS FOR UPPER COUNTER. ALL EDGES SHALL BE FACTORY POLISHED**.

27. Position the cursor at the workstation and type **ALL WOOD GRAIN SHALL RUN IN A NORTH TO SOUTH DIRECTION, TYP**.

28. Position the cursor at the grommet and type **2½ GROMMETS, TYP. MILLWORKER SHALL LOCATE IN FIELD**.

29. Start the Multileader command, position the cursor at the support, and type **METAL SUPPORT**.

Make sure the notes are organized so they are clearly legible on your drawing. Then, to add the elevation tags and the drawing name tag, do the following:

30. Set the current layer to A-Millwrk-Tags.

31. Insert the Elevation – Imperial block into the drawing, and then copy and manage these tags accordingly.

As previously mentioned, the following will be drawn for the workstation:

- One front elevation (front view).
- One side elevation (front view). This elevation will be used for both sides and keyed in the plan to reflect it as similar.
- One side elevation (inside view). This elevation will also be used for both sides and keyed in the plan to reflect it as similar.
- One front elevation (inside view).
- One vertical section.

All of these drawings will not fit on one page. Therefore, the following drawings will appear on MW-4:

- The Workstation plan – Drawing 1
- The Workstation horizontal plan – Drawing 2
- The Workstation side elevation (front view) – Drawing 3
- The Workstation side elevation (inside view) – Drawing 4

The following drawings will appear on MW-5:

- The Workstation front elevation (front view) – Drawing 1
- The Vertical section – Drawing 2

32. Insert the Drawing Title – Imperial block below the Reception Desk Plan Detail copy and manage this tag accordingly.

The Reception Area Workstation plan (Figure 10.5) will be drawing number 1 on sheet MW-4. You will draw the horizontal section of the workstation next.

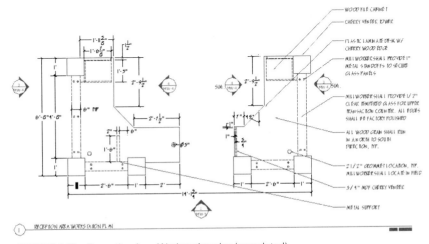

► **FIGURE 10.5:** The Reception Area Workstation plan (completed)

The Reception Area Workstation Horizontal Section Detail

To begin drawing the Reception Area Workstation horizontal detail (Figure 10.6), do the following:

1. Copy the previously drawn Reception Area Workstation plan to another location.
2. Set the Annotation Scale of the drawing to ¾" = 1'-0".

In order to draw the horizontal section, you will need to change some of the linetypes and erase some items of the Reception Area Workstation plan for clarity.

3. Erase the lines of the grommets and the metal standoffs.
4. Match the properties of the transaction counter with the properties of the solid lines already drawn in plan.

5. Match the properties of the desktop with the properties of the dashed lines already drawn in plan.

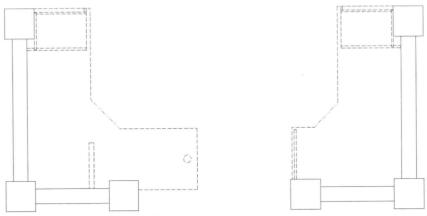

► **FIGURE 10.6:** The Reception Area Workstation horizontal section

The support wall for the workstation is the same as the reception desk's. However, the placement of the support wall with regard to the transaction counter is slightly different. The transaction counter is 6" thick The support wall is 4¾" thick and is recessed from the outside edge of the transaction counter at a distance of ⅝" on either side. The ¾" wood blocking will be added to the support wall at 1'-6" on center of block. To begin adding detail to the left-hand vertical support wall (Figure 10.7), do the following:

6. Offset the vertical lines of the transaction counter on the left-hand side to the inside at a distance of ⅝". Offset those lines once more in the same direction at a distance of ¾". Next, offset the left-hand line that was just previously offset to the inside at a distance of ¾".

Next, draw the wood panels on the front face. There are two equal rows of wood panels at this face, with a ½" reveal on either side at the towers and one midway between the two towers. To draw the wood panels, do the following:

7. Offset the horizontal lines of the towers on the left side of the workstation, toward the support wall, at a distance of ½", and trim the front face of the support wall to form the reveals on both ends.

8. Draw a horizontal line from the midpoint of the vertical line on the front face to the midpoint of the adjacent vertical line in the east direction. Offset that line in the north and south directions at a distance of ¼". Trim and erase the lines to form the middle ½" reveal.

9. Repeat the same procedure for the opposite vertical support wall. (See Figure 10.7.)

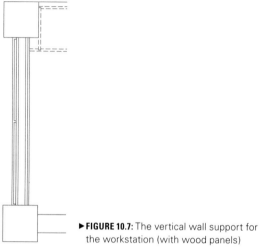

▶**FIGURE 10.7:** The vertical wall support for the workstation (with wood panels)

The wood panels located on the front walls that flank the entrance to the workstation also have the ½" reveal. The difference is that because of the width of these areas, only one panel is used. Therefore, repeat the same procedure to add the ½" reveals around the perimeter of the wood panel at the wall supports for the horizontal walls (in plan). (See Figure 10.8.)

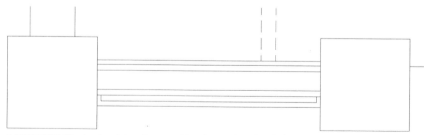

▶**FIGURE 10.8:** The horizontal wall support for the workstation (with wood panels)

To complete the detail of the wall support, add the ¾" wood blocking. Remember, this wood blocking is spaced 1'-6" on center of the block. Begin by placing the first piece at the midway point of the wall support and space the additional pieces from that point. Then display a piece directly adjacent to each tower.

Next, add hatching to the ¾" MDF wood panels and outside walls of the wall support (Figure 10.9). Refer to the Reception Desk details for the hatch pattern information.

Then, delineate the wall thickness for the towers, hatch them accordingly, and dimension the typical elements that were drawn.

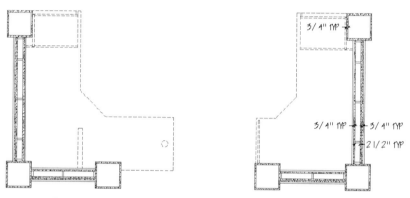

▶**FIGURE 10.9:** The Reception Area Workstation horizontal plan (with hatching and dimensions)

To add text, do the following:

10. Set the current layer to A-Millwrk-Text.

11. Start the Multileader command and add any pertinent notes.

Verify that the Caps Lock key is set to On and do the following:

12. Position the cursor at the tower and type **CHERRY VENEER TOWER WITH ¾" MDF.**

13. Start the Multileader command, position the cursor at the wood blocking, and type ¾" **WOOD BLOCKING SPACED 1'-6" ON CENTER, TYP.**

14. Position the cursor at the lower desktop and type **PLASTIC LAMINATE DESK WITH CHERRY WOOD EDGE.**

15. Start the Multileader command, position the cursor at the wood panels, and type **CHERRY VENEER PANELS AT BOTH SIDES OF WALL SUPPORT ON ¾" MDF, TYP.**

16. Start the Multileader command, position the cursor at the ½" reveal, and type **½" CHERRY VENEER REVEALS, TYP.**

Organize the notes so they are clearly visible on your drawing. Then, to add the drawing name tag, do the following:

17. Set the current layer to A-Millwrk-Tags.

18. Insert the Drawing Title – Imperial block below the Reception Area Workstation horizontal plan detail and manage this tag accordingly.

The Reception Area Workstation horizontal plan will be drawing number 2 on sheet MW-4 (Figure 10.10). You will draw the side elevation's front view of the workstation next.

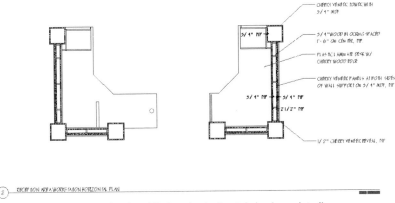

▶**FIGURE 10.10:** The Reception Area Workstation horizontal plan (completed)

The Reception Area Workstation Elevations – Front View Details

The front elevations of the workstation feature the same rectangular wood panels consistent with the design of the reception desk, with a ½" reveal around them at every corner. Both of the side elevations are the same. These elevations feature two equal columns of wood panels, while the front elevation features only one column on either side of the entrance.

The overall height of the desk to the glasstop transaction counter is 2'-10". There will be a 4" wood base. There will be three linear rows of wood panels. The top and bottom wood panels will measure 1'-10" wide × 10" high, and the middle row of wood panels will measure 1'-10" wide × 6" high. The woodtop counter thickness will be 1" thick, and placed on top of that will be a horizontal piece of ½" clear, tempered glass set off of the woodtop transaction counter by ½". Finally, the towers that flank the unit will be 3'-6" high.

In addition, the left-hand front elevation features a ¾" wood return desk surface with a circular metal post for support.

The Reception Area Workstation Side Elevation – Front View Detail

To begin drawing the left-hand elevation of the front view (Figure 10.11), copy the already drawn Workstation horizontal plan to a blank area and do the following:

1. Set the Annotation Scale of the drawing to ¾" = 1'-0".

2. Set the current layer to A-Millwrk-H.

3. Begin projecting vertical lines in the north direction from the boundaries of the plan.

Refer to the front view of the reception desk's front elevation for information to delineate this elevation. This is the elevation that details the entrance to the workstation.

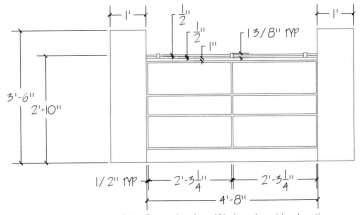

▶**FIGURE 10.11:** Front view of the Reception Area Workstation side elevation (delineated with dimensions)

To add text, do the following:

4. Set the current layer to A-Millwrk-Text.

5. Start the Multileader command and add any pertinent notes.

Make sure the Caps Lock key is toggled On, and do the following:

6. Position the cursor at the right-hand tower and type **CHERRY VENEER TOWER**.

7. Start the Multileader command, position the cursor at a metal standoff and type **1″ DIAMETER BY 1-⅜″ HIGH METAL STANDOFFS, TYP**.

8. Start the Multileader command, position the cursor at the glass panel, and type **½″ CLEAR, TEMPERED GLASS**.

9. Start the Multileader command, position the cursor at the transaction counter, and type **1″ CHERRY VENEER TOP**.

10. Start the Multileader command, position the cursor at a wood panel, and type **¾″ CHERRY WOOD VENEER PANELS**.

11. Position the cursor at the ½″ reveal of a wood panel and type **½″ CHERRY VENEER REVEALS, TYP**.

12. Position the cursor at a wood panel and type **ALL WOOD GRAIN SHALL RUN IN A NORTH TO SOUTH DIRECTION, TYP**.

13. Start the Multileader command, position the cursor at the wood base, and type **CHERRY VENEER BASE**.

Add the section detail markers for the two horizontal section tags, as you learned how to do by modifying dynamic blocks in Chapter 7, "Starting the Millwork Detail Drawings." Remember to strive for clarity in your drawings. Make sure the tags and notes do not overlap or conflict with one another. To add the section detail markers for the workstation, do the following:

14. Set the current layer to A-Millwrk-Tags.

15. Insert the Section Callout – Imperial block into the drawing.

Remember, this tag is a dynamic block. It has a parameter set to it that allows it to rotate the arrowhead and attributes. You will need to double-click this tag in order to access the parameter that you want to change.

16. Position this tag near the lower portion of the workstation and update the attributes.

This tag denotes the plan drawing of the workstation. It is drawing number 1 on sheet MW-4. Repeat the same procedure and add a section tag for the horizontal section of the workstation, which is drawing number 2 on sheet MW-4. You can insert another tag or copy the previously inserted tag.

To add the drawing name tag, do the following:

17. Insert the Drawing Title – Imperial block below the Reception Area Workstation Side Elevation – Front View detail and manage this tag accordingly.

The Reception Area Side Elevation – Front View will be drawing number 3 on sheet MW-4. (See Figure 10.12.) You will draw the inside, side elevation next.

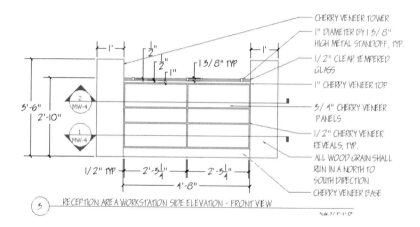

▶ **FIGURE 10.12:** Front view of the Reception Area Workstation side elevation (completed)

The Reception Area Workstation Elevations – Inside View Details

The inside elevations of the workstation feature basically the same elements that were drawn for the reception desk. The only difference is that the wood file cabinet is slightly larger than the wood file cabinets for the reception desk. There are two cabinets and both elevations are similar.

The elements that need to be drawn are the support wall section, the metal support, the grommet location, desk height, and the wood file cabinet.

The Reception Area Workstation Side Elevation – Inside View Detail

To begin drawing the left-hand elevation of the inside view, copy the Workstation horizontal plan that you have already drawn to a blank area and do the following:

1. Set the Annotation Scale of the drawing to ¾" = 1'-0".

2. Set the current layer to A-Millwrk-H.

3. Begin projecting vertical lines in the north direction from the boundaries of the plan.

Refer to the inside view of the Reception Desk front elevations for information to delineate this elevation. Remember that the wood file cabinet is slightly larger. Add the wall section on the left-hand side and include the metal support, grommet location, and removable panels below the desk. (See Figure 10.13.)

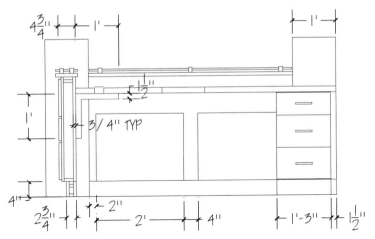

▶**FIGURE 10.13:** Inside view of the Reception Area Workstation side elevation (delineated with dimensions)

To add text, do the following:

4. Set the current layer to A-Millwrk-Text.

5. Start the Multileader command and add any pertinent notes.

Verify that the Caps Lock key is set to On, and do the following:

6. Position the cursor at the metal support and type **METAL SUPPORT**.

7. Start the Multileader command, position the cursor at the desktop, and type **PLASTIC LAMINATE DESK WITH CHERRY WOOD EDGE**.

8. Position the cursor at a tower and type **ALL WOOD GRAIN SHALL RUN IN A NORTH TO SOUTH DIRECTION, TYP.**

9. Start the Multileader command, position the cursor at the wood file cabinet, and type **¾" MDF ON CHERRY VENEER**.

10. Start the Multileader command, position the cursor at the removable panel, and type **REMOVABLE PANEL**.

Make sure to add the section detail markers for the two horizontal section tags and the vertical section tag for the section of the wood file cabinet, yet to be drawn. To add the section detail markers for the workstation, do the following:

11. Set the current layer to A-Millwrk-Tags.

12. Insert the Section Callout – Imperial block into the drawing.

13. Position this tag near the lower portion of the workstation and update the attributes.

This tag denotes the plan drawing of the workstation. It is drawing number 1 on sheet MW-4. Repeat the same procedure and add a section tag for the horizontal section of the workstation. It is drawing number 2 on sheet MW-4. You can insert another tag or copy the previously inserted tag. Repeat this procedure again to add the vertical-section detail marker. This will be drawing number 2 on sheet MW-5.

Then, to add the drawing name tag, do the following:

14. Insert the Drawing Title – Imperial block below the Reception Area Workstation Side Elevation – Inside View detail and manage this tag accordingly.

The Reception Area Side Elevation – Inside View will be drawing number 4 on sheet MW-4 (Figure 10.14). We will draw the front view of the front elevation next.

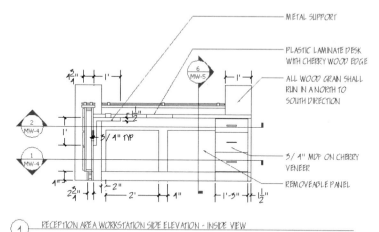

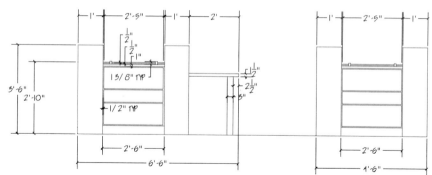

▶ **FIGURE 10.15:** Front view of the Reception Area Workstation front elevation (delineated with dimensions)

▶ **FIGURE 10.14:** Inside view of the Reception Area Workstation side elevation (completed)

The Reception Area Workstation Front Elevation – Front View Detail

To begin drawing the front-view elevation, copy the Workstation plan that you have already drawn to a blank area of your drawing and do the following:

1. Set the Annotation Scale of the drawing to ¾″ = 1′-0″.

2. Set the current layer to A-Millwrk-H.

3. Begin projecting vertical lines in the north direction from the boundaries of the plan.

To complete this elevation, refer to the front view of the Reception Desk front elevation (Figure 10.15). Add the ¾″-thick, wood work surface with the metal post beneath. You should be able to locate these items from the plan view of the workstation.

To add text, do the following:

4. Set the current layer to A-Millwrk-Text.

5. Start the Multileader command and add any pertinent notes.

Make sure the Caps Lock keyboard is toggled On, and do the following:

6. Position the cursor at the wood work surface and type ¾″ **CHERRY VENEER WORK SURFACE ON MDF.**

7. Start the Multileader command, position the cursor at the metal post, and type **3″ CIRCULAR METAL COLUMN.**

8. Start the Multileader command, position the cursor at the tower, and type **CHERRY VENEER TOWER.**

9. Start the Multileader command, position the cursor at the metal standoffs, and type **1″ DIAMETER BY 1-⅜″ HIGH METAL STANDOFFS.**

10. Start the Multileader command, position the cursor at the glass counter, and type ½″ **CLEAR TEMPERED GLASS.**

11. Start the Multileader command, position the cursor at the wood panel, and type ¾″ **CHERRY VENEER PANELS, TYP.**

12. Position the cursor at a tower and type **ALL WOOD GRAIN SHALL RUN IN A NORTH TO SOUTH DIRECTION, TYP.**

13. Start the Multileader command, position the cursor at the base, and type **CHERRY VENEER BASE**.

Don't forget to add the section detail markers for the two horizontal section tags. To add the section detail markers for the workstation, do the following:

14. Set the current layer to A-Millwrk-Tags.

15. Insert the Section Callout – Imperial block into the drawing.

16. Position this tag near the lower portion of the workstation and update the attributes.

This tag denotes the plan drawing of the workstation. It is drawing number 1 on sheet MW-4. Repeat the same procedure and add a section tag for the horizontal section of the workstation. That is drawing number 2 on sheet MW-4. You can insert another tag or copy the previously inserted tag. Repeat this procedure again to add the vertical section detail marker. This will be drawing number 2 on sheet MW-5.

Then, to add the drawing name tag, do the following:

17. Insert the Drawing Title – Imperial block below the Reception Area Workstation Front Elevation – Front View detail and manage this tag accordingly.

The Reception Area Front Elevation – Front View will be drawing number 1 on sheet MW-5 (Figure 10.16). You will draw the vertical section next.

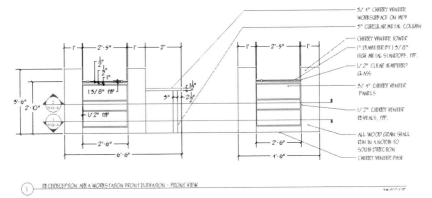

▶ **FIGURE 10.16:** Front view of the Reception Area Workstation front elevation (completed)

The Reception Area Workstation Vertical Section Detail

Before you begin drawing the new elements, copy the Reception Area Side Elevation inside view and the plan view to a blank area of your display and modify the elements to re-create the elevation of the wall support, transaction counter, desk, wood file cabinet side view etc. Remember to include the tower, file drawers, fronts, etc. (See Figure 10.17.)

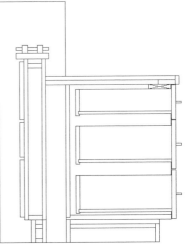

▶ **FIGURE 10.17:** The vertical section of the wood file cabinet (delineated)

To continue drawing, do the following:

1. Set the Annotation Scale of the drawing to 1½" = 1'-0".

2. Set the current layer to A-Millwrk-H.

Refer to the instructions in Chapter 9 regarding which hatch patterns to use, blocking, etc (Figure 10.18). Remember, there is 1" gap between the inside face of the back of the cabinet and the outside back face of the drawer. Also, because these drawers are larger than the drawers for the reception desk, you will need to insert a larger drawer slide. To add the larger drawer slide, do the following:

3. Insert the Drawer Slide block into the drawing, and place the midpoint of the right-hand side of the block at the midpoint of the inside line of the drawer front. Then copy and repeat for the other drawers.

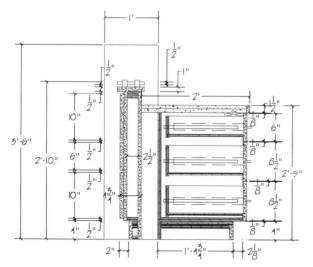

▶**FIGURE 10.18:** The Reception Area Workstation – Vertical Section at Wood File Cabinet (with hatching and dimensions)

Next, add the text.

4. Set the current layer to A-Millwrk-Text.

5. Start the Multileader command.

Several notes need to be added to the right side of the section. Make sure the Caps Lock key is set to On, and do the following:

6. Position the cursor at the tower and type **TOWER: CHERRY VENEER ON ¾″ MDF**.

7. Position the cursor at the glass panel and type **½″ CLEAR, TEMPERED GLASS WITH FACTORY POLISHED EDGES**.

8. Start the Multileader command, position the cursor at the metal standards, and type **1″ DIAMETER METAL STANDOFFS**.

9. Start the Multileader command and position the cursor at the desk and type **DESK TOP: PLASTIC LAMINATE DESK ON (2) LAYERS OF ¾″ PARTICLE BOARD WITH ¾″ X 1½″ CHERRY WOOD EDGE**.

10. Start the Multileader command, position the cursor at a drawer pull, and type **DRAWER PULL**.

11. Start the Multileader command, position the cursor at a drawer, and type **DRAWER: CHERRY VENEER ON ¾″ MDF WITH VENEER EDGES, DRAWER**

FRONT: ¾″ CHERRY VENEER (SIDES & BACK), DRAWER BOTTOM: ½″ CHERRY VENEER.

12. Start the Multileader command, position the cursor at the cabinet, and type **CABINET CONSTRUCTION: ¾″ CHERRY VENEER**.

13. Start the Multileader command, position the cursor at the wood base, and type **4″ CHERRY VENEER BASE**.

The following notes should appear on the left side of the section.

14. Start the Multileader command, position the cursor at the tower, and type **ALL GRAIN DIRECTION SHALL RUN IN A NORTH–SOUTH DIRECTION, TYP.**

15. Start the Multileader command, position the cursor at a reveal, and type **1½″ CHERRY VENEER REVEALS, TYP.**

16. Start the Multileader command, position the cursor at a wood panel on the front face, and type **WOOD PANELS: CHERRY VENEER ON ¾″ MDF WITH VENEER EDGES (CHERRY VENEER ON TWO LAYERS OF ⅜″ FLEXBOARD AT CURVE ONLY)**.

Then, to add the drawing name tag, do the following:

17. Set the current layer to A-Millwrk-Tags.

18. Insert the Drawing Title – Imperial block below the Reception Area – Vertical Section at the Wood File Cabinet detail and manage this tag accordingly.

The Reception Area – Vertical Section at the Wood File Cabinet will be drawing number 2 on sheet MW-5. (See Figure 10.19.)

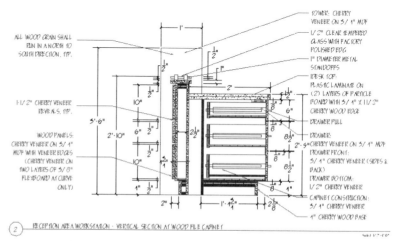

▶**FIGURE 10.19:** The vertical section of the wood file cabinet (completed)

Arranging the Details in Layout Space

The Millwork-Details.dwt drawing template that was used to create this drawing had several viewports and a generic title block inserted into the Layout 1 and Layout 2 tabs. Now that you've completed the detail drawings for MW-4 and MW-5, you need to organize all of your drawings to fit within the viewports.

You may need to modify some of the notes or dimensions that you added to the drawing. Be sure to arrange the detail drawings in some sort of order. Take special care in aligning your drawing titles, etc. Figures 10.20 and 10.21 show all of the detail drawings for MW-5 assembled within the Layout 1 tab.

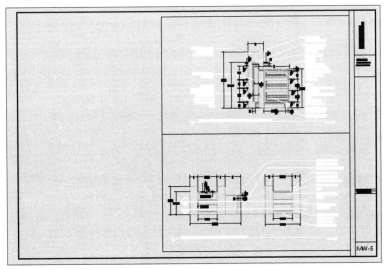

▶ **FIGURE 10.21:** The Layout 2 tab – MW-5 (assembled)

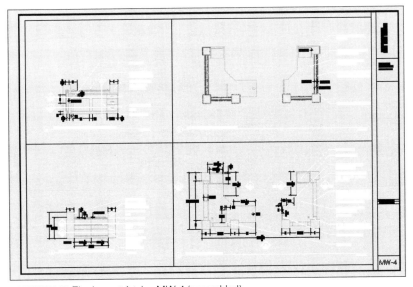

▶ **FIGURE 10.20:** The Layout 1 tab – MW-4 (assembled)

Index

About the DVD-ROM

Introduction

This appendix provides you with information on the contents of the DVD that accompanies this book. For the latest and greatest information, please refer to the ReadMe file located at the root of the DVD.

System Requirements

AutoCAD or AutoCAD LT 2008 or Higher—(Windows)

For 32-bit

- Intel Pentium 4 processor or AMD Athlon, 2.2 GHz or greater

  Or

- Intelor AMD Dual Core processor, 1.6 GHz or greater
- Microsoft Windows Vista, Windows XP SP2 operating systems for Microsoft
- Windows XP SP2
- 1 GB RAM
- 750 MB free disk space for installation
- 1024 x 768 VGA with true color
- Microsoft Internet Explorer 6.0 (SPI or higher)

For 64-bit

- Windows XPProfessional x64 Edition or Windows Vista 64-bit
- AMD 64 or Intel EM64T processor
- 2GB RAM
- 750 MB of free disk space for installation

For Use with a Mac

To use AutoCAD or AutoCAD LT 2008 or higher, **Boot Camp** with Mac OS x 10.5 is required

- An Intel Based Mac
- A Mac OS x 10.5 Leopard installation disc
- A USB keyboard and mouse, or a built-in keyboard and trackpad
- At least 10 GB of free space
- Boot Camp Assistant
- A DVD-ROM drive

NOTE: Many popular word processing programs are capable of reading Microsoft Word files. However, users should be aware that a slight amount of formatting might be lost when using a program other than Microsoft Word.

Using the DVD with Windows

To install the items from the DVD to your hard drive, follow these steps:

1. Insert the DVD into your computer's DVD-ROM drive.
2. The DVD-ROM interface will appear. The interface provides a simple point-and-click way to explore the contents of the DVD.

   If the opening screen of the DVD-ROM does not appear automatically, follow these steps to access the DVD:

1. Click the Start button on the left end of the taskbar and then choose Run from the menu that pops up.
2. In the dialog box that appears, type *d*:\start.exe. (If your DVD-ROM drive is not drive d, fill in the appropriate letter in place of *d*.) This brings up the DVD Interface described in the preceding set of steps.

What's on the DVD

The following sections provide a summary of the software and other materials you'll find on the DVD.

Content

Material from the book are in the folder named "Content".

Video Tutorials:

AutoCAD® 2009

AutoCAD® 2010

Chapter Review Questions and Answers (PDF format)

Practice Tutorial Exercises

AutoCAD Drawing and Template Files (in order to complete exercises in book)

Applications

The following applications are on the DVD:

ADOBE READER

Adobe Reader is a freeware application for viewing files in the Adobe Portable Document format.

WORD VIEWER

Microsoft Word Viewer is a freeware viewer that allows you to view, but not edit, most Microsoft Word files. Certain features of Microsoft Word documents may not display as expected from within Word Viewer.

Shareware programs are fully functional, trial versions of copyrighted programs. If you like particular programs, register with their authors for a nominal fee and receive licenses, enhanced versions, and technical support.

Freeware programs are copyrighted games, applications, and utilities that are free for personal use. Unlike shareware, these programs do not require a fee or provide technical support.

GNU software is governed by its own license, which is included inside the folder of the GNU product. See the GNU license for more details.

Trial, demo, or evaluation versions are usually limited either by time or functionality (such as being unable to save projects). Some trial versions are very sensitive to system date changes. If you alter your computer's date, the programs will "time out" and no longer be functional.

CUSTOMER CARE

If you have trouble with the CD-ROM, please call the Wiley Product Technical Support phone number at (800) 762-2974. Outside the United States, call 1(317) 572-3994. You can also contact Wiley Product Technical Support at **http://support.wiley.com**. John Wiley & Sons will provide technical support only for installation and other general quality control items. For technical support on the applications themselves, consult the program's vendor or author.

To place additional orders or to request information about other Wiley products, please call (877) 762-2974.

CUSTOMER NOTE: IF THIS BOOK IS ACCOMPANIED BY SOFTWARE, PLEASE READ THE FOLLOWING BEFORE OPENING THE PACKAGE.

This software contains files to help you utilize the models described in the accompanying book. By opening the package, you are agreeing to be bound by the following agreement:

This software product is protected by copyright and all rights are reserved by the author, John Wiley & Sons, Inc., or their licensors. You are licensed to use this software on a single computer. Copying the software to another medium or format for use on a single computer does not violate the U.S. Copyright Law. Copying the software for any other purpose is a violation of the U.S. Copyright Law.

This software product is sold as is without warranty of any kind, either express or implied, including but not limited to the implied warranty of merchantability and fitness for a particular purpose. Neither Wiley nor its dealers or distributors assumes any liability for any alleged or actual damages arising from the use of or the inability to use this software. (Some states do not allow the exclusion of implied warranties.)